The Kemsleys

A Socialist Anthology

AND THE MEN WHO MADE IT

Compiled with an historical
Introduction

by

Norman Longmate

Phoenix House Ltd
LONDON

Printed in Great Britain by
Western Printing Services Ltd of Bristol for
Phoenix House Ltd, 38 William IV Street, Charing Cross, W.C.2

First published 1953

Foreword

by Michael Foot, M.P.

SINCE SEDGEMOOR no great battle has been fought on English soil. Since the days of the first Queen Elizabeth Englishmen have settled by the arts of negotiation many issues which in other lands were only decided by the sword. The English tradition of parliamentary institutions is longer and stronger than that of any other country. Hence most of the English heroes lauded by the English historians have been the men who seemed to know how far they could go and how much they must concede if convulsion was to be avoided. We never cease to congratulate ourselves on the English genius for compromise. One result of this complacent theme has been that proper credit has never been given to the others who have supplied so much of the motive power in our history—the rebels, the revolutionaries, the heretics who risked their neck, the prophets who understood more than the statesmen, the far-seeing, the eccentrics and the men of no-compromise. They were not blessed by success in their own generation and their historical stature is made to suffer in consequence.

And yet the story could be written so differently and many names should possess a glory of which they are now cheated. The boldest revolutionaries in Cromwell's armies had a wonderful logic on their side and the demand of Colonel Thomas Rainborough that 'the poorest he that is in England has a life to live, as the greatest he' still resounds across the centuries. A good case can be made for the view that Thomas Paine was the greatest Englishman of the eighteenth century; certainly he had a better understanding of his age than the rulers who hunted him for treason and burnt his books. He was proclaiming the age of democracy in far better prose than Dr. Johnson's and building a new nation across the seas while his triumphant enemies spent their best exertions to restore the Bourbons. Today the works of Paine still sell steadily at the bookstalls; no such claim can be made even for Edmund Burke.

In the years that followed, the intrepid radicalism of the early nineteenth century—of William Cobbett and William Hazlitt, of Shelley and Godwin, of Francis Place and Orator Hunt—was swallowed up by the industrial revolution. The smug champions of that conquest have

3

received their full meed of fame. 'What has never been adequately written,' says Professor Tawney, 'is the history of the political philosophy which failed. For the victory of the panegyrists of the new industrial order was so complete as to obliterate the very remembrance of its critics, and to create the impression that Utilitarianism spoke with the voice of reason itself.' The reputations of writers like Gray, Thompson, Hodgskin and Bray seemed sunk without a trace. Even Sidney Webb writing the historical view of Socialism in the first Fabian Essays published in the year 1889 managed to achieve the feat without once mentioning the Chartists!

But a great revenge was in store. The ruthlessness, the squalor, the ugliness and the unpitying disorder of the industrial revolution gave birth to modern socialism. A splendid array of new prophets arose to protest against the horror they saw around them and to search out a new path for mankind. They appeared in many lands, but England, Scotland and—let us not forget to our shame—Ireland supplied many among the foremost. They laid the foundations of a new party which was soon to change the face of British politics and offer the Britain of the twentieth century a new prospect of survival and resurgence once the old capitalism had lost its virility.

Even the snobbish historians who worship success should be impressed and prepared to pay tribute to the men who did it. But they rarely do. And sometimes they are assisted in their neglect by Socialists whose arteries have hardened, who have grown too 'responsible', and who fear to recall the idealism which brought the Labour Party into being. They like to pretend that the contrast between any real society and the millennial dreams of the Utopian revolutionaries are too sharp for any relevant instruction to be derived from such sources.

There are no grounds for such contempt. Socialism, for many of the pioneers, meant a golden sunrise in a matchless Elysium, and it is no complaint against the Labour Government of 1945 that they did not succeed in creating that atmosphere overnight in Stoke-on-Trent or Warrington. Nor should it be a complaint against the pioneers that they spoke and wrote in such terms. Nothing is chipped off the grandeur of Moses as a world figure because of a pardonable exaggeration about the milk and the honey. In fact, for those who re-read the works of the early Socialist writers today, more remarkable than the falsification of their hopes is the persistence with which they discussed many of the real problems hanging round our necks today. Let the cynics save their jeers! Keir Hardie and William Morris have much more to say to the world of 1953 than, say, Arthur Balfour and Rudyard Kipling; Robert

Blatchford, who wins a just pride of place in this volume, has left a name in journalism which stands a good deal higher than Lord Northcliffe's.

Norman Longmate has here collected an anthology from this rich storehouse. On one major issue I would quarrel with him. He claims to exclude those who preached 'the doctrines of Marxism and class war'. Why, in heaven's name? Karl Marx should not be held guilty of the crimes of Joseph Stalin and many English Socialists owed to him much more than they were ever ready to acknowledge. He still remains a towering figure in the history of Socialism; no modern witch-hunt will ever knock him from his pedestal. As for class war, it is, in the words of H. G. Wells, nothing more than an old pastime of the British ruling classes.

There are other omissions, but that is inevitable. Here in this anthology Socialists may learn something of their proud ancestry, of the great men who were truly so much greater than their more famous contemporaries, of those who still stand with us as allies in the fight to 'enlarge the empire of the human mind'.

MICHAEL FOOT

May 1953

Preface

THE PURPOSE of this Anthology is to provide in one volume a selection of documents illustrating the development of Socialism in this country, together with an account of the rise to power of the Labour Party. Since Socialism in this country has been essentially political, and not industrial, in its expression, I have dealt but briefly with Trade Union history and the Co-operative Movement. British Socialism owes nothing to the doctrines of Marxism and class-war; extracts concerning these would be appropriate to a Communist Anthology; they would be wholly out of place here.

Most of the books which have been influential in making converts to the Socialist faith are quoted in these pages, even though, in one or two cases, the author was not himself a Socialist. For the same reason, certain passages are taken from works of fiction.

I am indebted for assistance with the Christian Socialist section of the book to the Rev. W. W. and Mrs Meadows, of St Mary's Vicarage, Newbury.

It is in the belief that the Labour Movement will profit at this moment of its history from a reminder of the uncompromising beliefs of those who founded it and the unwearying sacrifices of those who built it up, that this book has been compiled.

N.R.L.

General Election Day, 1951

Contents

Acknowledgments

*The publishers are grateful to the following for permission
to include coypright material:*

Miss Winifred Blatchford for extracts from *Merrie England, Not Guilty:
A Plea for the Bottom Dog*, and *My Eighty Years* by Robert Blatchford;
Colonel Booth for *The Life and Labour of the People in London* by Charles
Booth; Miss D. E. Collins for G. K. Chesterton's *Notebooks*; Mr S. R.
Elliott for *England, Cradle of Co-operation*; Miss M. Graham Wallas for
Human Nature in Politics by Graham Wallas; Emrys Hughes, M.P., for
Keir Hardie's *Speeches and Writings*; Dr Edith Summerskill, M.P., for
the extract from her broadcast; The Society of Authors and the Public
Trustee for *Essays in Fabian Socialism* edited by Bernard Shaw; Messrs
George Allen & Unwin Ltd for *Towards a Christian Democracy* by Sir
Stafford Cripps, *Hyndman, Prophet of Socialism* by E. J. Gould, *The Life
of Francis Place* by Graham Wallas, and *Christ and Society* by Charles
Gore; Messrs Jonathan Cape Ltd for *Love on the Dole* by Walter Green-
wood; Messrs Collins, Publishers, for *South Riding* by Winifred Holtby,
and Mr Howard Spring for *Fame is the Spur*; the Co-operative Union
Ltd for *Co-operation* by F. Hall and P. Watkins; the *Daily Herald* for
extracts dated 2 August 1945; The Fabian Society for Fabian Tracts *The
Labour Party on the Threshold, The Life of William Cobbett, The Life of
Thomas Paine*, and *Socialism and the Standardised Life*; Messrs Faber
& Faber Ltd for *The Socialist Case* by Douglas Jay; Messrs Victor
Gollancz Ltd and Miss Vera Brittain for *Testament of Youth*, and Profes-
sor G. D. H. Cole for *The Simple Case for Socialism*, and Miss Lettice
Cooper for *National Provincial*, and the Rt. Hon. John Strachey, M.P.,
for *A Faith to Fight For* and *Why You Should be a Socialist*, and Miss
Anne E. Wilkinson for *The Town that was Murdered* by Ellen Wilkinson;
Messrs George G. Harrap & Co. Ltd for *My Life of Revolt* by David
Kirkwood; Messrs William Heinemann Ltd for *The Life of Charles Gore*
by G. L. Prestige, *Mr Attlee* by Roy Jenkins, and *Press, Parliament, and
People* by Francis Williams; Messrs Michael Joseph Ltd for *My Quest
for Peace* by George Lansbury; Messrs John Long Ltd for *Memories and
Reflections* by Ben Tillett; Messrs Longmans, Green & Co. Ltd for *The
Village Labourer 1760–1832* and *The Town Labourer 1760–1832* by J. L.

and B. Hammond, *William Morris and the Early Days of the Socialist Movement* by R. B. Glasier, and the Trustees of the late Lord Passfield for *The History of Trade Unionism* by Sidney and Beatrice Webb and *My Apprenticeship* by Beatrice Webb; Messrs Methuen & Co. Ltd for *The Rise of Modern Industry* by J. L. and B. Hammond, and *The Common People* by G. D. H. Cole and R. Postgate; Messrs A. R. Mowbray & Co. Ltd for *The Life of F. D. Maurice* by C. F. G. Masterman; The Oxford University Press for *William Temple, His Life and Letters* by F. A. Iremonger; Penguin Books Ltd for *Christianity and Social Order* by William Temple; The Richards Press Ltd for *The Ragged Trousered Philanthropists* by Robert Tressall; Messrs Sampson Low, Marston & Co. and Mrs Mary Agnes Hamilton for *Sidney and Beatrice Webb*; Messrs Martin Secker & Warburg Ltd for *Tom Paine* by W. E. Woodward; *The Times* for the extract dated 2 August 1945.

Every effort has been made to trace the owners of copyright material used in this book. Should any material have been included inadvertently without the permission of the owner of the copyright, acknowledgment will be made in any future edition.

Historical Introduction

THE ROOTS IN HISTORY

THE DEFINITION OF Socialism which I have adopted for the purposes of this anthology is that 'Socialism is a belief in a fundamental reorganization in the structure of society, based on the common ownership of the means of production, distribution, and exchange, the political liberty of the individual, and the replacement of the motives of profit and competition by those of service and co-operation'. This is a definition which would have been acceptable to all those whose writings appear in this book and should be acceptable to all who can justly be called Socialists in Britain to-day.

No form of Socialism which would answer to this definition appears in England before the nineteenth century, when the word was itself first coined. Certain aspects of Socialistic belief are, however, almost as old as man. It may be assumed that in the primitive tribes which were the first form of political society, the strong accepted some kind of responsibility for those wounded in battle or attacked by illness, and the law of Moses lays down that the prosperous must make adequate provision for the needy. Plato, who was born in 425 B.C., proposed in *The Republic* a society in which all private property would be abolished and all activity would be for the common benefit, but his beliefs as a whole are more characteristic of modern Fascism than of any other system.

The coming of Christianity is the first great milestone in the development of Socialist thought, though it is untrue to suggest that the New Testament is in any sense a political textbook. Christ himself repeatedly condemned the idea of money-making and stressed the obligation of all men towards their neighbours, but the poor man was not to be excused blame for being covetous any more than the rich man. The parable of the workers in the vineyard is perhaps the first recorded instance of the classic Socialist doctrine of 'To each according to his need' but would be wholly unacceptable to a modern trade union. St Luke reveals that the early Christians realized in their scattered congregations the idea of co-operation between members, even to the extent of holding all their property in common. St Paul is equally outspoken on unnatural class divisions; there was to be 'neither bond nor free' in the Christian state and the Christians were exhorted to be 'members one of another'. When Christianity became the official religion of the Roman Empire these doctrines were propagated all over Europe with the rest, but the medieval Church seems to have seen nothing wrong in the profit motive as such, though usury—making money out of the mere ownership or manipulation of money—was forbidden to Christians and remained so until the Reformation.

It is perhaps significant that the first known English Socialist was a priest, John Ball, whose preaching on the injustice of the poor man's lot and the necessity for property to be held in common was one of the causes of the unsuccessful Peasants' Revolt of 1381. The idea of common ownership of property recurs in Sir Thomas More's *Utopia*, which appeared in 1515, and which vigorously condemned the existing condition of the world in which each man was in a state of constant war with his neighbour. *Utopia* however can have had little effect; it was in Latin, the common people were illiterate, and More himself, like John Ball, though for other reasons, was later executed; nor is there any evidence that he himself held the opinions which he put into the mouths of his characters.

The seventeenth was the first century in which political discussion became general in England. The war of Parliament against King Charles, and his execution in 1649, provoked a tremendous wave of speculation, and during the ten years of Cromwell's rule every kind of new proposal was discussed and circulated, among them the suggestion from the Levellers for universal franchise among adult males and the abolition of the aristocracy, and from the much less important and far less numerous Diggers the demand that all land should be held in common and men should work together upon it in co-operation and harmony. None of these ideas established themselves and England sank into political quiescence, as far as the reorganization of society was concerned, for over a century.

The French Revolution in 1788 worked upon the imagination of many of the population as had the execution of the king a hundred and forty years before. Revolutionaries such as Tom Paine sprang up who challenged the existing order, but most of these protests were directed to obtaining political power for the working class, and there seems to have been little idea of what was to be done when the machine of government had been captured. Meanwhile the progress of the Industrial Revolution was creating a large working population possessing nothing but their labour power, and herded together in great new cities, often under disgusting conditions and with no regard for their well-being.

A notable exception to the general indifference of the manufacturing class was Robert Owen, who has been described as 'the first British Socialist'. The community which he created at New Lanark in the years following 1800 became a wonder, but not a model, to the men of his time. His workers were properly housed and cared for; the clothes, food, and other possessions they needed were bought in bulk by Owen and sold to them on the co-operative system, at an enormous saving, and their children were educated in a common nursery, run on principles which would be approved even to-day. But the example provided by New Lanark proved merely that a mill could be run efficiently, even though its workers were treated as human beings; it was as much an example of enlightened and successful capitalist enterprise as of embryonic Socialism, and Owen had few imitators and no successors.

In the next few years, against the bitter opposition of the Conservatives, then, as now, ready to defend their privileges with the argument that disaster would result from any interference with their freedom to manage their affairs as they chose, the first feeble Factory Acts were passed, restricting the hours of labour worked by children and, later, women; they were often evaded, but their importance lies not in themselves but in the principle that they established, that the state had a duty to interfere to protect its weakest citizens, and that private benevolence could not be relied on to perform this task.

The Reform Bill of 1832, which removed the rotten boroughs and gave part of the middle class the franchise, disappointed the working classes, and there was a period of great political agitation in the following years. Many of the movements of this time tended to look back to the land as the salvation of the oppressed factory worker, and even the most elaborate, such as the Chartists, thought solely in terms of obtaining political power for the disfranchised classes, and had no programme to be realized once that had been won. They are important as helping to obtain the means to Socialism—the vote—but show no knowledge or understanding of the end—a new type of society.

THE PATH TO POWER

IN 1867 Disraeli's Reform Act extended the franchise to some 900,000 working men, thus almost doubling the electorate. In the following year the London Working Men's Association, whose ancestor was the Chartist Movement which had collapsed twenty years before, issued a manifesto proposing certain social reforms and suggesting that the interests of labour might best be served by the election of working-men candidates to Parliament. In the General Election of 1869 three working men stood as candidates with this programme and were defeated.

During the next few years various other contesting groups with similar programmes were founded and eventually in 1874 two miners were returned as the first working-men M.P.s. They supported the Liberals in Parliament and were certainly not Socialists. For the next twenty-five years the working classes continued to support the Liberal Party, either in name or in disguise, as 'liberal-labour'. It was not the arrival of these working men, who tended merely to attempt to outvie the Liberals in respectability and orthodoxy at Westminster, which was the real portent of the future, but the eruption into English political life of two widely different figures. The first was the atheist Bradlaugh, who was elected in 1880 and allowed to take his seat six years later. The influence of his new and more vigorous Radicalism on the Liberal Party was considerable, though he tended to discredit progressive ideas, because his religious views were anathema to the great class of non-conformist workmen, from whom a working-class movement would have to draw its main support.

The second figure was the Mayor of Birmingham, Joseph Chamberlain, who became the advocate of what was later known as 'gas and water Socialism'. He stood for, and in Birmingham carried out, a large-scale intervention of the state, not only in housing and sanitation, but in the provision of water and other essential services. To him must belong the credit of being the first great Liberal to perceive the tendency of the times. Socialism, he declared, 'was not a stigma, but a modern tendency pressing for recognition. The path of legislative progress in England had been for years, and must continue to be, distinctly Socialistic.' But Chamberlain did not envisage the ownership of industry not merely on a municipal but on a national scale.

THE SOCIAL DEMOCRATIC FEDERATION

THIS HOWEVER was beginning to be suggested by certain active Radicals who in 1881 banded together to form the Democratic (later, Social Democratic) Federation, to which, in spite of its later decline and humiliation, must belong the credit of being the first Socialist political organization in England. The S.D.F. frankly declared its opposition to 'landlord and capitalist parties' and Hyndman, who presided over the inaugural conference, professed himself a Socialist. The Federation was largely discredited after two candidates had been admitted to have been financed by the Conservative Party in the election of 1885. The votes cast for these two candidates—27 and 32 respectively—show how far from accepting Socialist ideas were the voters of the day, and as Bernard Shaw commented shortly afterwards, 'It is hard to say which cut the more foolish figure, the Tories who had spent their money for nothing—at a cost of eight pounds a vote—or the Socialists who had sacrificed their reputation for worse than nothing'.

In the Social Democratic Federation itself three groups of thinkers were to be found—those who thought Parliament useless, those who thought Parliament might be useful, but favoured concentrating for the present on the education of the working classes, and those who believed in gradual permeation of all parties. Similar difficulties overtook Labour Electoral Associations which were set up by the Trades Union Congress, some members arguing that membership should be confined to working men, whatever their political views, others arguing that co-operation with the middle classes was desirable, and a third group pressing for a distinctively Socialist movement. In the midst of these dissensions came the election of Keir Hardie to Parliament. The son of a miner, he had been brought up in a one-roomed cottage amid every circumstance of degrading poverty, and had been dismissed from his work for presiding over a meeting called to agitate for better working conditions. In consequence no mine-owner in Scotland would give him work and Hardie learned by his own experience that Liberal claims to be concerned with the liberty of the working man were the merest hypocrisy. He perceived, long before the majority of contemporary Socialists, that 'what the capitalist class fears is not neurotic shouting, but steady, plodding, undermining work, which will bring the whole structure about their heads'.

KEIR HARDIE GOES TO PARLIAMENT

BY 1888, when Hardie first stood, unsuccessfully, for election to Parliament, the working class were being driven into that very class consciousness that their employers feared. In 1886 had occurred the famous attack on the windows of London clubs, whose members had jeered at a procession of unemployed passing below. In 1887 came 'Bloody Sunday' when a demonstration in Trafalgar Square was charged by the police. The great Dock Strike, when for the first time the prosperous half of London learned how the other half lived, assisted the process of conversion. In 1892 Keir Hardie was elected as the first Independent Labour M.P. His arrival in a cloth cap at Westminster horrified the governing classes, and rightly; the day of the Lib-Labs and the Tory working man was past; the working-class M.P. with a working-class programme had arrived.

THE INDEPENDENT LABOUR PARTY

It was Keir Hardie who in 1893 presided over the conference which
created an organization much more challenging than the S.D.F. which
had by this time already embarked on its career of internal division. This
organization was the Independent Labour Party, which deliberately
restricted membership to those who subscribed to its principles, defined
in the classic Socialist phrase as 'to secure the collective ownership of the
means of production, distribution, and exchange'. The practical programme of the I.L.P. called for an eight-hour working day and public
provision for the sick and aged, with educational opportunities right up
to the university for poor children. Where the London Working Men's
Association and the Social Democratic Federation had been vague about
their beliefs, and had tended to be diverted into the profitless channels
of speculation about land taxation, and where Chamberlain and Bradlaugh
had never been more than advanced radicals, the I.L.P. was firm and
definite. It was a Socialist Party, and as such it attracted some 11,000
members in the following five years. By 1899, however, it was obvious
that it would never be able to secure the election of candidates to Parliament without the help of a much larger and wealthier body; that body
could only be the Trades Union Congress.

The I.L.P. did achieve some successes. It was responsible for securing
the election of some sixty progressives as town councillors and another
considerable body to the newly created School Boards. In these positions
the new members proved effective both as propagandists and reformers,
for they were supplied with irrefutable facts and with practical and well-
drafted policies from the newly created research and discussion group
known as the Fabian Society.

THE FABIAN SOCIETY

The Fabians are the third of the Socialist groups whose fusion with the
Trades Union Congress created the Labour Party. They took their name
from that of the Roman general who had won his battles by cautiously
waiting until his enemy's defences were undermined and then striking
hard. The society was originally founded, though with different aims,
in 1883. The young Bernard Shaw joined it in the following year and,
in his own phrase, 'roped in' a highly-gifted sociologist, Sidney Webb.
The Fabians were at first no more than forty strong since from the beginning the Fabians insisted they were a discussion group of intellectuals and
not a mass political organization. While agreeing with Marx that econo-

mic development was inevitably socializing society, they opposed revolution and class war, and looked to the capture rather than to the overthrow of the existing system. They favoured two lines of approach to the problem of socializing Britain—first, by permeation of all existing parties and groups, especially those, such as local councils, with remedial powers, but also to a lesser extent avowedly hostile societies such as the Conservative Party. Second, they desired the creation of a specifically workers' party, not necessarily collectivist, but expressing the workers' point of view. Although right up to 1900 the Fabians never numbered more than a thousand, their influence as a formative agent on British Socialism was overwhelming. Their great advance was not only in openly professing collectivism—'The Fabian Society is composed of Socialists' declared their leaflets—but also in advancing practical programmes which local, and especially London, councils could carry into effect. To the fire and enthusiasm of the S.D.F. and the I.L.P. were now added the searching logic and incomparable knowledge of the Webbs. They studied the existing machinery of government, and pointed out exactly what could be done without legislative action; they explored to the full the limits of existing laws, and where present legislation was inadequate they prepared tracts which contained a summary of the existing machinery and definite proposals so drafted that they could be carried to the statute book without a word of amendment. From 1889 these valuable tracts began to appear. Their changing titles are an indication of the strengthening of resolve in the Fabian ranks. Tract number 1 asked the searching question: 'Why are the many poor?' Later tracts—number 5, with 'Facts for Socialists', number 9 with 'The Eight Hours Bill', number 39, with 'A Democratic Budget' —gave the answer and provided the remedy.

Nor were the Webbs mere statisticians. Their tracts often became indignant and eloquent. Both the Liberal and Conservative Parties, they declared, were 'guilty of the conspiracy of hypocrisy' in governing in the interest of the same class. They spoke of the tendency of the governing class to 'screw revenue out of the poor before the idle rich are touched' and, in pleading for land nationalization, appealed to the Biblical strain in many of the early Socialists with a phrase used by the Levellers of the seventeenth century, 'The earth is the Lord's and therefore not the landlord's'. The Fabians saw, long before most other reformers of the time, that to secure reform the workers must found their own party. It was a conclusion to which the Independent Labour Party was slowly being driven; it was a view which the Social Democratic Federation had come near to accepting, and now, at the very end of the nineteenth century, the new party came into being.

THE SCENE IN THE NINETIES

CONDITIONS WERE ripe for this act of creation. The death of Gladstone had removed from working-class voters one great reason for supporting the Liberal Party; Joseph Chamberlain had drifted into the ranks of the Conservatives, and among the vast mass of trade unionists there was general discontent with the invariable succession of booms and slumps which marked the course of the last decades of the nineteenth century. Among the intellectuals of all parties the Fabians had done their magnificent work; among the working classes, Robert Blatchford's *Clarion* had made politics comprehensible, had made them personal, had made them a matter of immediate concern to everyone who could read. 'Clarion Clubs' formed of young Socialist cyclists spread across the countryside the message of good fellowship for the present and a new hope for the future. Blatchford's 'Letters to John Smith', an imaginary workman, which appeared week by week in the *Clarion*, form the best simple statement of Socialist doctrine which has ever been written, and reprinted as *Merrie England* sold a million copies in little more than a year. Among the literary classes William Morris's plea for a more just and beautiful social order had a comparable effect; the passionate sincerity of the early Socialists, pleading not for their personal advancement but for the improvement of their fellow men, inevitably had its effect upon all those open to conversion. The followers of Henry George, whose book *Progress and Poverty*, appearing in 1879, traced the injustice of present society to the private ownership of land, helped to swell the Socialist ranks. The Christian Socialist Movement was another ally, the more important in that it could reach those who might have been frightened by purely political arguments. Individual Anglican priests in all parts of the country testified to their faith that the doctrines of the New Testament were the doctrines of Socialism—that there was a hope for man not only in the next world, but also in this, while the 'pleasant Sunday afternoons' in which the nonconformist churches delighted became a valuable instrument of political education. Among Roman Catholics, the influence of Cardinal Manning, who worked so heroically on the side of the strikers during the great Dock Strike of 1889, had left its mark. It was a cardinal belief of the early Socialists that the truths of their faith were so obvious and their superiority to all others, on moral as well as on economic grounds, so apparent, that once the voter had been persuaded to think for himself the battle was won.

While this campaign of intellectual enlightenment had a great effect, it would have been powerless without more practical lessons; these also

were to be seen in the history of the fifteen years since the Social Democratic Federation had first exposed its frail being to the light. The great
Dock Strike had left among the working classes a great confidence in
their own powers of bargaining; Blatchford, Keir Hardie, MacDonald,
and the Webbs had driven home the lesson that bargaining could better
be done on the floor of the House of Commons with a great body of
voters behind the working-class representatives than in the employer's
room at some factory with only the workers' own immediate labour to
strengthen their arguments. The Liberal Party was fatally split by the
great division of opinion first over Home Rule and then over the South
African War. The Lib-Labs had proved that working men could reach
Parliament, but had demonstrated that so long as they were not really
independent they could do little but support the measures proposed by
the majority of the Liberal Party. Thus it came about that in 1889 the
Trades Union Congress carried a motion to empower its Parliamentary
Committee to hold a conference of all interested bodies with a view to
increasing working-class representation in Parliament.

THE LABOUR REPRESENTATION COMMITTEE

THE CONFERENCE so convened consisted of 139 representatives from
various trade unions, numbering about 376,000 affiliated members, and
from the three Socialist societies—the S.D.F., the I.L.P., and the Fabians,
whose membership totalled about 23,000. The conference was faced with
the familiar difficulty as to whether it should whole-heartedly support a
class war, whether it should co-operate with sympathizers of all classes
and all parties, or whether it should support only those who belonged to
organizations affiliated to the conference. The third course, which was
advocated by Keir Hardie, was the one adopted. It was also decided that
membership of the organization, and service in Parliament, should not
be restricted to those of working-class origin. The new movement was
thus from the beginning to be based on all classes, though, as with all
political parties, its main voting strength would have to be drawn from
the working class. The doctrine of the class war was rejected by the conference, which adopted the characteristically English belief in democratic
methods held by the other two parties. A resolution that the party should
have as its ultimate aim the 'socialization of the means of production,
distribution, and exchange' was also rejected, and Keir Hardie's alternative accepted—that the party would strive to promote and support
legislation in the direct interest of labour.

With the ground thus cleared, the conference proceeded to create a new body called the Labour Representation Committee, which six years later adopted the name of the Labour Party. This Committee consisted of seven trade union representatives, two delegates each from the Independent Labour Party and the Social Democratic Federation, and one from the Fabians, and thus represented that happy fusion of the Socialist societies with the voting power of the trade unions which has continued ever since. Ramsay MacDonald was elected first secretary of the Committee. Thus on the 27th of February 1900, in the Memorial Hall, Farringdon Street, London, the Labour Party came into being, with a leadership of twelve (later reduced to eleven by the defection of the S.D.F., which retired to pursue arid Marxist speculation) and a membership of less than 400,000, of whom fewer than 25,000 acknowledged themselves to be Socialists.

Ramsay MacDonald, who was thus launched on his career as the first, and so far the last, man of working-class origins to reach Downing Street, was brought up in extreme poverty as the illegitimate son of a Scottish farm labourer and was rescued by an intelligent schoolmaster, who sent him to be trained as a pupil teacher. Since that time he had elevated himself by his own efforts—first, by becoming secretary to a Liberal M.P., second, by marrying a woman of intelligence and social position, and third, by fighting an election as an unsuccessful Independent Labour Party candidate. He was present at the Conference as one of the I.L.P. delegates and attracted attention by his fine speaking voice and remarkable platform presence, on which there is general agreement, even among his most hostile critics. The deliberate imprecision of his talk, which proved so infuriating in later years, perhaps helped to conceal from those present at the Conference on the one hand that he was much less Socialistic than the Socialists would have liked, and on the other, that he was far more Socialistic than the trade unions would have approved.

The new party's appearance was greeted by a notable lack of enthusiasm. The newspapers ignored the occasion and the trade unions tended in many cases to continue to believe that their business was to better the conditions of their own members without indulging in political activity, except in so far as it furthered that end, and then only through the innocuous Lib-Lab M.P.s who were themselves virtually Liberals. There was also considerable hostility to all officials who were not of working-class origin.

The two leading members of the new Labour Representation Committee were however unquestionably Socialists, as were the I.L.P. members and the Fabians, but the process of converting the trade unions to any programme more ambitious than one of selfish sectional advancement seemed likely to be a long one. At this point the House of Lords intervened. Acting in its judicial capacity, it decided by the Taff Vale decision of 1901 that trade unions were financially liable for any acts committed by their members. This verdict had the effect of making the trade unions, if not illegal, at least powerless; it deprived them of the strike weapon, and left them in a position more defenceless than any they had occupied since 1870. In consequence, membership of the L.R.C. leapt up at a remarkable speed. Organized Labour found itself compelled to fight for its existence at the polls, and took as its instrument the humble Committee which it had so far largely despised. That which no Socialist writer or orator could achieve was effected by the judges. They called into existence the Parliamentary Labour Party.

At the election of 1900 the L.R.C. had put up two successful candidates —one of them Keir Hardie, the other a man who later joined the Liberals —who served in a House containing no fewer than 402 Conservatives, against only 176 Liberals and 8 Lib-Labs. In the General Election six years later the L.R.C. was able to make an understanding with the Liberals by which L.R.C. and Liberal candidates united for the moment, the Liberals agreeing to support the Labour movement for legislation to annul the effects of the Taff Vale decision. The great landslide of this year is famous in electoral history; 130 Tories returned to Westminster, 375 Liberals, 83 Irish Nationalists, 24 Lib-Labs, of whom 13 could be relied on to support the Labour members, and 29 L.R.C. members. It is significant however that of this twenty-nine only five had been engaged in anything other than a straight fight with the Conservatives; nor had the Labour Party fought the election on a Socialist programme, and the old S.D.F., which did so, as it was by this time independent, put up thirteen candidates, all of whom were decisively defeated.

The Annual Report of the Labour Representation Committee presented at the 1906 conference was justly jubilant. 'The wage-earners', it stated, 'have at last declared in favour of definite, united, independent political action, and we can rejoice in an electoral triumph which, having regard to all the circumstances, can safely be pronounced as phenomenal. We can congratulate ourselves to-day that a real, live, independent Labour Party, with its own chairman and its own Whips, is now an accomplished fact in British politics.' This confidence would seem to have been justified. There were forty-two reliable Labour members in the 1906 House of Commons against two in that of 1900, and the membership of the L.R.C. itself had risen to 900,000—or more than double what it had been six years before. In this year the Labour Representation Committee officially adopted the name of 'Labour Party'.

THE LABOUR PARTY 1906–14

THE FOLLOWING eight years, 1906–14, however, proved difficult for the new party. In the great Liberal reforming ministries the Labour members were divided; the social legislation which Lloyd George was determined to carry through, and notably the National Insurance Act of 1911, seemed to some the first instalment of Socialism, and to others the first step towards the 'servile state'. They argued that unemployment and health insurance should be effected at the cost of heavier taxation on the wealthy and not by means of contributions from the poor. The more extreme Socialists argued that Lloyd George, by removing the worst effects of the capitalist system, was making it more difficult for them to bring in a really drastic programme of reform. These difficulties were intensified after the elections of 1910, when the Liberals and Tories had almost exactly equal strength, and the Labour members, forty-two strong, held the balance of power. They dared not vote against the government for fear that they might let in the Tories and prevent the passing of the Parliament Act—though they did make use of the occasion to attempt to abolish the House of Lords altogether. The presence of a small and active group of Socialists, ably led, acted as a spur to the Liberal Party, which until the advent of organized labour had slumbered happily in the belief that the reforms of Mr Gladstone were the final concessions necessary to content the working classes. The Trade Disputes Act gave the unions their cherished rights of protection of the funds and of the right to strike, and this victory enormously increased the prestige of the Labour Party inside the Trade Union Movement. Some beginnings were also made in setting up machinery for unemployment relief, for workmen's compensation, old-age pensions, and school meals, and one of the remaining points of the Chartists' old programme was carried into law with the passing of the Bill to secure the payment of members.

Nevertheless the Labour Party did not continue the electoral gains which it had made up to 1906, and in 1914 its numbers in the Commons had been slightly reduced, to thirty-eight. This was partly due to the decision of the Liberals from December 1910 to treat Labour in the country, though not in the House, as a hostile party, and hence to end the electoral alliance on which the Labour Party had risen to its respectable membership in the Commons. Another factor was a second judicial judgment, second in importance only to Taff Vale—that named after Osborne, a foreman railway porter at Clapham Junction, who contested the right of his trade union to provide funds for the Labour Party, of which he strongly disapproved. The case, financed on Osborne's side by outside interests, was fought through every court to the House of Lords, who expressed the opinion that trade unions had no right to use their members' funds for political purposes. The immediate consequence was a series of law-suits against certain trade unions, with a drop, speedily regained, in Labour Party membership. The effects of the Osborne Judgment were redressed by the Trade Union Act of 1913, but the necessary loyalty of the Labour members to the minority Liberal Government tended to obscure its separate identity and distinctive programme. There was also a general increase in disillusionment with the achievements of the Labour Party, which did not seem to have fulfilled the high hopes expressed in the flush of success in 1906. A large number of Socialists in the Labour Party thought alliance with the trade unions would result in the programme adopted being always too timid to deserve the name of Socialist, while many trade unionists were profoundly suspicious, not merely of the party's intellectuals, but of all parliamentary action, which seemed to have done less for the working classes than direct industrial action by the unions. The party was also divided on the question of the German menace, about which Blatchford began to agitate, thus offending the many pacifist members, and on that of support for the militant suffragettes. Most serious of all, the leadership was either not suited to parliamentary work, as was the case with Keir Hardie, or not genuinely Socialist, as was already the case with MacDonald. As anyone who has listened to a supposedly 'Right-wing' Labour candidate trying to present the Socialist case will realize, this was a grave defect, for passionate sincerity and an idealistic belief in the goodness of man and the possibility of transforming, and not merely reforming, his life by parliamentary action are, quite apart from their moral worth, valuable electoral assets. These factors produced in the Labour Party a dangerous spirit of frustration, and the enormous increase in numbers which took place during these years must not be taken as evidence of a sudden and startling conversion to Socialism of the mass of the working class. In 1907 trade union membership of the Labour Party was over a million and that of the Socialist societies, although the S.D.F. had long since withdrawn, 22,000. By 1912 trade union membership had risen to 1,858,000 and 31,000 from the societies, and in 1915 the total membership of the Labour Party was 2,093,000, of whom the Socialist societies—the Fabians and the Independent Labour Party—were 33,200, a body whose importance was out of all proportion to their numbers. (In 1949 the total membership was 5,700,000, of whom individual members and Socialist and Co-operative Societies formed 770,000.)

In 1918, the year in which the first declaration of its Socialist objectives was written into the constitution of the party, and thus made an essential article of the faith to be accepted by every Labour candidate, the Labour Party was successful in only fifty-seven constituencies, in spite of the widening of the suffrage which had almost doubled the electorate. In 1922 it won 142 seats and in 1923, 191, thus definitely eclipsing the Liberals with their 158, though still second to the Conservatives. Early in 1924 the first Labour Government took office, dependent for its day-to-day existence on Liberal support. It fell a few months later, after accomplishing some useful but minor reforms, and in the resulting election its parliamentary strength was reduced to 151, the Liberals at last being swept off the political stage, on which they had ceased to have any part to play, and reduced to a trivial rump of forty-two members—the exact number of supporters of the Parliamentary Labour Party in 1906, when it had first begun its rapid climb to power. The main issue in the election was the 'Zinoviev letter'—a document purporting to show that the Russian Government, with whom the Labour Government had had close relations, was intending to organize revolution in Britain. The Government's domestic policy was not largely in dispute. Five years later, in 1929, the Labour Party was returned as the largest single party in the House of Commons, with 288 seats, while the Liberals could summon up only fifty-seven members. Two years later MacDonald betrayed his colleagues and his party, throwing away the position it had won and its hopes of applying effective, since Socialist, measures to the grave economic situation, in exchange for a few more months of office for himself. MacDonald may well have believed, as did many of his contemporaries, that he had destroyed the Labour Party by his desertion of it. He was mistaken; he had only destroyed himself and a few years later was driven from office by his new allies.

The catastrophic election of 1931 swept the number of Labour M.P.s back to an almost pre-war figure—forty-six, but this was increased in the election of 1935 to 154, and a further ten years later, in 1945, to 393, a number making it possible for the Labour Party for the first time to govern as it wished. This figure was reduced in 1950, partly as a result of an unfavourable redistribution of seats, to 315, although the Labour Party remained in power, with a clear majority over all other parties combined—the Liberals by this time being a trivial and divided remnant of nine.

The increase in the number of votes cast for Labour candidates is perhaps a better indication of increasing strength than the number of members returned. The Labour vote was 63,000 in 1900, 320,000 in 1906, 500,000 in January 1910, 2,500,000 in 1918, 4,250,000 in 1922, 4,300,000 in 1923, and, in spite of the great decrease in the number of Labour candidates returned in 1924, it increased in that year to 5,500,000, climbing in 1945 to just over 12,000,000, and in 1951 achieving a peak of 13,950,000—the largest number of votes ever cast for any party in any British General Election.

LABOUR IN POWER

THE PARLIAMENTARY LABOUR PARTY met in 1945 in an atmosphere of enthusiasm and hope, which was to be largely justified by its enormous achievements in the next five years. The economic principles of Socialism were vindicated by the nationalization of many basic industries, including coal, transport, and electricity, while its moral principles were demonstrated by the creation of a Health Service in which class barriers had no place and need was for the first time the only criterion of treatment. Equality of opportunity was to a limited extent established by far-reaching educational reforms, and the declaration of St Paul that Christians were 'members one of another' found practical expression in insurance schemes in which the fit helped the sick, in taxation by means of which the rich parent paid for the poor man's child to reach the university. The Government which in February 1950 'went to the country' had served the nation well. Its reforms had been more numerous and more extensive than those of any previous ministry and it had proved that the Labour Party could govern much more competently than the capitalist parties, that state intervention, by abolishing unemployment and poverty, was not the enemy of liberty but its protector. It was as important a discovery on the political plane as that of Francis Thompson in *The Hound of Heaven* had been on the religious one—that the hand of God was outstretched over the individual not to stifle and destroy but to strengthen and console. Not the least of the Government's achievements was the conversion of the other two parties to a degree of belief in Socialism which would have been impossible only a few years before; the Liberal and Conservative Parties vied with each other in claims to have created the Welfare State, which they had failed to develop when in office and had largely opposed when the Labour Party at last obtained power.

Inevitably there were failures: the newly nationalized industries were saddled with vast burdens towards the former shareholders, who continued to enjoy a revenue from other men's labour, without even the most nominal risk attaching to the security of their possessions, and who were awarded compensation on the un-Socialist principle not of need but of the size of their former holdings; the rich continued to be able to buy a special type of education for their children, thus gravely retarding the destruction of the old barriers between the classes; most surprising of all, despite a feeble and complicated substitute measure, the land was left in private hands, so that those in most urgent need of new homes sometimes found the rent beyond their means, because of large sums paid to those who claimed to own the land on which the houses were to be built —a claim which would have been incomprehensible to all the early Socialists.

The results of the General Election of 1950 were disappointing, largely as a result of a redistribution of seats which the Government had made to its own grave disadvantage, and the 315 Labour members returned enjoyed a majority of only five over the other parties, the Liberals holding nine seats and the Conservatives 298. In spite of all the resulting difficulties the Government rightly carried out its promise to nationalize the iron and steel industry.

Memories of 1924 and 1931 were too recent for the Labour Party to feel at ease in a situation in which it possessed office without real power. It was no surprise when after only eighteen months the Government went to the country. Its decision was, however, taken at an unfortunate time for the party; failures in foreign affairs had clouded the preceding weeks and the undertaking of a huge rearmament programme, partly financed by a violation of the essential Socialist principle of a free health service, had led to the resignation of several ministers and to divisions within the party. Among the electorate there was a widespread feeling of irritation at the continuing shortages and restrictions produced by the world situation, and the fact of Labour's defeat was less surprising than the smallness of the Conservative majority—seventeen over all other parties. The Liberals held six seats, the Labour Party 294. In spite of this serious setback, the Labour Party had achieved the highest poll in its history— close on fourteen million votes—a total which surpassed that of the victorious Conservatives.

A notable feature of the election was that marginal seats held by the so-called 'Left-wing rebels' were retained without exception, although 'orthodox' members, with similar majorities, were going down before the storm. Foreign commentators pointed out that as the campaign progressed more and more candidates adopted what had been supposed to be a specifically 'Left-wing' point of view and on the morrow of the election there was general agreement that the Labour Party would now come to adopt as its official policy those opinions which had so recently been branded as heresies. These expectations are likely to be fulfilled: as early as the 1906 election it had been pointed out that timidity on the hustings was fatal to a Labour candidate and that the attempt to please all the electors merely resulted in the alienation of one's own loyal supporters. The people appreciate a 'connected' politician and when, as in October 1951, they desire an unadventurous government they will turn to the Conservative Party. It would be disastrous for the future of Socialism in Britain if this defeat were to be made the occasion for any dilution of the Socialist faith.

For it is impossible for a Socialist to evade the conclusion he must draw from the study of the rise of the Labour Party in the last fifty years, unpalatable as it must be to those of other views—namely that the main reason for the triumph of Socialism has been that Socialism was right. Gladstone spoke as far back as 1866 of the social forces 'which move onward in their might and majesty and which are marshalled on our side'. He could hardly have foreseen that within less than a century those forces would destroy his party and sweep another into office in its place. Keir Hardie was more clear-sighted; his verdict, true of that devoted handful who elected him in 1892, is no less true to-day, if we hold firm to the faith to whose service he devoted his life. For the Labour Party is, as Hardie said of those who held its views, eight years before it came into being: 'Simply a straightforward, honest, dignified movement, self-supporting and self-contained, marching forward irresistibly to a self-assured triumph.'

1. The Growth of an Idea

When Adam delved and Eve span,
Who was then the gentleman?

John Ball

THE FIRST SOCIALIST MEETINGS? (1381)

THE UNHAPPY PEOPLE of these said counties [Kent, Sussex, Essex, and Bedfordshire] began to stir, because they said they were kept in great bondage, and in the beginning of the world, they said, there were no bondmen, wherefore they maintained that none ought to be bond, without he did treason to his lord; but that they were men formed to the similitude of their lords, saying why should they then be kept so under, like beasts; the which they said they would no longer suffer, for they would be all one. . . . And of this imagination was a foolish priest in the county of Kent, called John Ball. For this priest used oftentimes on the Sundays after mass, when the people were going out of the minster, to go into the cloister and preach, and make the people to assemble about him, and would say thus:

'My good people: Things cannot go well in England, nor ever will, until all goods are held in common, and until there will be neither serfs nor gentlemen, and we shall all be equal. For what reason have they, whom we call lords, got the best of us? How did they deserve it? Why do they keep us in bondage? If we all descended from one father and one mother, Adam and Eve, how can they assert or prove that they are more masters than ourselves? Except perhaps that they make us work and produce for them to spend! They are clothed in velvet and in coats garnished with ermine and fur, while we wear coarse linen. They have wine, spices, and good bread, while we get rye-bread, offal, straw and water. They have residences, handsome manors, and we the trouble and the work, and must brave the rain and the wind in the fields. And it is from us and our labour that they get the means to support their pomp; yet we are called serfs and are promptly beaten, if we fail to do their bidding.'

Thus John Ball said on Sundays, when the people moved out of the churches in the villages. Wherefore many of the mean people loved him, and such as intended to no goodness, said how he said truth; and so they

28

would murmur one with another in the field and in the ways as they went
together; affirming how John Ball said truth.

Froissart's Chronicles

SOCIALISM IN UTOPIA

Now I have declared and described to you, as truly as I could, the form
and order of that commonwealth, which truly in my judgement is not
only the best, but also that which alone of good right may claim and take
upon it the name of a commonwealth or state. For in other places they
speak still of the commonwealth; but every man procures his own private
wealth. Here where nothing is private, the common affairs be earnestly
looked upon. And truly on both parts they have good cause so to do as
they do. For in other countries who knows not that he shall not starve
for hunger, unless he makes some several provision for himself, though
the commonwealth flourish never so much in riches? And therefore he is
compelled, even of very necessity, to have regard to himself rather than
to the people, that is to say, to others. Contrariwise, there where all things
be common to every man, it is not to be doubted that any man shall lack
any thing necessary for his private uses, so that the common store houses
and barns be sufficiently stored. For there nothing is distributed after a
niggardly sort, neither there is any poor man or beggar. And though no
man have anything, yet every man is rich. For what can be more rich
than to live joyfully and merrily without all grief and pensiveness; not
caring for his own living, nor vexed or troubled with his wife's impor-
tunate complaints, nor dreading poverty for his son, nor sorrowing for
his daughter's dowry? Yea, they take no care at all for the living and
wealth of themselves and all theirs; or their wives, their children, their
nephews, their children's children and all the succession that ever shall
follow in their posterity. And yet, besides this, there is no less provision
for them that were once labourers and be now weak and impotent, than
for them that do now labour and take pain.

Here now would I see if any man dare be so bold, as to compare with
this equity the justice of other nations. Among whom, I forsake God, if
I can find any sign or token of equity and justice. For what justice is this,
that a rich goldsmith or a usurer, or, to be short, any of them, which
either do nothing at all; or else that which they do is such, that it is not
very necessary to the commonwealth; should have a pleasant and a wealthy
living, either by idleness or by unnecessary business? When in the meantime poor labourers, carters, ironsmiths, carpenters and ploughmen by so
great and continual toil, as drawing and bearing beasts be scarcely able to

sustain; and again so necessary toil that without it no commonwealth were able to continue and endure one year; do yet get so hard and poor a living and live so wretched and miserable a life, that the state and condition of the labouring beasts may seem much better and wealthier. For they be not put to so continual labour, nor their living is not much worse; yea, to them much pleasanter; taking no thought in the meantime for the time to come. But these silly poor wretches be presently tormented with barren and unfruitful labour. And the remembrance of their poor indigent and beggarly old age killeth them up. For their daily wage is so little that it will not suffice for the same day; much less will it yield any over-plus, that may daily be laid up for the relief of old age.

Is not this an unjust and an unkind state, which gives great fees and rewards to gentlemen as they call them, and to goldsmiths, and to such other, which be other idle persons or else only flatterers, and devisers of vain pleasures; and on the other hand makes no gentle provision for poor ploughmen, colliers, labourers, carters, ironsmiths and carpenters; without whom no commonwealth can continue. But when it has abused the labours of their lusty and flowering age, at the last, when they be op-pressed with old age, and sickness, being needy, poor and indigent of all things; then, forgetting their so many painful watchings, not remember-ing their so many and so great benefits; recompenseth and acquitteth them most unkindly with miserable death. And yet besides this the rich men not only by private fraud, but also by common laws, do every day pluck and snatch away from the poor some part of their daily living. So, where as it seemed before unjust to recompense with unkindness their pains that have been beneficial to the state, now they have to this their wrong and unjust dealing (which is yet a much worse point) given the name of justice, yea and that by force of a law.

Therefore when I consider and weigh in my mind all these states which nowadays anywhere flourish, so God help me, I can perceive nothing but a certain conspiracy of rich men, procuring their own commodities under the name and title of the state. They invent and devise all means and crafts, first how to keep safely without fear of losing what they have un-justly gathered together; and next how to hire and abuse the work and labour of the poor for as little money as may be. These devices when the rich men have decreed to be kept and observed . . . then they be made laws.

Sir Thomas More, *Utopia*, 1515

THE POOREST HE . . .

I hear it said that it's a huge alteration in bringing in of new laws, and that this kingdom hath been under this government ever since it was a kingdom. If writings be true there have been many scufflings between the honest men of England and those that have tyrannised over them; and if it be true what I have read, there is none of those just and equitable laws that the people of England are born to but are entrenchments on the once enjoyed privileges of their rulers altogether. . . . But even if they were those which the people have been always under, if the people find that they are not suitable to freemen as they are, I know no reason that should deter me, either in what I must answer before God or the world, from endeavouring by all means to gain anything that might be of more advantage to them than the government under which they live. . . .

. . . For really I think that the poorest he that is in England has a life to live, as the greatest he; and therefore truly, sir, I think it's clear that every man that is to live under a government ought first by his own consent to put himself under that government and I do think that the poorest man in England is not at all bound in a strict sense to that government that he hath not had a voice to put himself under. . . .

Thomas Rainborough, Colonel in Cromwell's Army, during the debate at Putney, October 1647

NO POWER BUT THE PEOPLE

The only and sole legislative law-making power is originally inherent in the people, and derivately in their commissions chosen by themselves by common consent and no other. In which the poorest that lives hath as true a right to give a vote as well as the richest and greatest.

John Lilburne, December 1646

AN EXPERIMENT IN SOCIALISM, 1800

When to my friends and nearest connections I mentioned that my intentions were to commence a new system of management on principles of justice and kindness . . . they one and all smiled at what they called my simplicity.

I entered upon the government of New Lanark in 1800—I say 'government', for my intention was not to be a mere manager of cotton mills, as such mills were at the time generally managed, but to introduce principles in the conduct of the people . . . and to change the conditions of the people, who I saw were surrounded by circumstances having an injurious influence upon the character of the entire population of New Lanark.

[By 1816] I was making great and substantial progress with my New Lanark experiment. I had now completed . . . the first institution for the formation of the infant and child character—the infants being received into it at one year old. . . . In addition there were day schools for all under 12 years old.

I also organised arrangements to supply all the wants of the population, buying everything for money on a large scale in the first markets, and supplying them at first cost and charges. They had previously been necessitated to buy inferior articles, highly adulterated at enormous prices, making their purchases at small grocery and grog shops, chiefly on credit; and their butcher's meat was generally little better than skin and bone. By the time the arrangements to provide for the whole circle of their wants in food, clothing, etc, were completed, some of the larger families were earning two pounds per week, and the heads of these families told me that my new arrangements to supply their wants saved them in price ten shillings weekly; beside the great difference between deteriorated and the most inferior qualities and the best unadulterated articles.

The Life of Robert Owen, by Himself, 1857

HANDS OFF FREE ENTERPRISE!

Children at this time [1815] were admitted into the cotton, wool, flax and silk mills at six and sometimes at five years of age. The time of working, winter and summer, was unlimited by law, but usually it was 14 hours per day—in some 15, and even, by the most inhuman and avaricious, 16 hours—and in many cases the mills were artificially heated to a high state most unfavourable to health.

The first plea of the objectors to my Bill [to regulate hours of work] was that masters ought not to be interfered with by the legislature in any way, in the management of their business.

The Life of Robert Owen, by Himself, 1857

A SOCIALIST MAKES HIS WILL

. . . These are my views and feelings in quitting an existence that has been chequered with the plagues and pleasures of a competitive, scrambling, selfish system; a system by which the moral and social aspirations of the noblest human beings are nullified by incessant toil and physical deprivations; by which, indeed, all men are trained to be either slaves, hypocrites

or criminals. Hence my ardent attachment to the principles of that great
and good man—ROBERT OWEN. I quit this world with a true conviction that his system is the only true road to human emancipation; that
it is, indeed, the only just system for regulating the affairs of honest,
intelligent human beings—the only one yet made known to the world,
that is based on truth, justice and equality. While the land, machines,
tools, implements of production, and produce of man's toil, are exclusively in possession of the do-nothings; and labour is the sole possession
of the wealth-producers—a marketable commodity, bought up and
directed by wealthy idlers—never-ending misery must be their inevitable
lot.

Henry Hetherington, *Last Will and Testament*, 1849

THE PROFIT MOTIVE, 1835

1835. It was a terrible winter. . . . The scenes I witnessed then made an
indelible impression on my mind. I have often told the Tories 'You
caused the iron to enter into my soul very young, and you will never
draw it out. . . . It will remain there till I die.'

There was corn enough for everybody, that was the hard, cruel part of
it, but those who owned it would not sell out when it was so sorely
needed. They kept it back, they locked it up; and all the time the folk
were crying out in their extremity for bread—crying out to men who
hardened their hearts and turned deaf ears to the hungry cries of their
starving fellow-creatures. To make as much money as they could, by
letting corn rise to famine prices, was all the owners of it cared about.
'Make money at any price' was their motto. They belonged to the class
of men who always try to turn to their own profit the miseries, the misfortunes, and the helplessness of their poorer neighbours. They grew
fat at the expense of their fellows. Those who ruled in high places, and
had the making of the laws in their hands, were chiefly rich landowners
and successful traders, and instead of trying to raise the people, create a
higher standard of comfort and well being, and better their general condition, they did their best—or worst—to keep them in a state of poverty
and serfdom, of dependence and wretchedness. Those who owned and
held the land believed, and acted up to their belief as far as they were
able, that the land belonged to the rich man only, that the poor man had
no part nor lot in it, and had no sort of claim on society.

If a poor man dared to marry and have children, they thought he had
no right to claim the necessary food wherewith to keep himself and his
family alive. They thought, too, every mother's son of them, that, when

B

a labourer could no longer work, he had lost the right to live. Work was all they wanted from him; he was to work and hold his tongue, year in and year out, early and late, and if he could not work, why, what was the use of him? It was what he was made for, to labour and toil for his betters, without complaint, on a starvation wage. When no more work could be squeezed out of him he was no better than a cumberer of other folk's ground, and the proper place for such as he was the churchyard, where he would be sure to lie quiet under a few feet of earth, and want neither food nor wages any more. A quick death and a cheap burying—that was the motto of those extortioners for the poor man past work.

Joseph Arch, *The Story of his Life, by Himself*, 1898

THE RIGHTS OF 'ROBBERY'

What seek the Trades Unions? Increases of wages and a diminution of the hours of labour; that is to say, to work less, and to get more for it. . . . Who does not see that this is to attack 'property'? . . . Common sense tells us that the more the producers get, the less is left for the men of profits. . . . But do *we* find fault with this? Far from it! To attack 'property' is to attack robbery . . . how are we to attack him in the safest and most expeditious manner? . . . we cannot attack him by law, for he holds the 'law' in his own hands. . . . In our opinion the Trades Unions have hit upon the best way of striking property on the head, provided only that they add Universal Suffrage to their present avowed objects.

The Poor Man's Guardian, December 1833

IN STEPS THE CAPITALIST

Betwixt him who produces food and him who produces clothing, betwixt him who makes instruments and him who uses them, in steps the capitalist, who neither makes nor uses them and appropriates to himself the produce of both. With as niggard a hand as possible he transfers to each a part of the produce of the other, keeping to himself the larger share. Gradually and successively has he insinuated himself betwixt them, expanding in bulk as he has been nourished by their increasingly productive labours, and separating them so widely from each other that neither can see whence that supply is drawn which each receives through the capitalist. While he despoils both, so completely does he exclude one from the view of the other that both believe they are indebted to him for subsistence. He is *middleman* of all labourers; and when we compare what the skilled labour of England produces, with the produce of the untutored labour of the Irish peasantry, the middlemen of England cannot be considered as inferior in their exactions to the middlemen of Ireland. They have been more fortunate, however, and while the latter are stigmatized as oppressors, the former are honoured as benefactors. Not only do they appropriate the produce of the labourer; but they have succeeded in persuading him that they are his benefactors and employers. At least such are the doctrines of political economy; and capitalists may well be pleased with a science which both justifies their claims and holds them up to our admiration, as the great means of civilising and improving the world. . . .

Thomas Hodgskin, Labour Defended, 1825

THE LIFE OF TOM PAINE

No-one could have prophesied a great future for Paine when he arrived in America in 1774. He was already 37 years old and his career had been singular but not promising. . . . He had been a sailor, a maker of ladies' stays, an exciseman, a schoolmaster; he had tried his hand at the evangelical novelty of lay preaching and appears to have been prevented from taking holy orders only by his ignorance of Latin. He had been a shopkeeper and gone bankrupt and had lost one wife. . . . In 1771 he married a second time and joined with his wife and her widowed mother in keeping a small shop and 'tobacco mill'. He spent much of his time in the White Hart tavern with a group of friends, with whom he composed humorous verses and patriotic songs. For the first time his ability seems to have been discovered, and he was chosen by his fellow excisemen to act as their spokesman in an agitation for higher wages and an improved status. . . . In 1787 Paine returned to Europe. . . . Early in 1791 Paine again crossed to France leaving the publication of the first part of the *Rights of Man* in the hands of his radical friends, Godwin, Holcroft and Holles. . . . He returned to England with Horne Tooke and other English Radicals and proceeded to organise meetings in favour of Republican principles and social reform. In 1792 the second part of the *Rights of Man* appeared. It was an elaboration and expansion of the principles laid down in Part I. Man's rights were of two kinds: some of them, such as the right to free thought and its expression, ought never to be interfered with in any way; others, such as the right to property whose value a man had enhanced by his labour, can only be secured by government regulation. Government, therefore, is an organisation for the control and security of those rights which men cannot secure for themselves without regulation. All governments except democratic republics are in the interests of a few. . . . Paine proceeded to an amazingly bold series of practical suggestions for a peaceful English revolution. Spence and Ogilvie had already put forward schemes of land nationalisation. Paine was less socialistic perhaps but more practical and he did not consider the landowner the only source of social evil.

He computed the population of England at about 7 million, and believed that if the Poor Law was abolished, the 4 million pounds thus saved would be sufficient for a grant of £4 per head to each child under 14 and a pension, beginning at £6 per annum for workers after the age of 50. The residue of the money saved could be spent in a grant for education, a maternity benefit of £1 at the birth of each child and the setting up of government work for the unemployed. This however was only a beginning. The abolition of sinecure offices and ultimately of kings and their courts would bring further revenue. Most productive of all, however, would be a graded estate duty which, beginning with an annual tax of 3d per pound on estates worth £500 a year would rise on each thousand pounds till it reached 20 shillings in the pound for all annual revenue over £23,000 a year. Thus an estate which brought in this sum annually would be taxed £10,630 by the State. Taxation of this kind would make indirect taxes unnecessary and ensure the property of the people. . . . What possible arguments, he asks, could his opponents bring against him? Would they dare to say that to 'provide against all the misfortunes to which human life is subject' by devoting the national revenue to their prevention 'is not a *good thing*'? Europe, in any case, had reached the end of aristocratic government which alone stood in the way of reform. But 'reason and discussion will soon bring things right, however wrong they may begin' and 'if the good to be obtained be worthy of a . . . rational and costless revolution, it would be bad policy to prefer waiting for a calamity which should force a violent one' . . . .

The book was an immediate success. Cheap editions were demanded by working class societies all over the country. Paine was burnt in effigy by upper class mobs in Plymouth and other places. . . . Pitt took alarm and decided to prosecute. Paine appeared, and pleaded not guilty at the first summons but, prompted, it is said, by William Blake, who had heard a rumour of his impending arrest, did not wait his trial and fled to France. . . . In his absence, Paine was pronounced guilty by a jury which did not even wait for the judge to sum up against him. Paine was never able again to visit England. He died in 1809 at the age of 72.

Kingsley Martin, *Thomas Paine*, 1925

PAINE'S VIEW OF MONARCHY

(Paine's greatest book, *The Rights of Man*, was written in 1791 as
an answer to Burke's bitter attack on democracy and the French
people, *Reflections on the Revolution in France*.)

Why does Mr Burke talk of his house of peers, as the pillar of the landed
interest? Were that pillar to sink into the earth, the same landed property
would continue, and the same ploughing, sowing and reaping would go
on.

The aristocracy are not the farmers who work the land, and raise the
produce, but are the mere consumers of the rent; and when compared
with the active world, are the drones, a seraglio of males, who neither
collect the honey, nor form the hive, but exist only for lazy enjoyment.
. . . Certain it is that what is called monarchy always appears to me a silly,
contemptible thing. I compare it to something kept behind a curtain
about which there is a great deal of bustle and fuss, and a wonderful air
of seeming solemnity; but when, by any accident, the curtain happens to
be open and the company see what it is, they burst into laughter.

In the representative system of government, nothing like this can
happen. Like the nation itself, it possesses a perpetual stamina, as well of
body as of mind, and presents itself on the open theatre of the world in a
fair and manly manner. Whatever are its excellencies or its defects, they
are visible to all. . . .

As the republic of letters brings forward the best literary productions,
by giving to genius a fair and universal chance; so the representative
system of government is calculated to produce the wisest laws, by
collecting wisdom where it can be found. I smile to myself when I
contemplate the ridiculous insignificance into which literature and all the
sciences would sink, were they made hereditary, and I carry the same
idea into governments. An hereditary governor is as inconsistent as an
hereditary author. . . .

We have heard the rights of man called a levelling system; but the only
system to which the word levelling is truly applicable, is the hereditary
monarchical system. It is a system of mental levelling. It indiscriminately
admits every species of character to the same authority. Vice and virtue,
ignorance and wisdom, in short every quality, good or bad, is put on the
same level.

Kings succeed each other, not as rationals, but as animals. Can we then
be surprised at the abject state of the human mind in monarchical countries
when the government itself is formed on such an abject levelling system?

It has no fixed character. Today it is one thing; and tomorrow it is something else. It changes with the temper of each succeeding individual, and is subject to all the varieties of each.

It is government through the medium of passions and accidents. It appears under all the various characters of childhood, decrepitude, dotage, a thing at nurse, in leading strings, or on crutches. It reverses the wholesome order of nature.

It occasionally puts children over men, and the conceits of nonage over wisdom and experience. In short, we cannot conceive a more ridiculous figure of government, than hereditary succession, in all its cases, presents. . . .

Mr Burke, in speaking of the aristocratical law of primogeniture, says 'It is the standard law of our landed inheritance; and which, without question, has a tendency and I think', continues he, 'a happy tendency to preserve a character of weight and consequence'.

Mr Burke may call this law what he pleases, but humanity and impartial reflection will pronounce it a law of brutal injustice. Were we not accustomed to the daily practice, and did we only hear of it, as the law of some distant part of the world, we should conclude that the legislators of such countries had not arrived at a state of civilisation.

Thomas Paine, The Rights of Man, 1791–92

COBBETT PAYS HOMAGE

To William Cobbett the thought of Paine lying under the ground of a country hillside was unendurable, for in Cobbett's world of fact and fancy, Tom Paine was a saint and a martyr—a saint in the righteousness of his ideas, and a martyr in the suffering that had been inflicted upon him. He resolved to do something about it.

When Paine died [1809] Cobbett had been in England for seven years and he remained there until 1817, when he came again to America and lived on his farm on Long Island.

Paine's grave was at the side of a road that runs north out of New Rochelle. The people who lived near by, came to know William Cobbett by sight, for during 1818 and the following year he would visit the grave once or twice a month, and stand near it, bareheaded and bowed in an attitude of reverence, as if he were paying homage to the man buried there. . . .

One night in October of that year he drove to New Rochelle from New York in a wagon accompanied by a couple of men. They dug up Paine's body—in its coffin—and drove away in the direction of the city. . . .

After a considerable delay a sheriff's posse set out on horseback to pursue the grave robbers, but it was too late; they had escaped. Evidently no further effort was made to capture Cobbett and those who assisted him, and soon thereafter he shipped Paine's body to England, concealed in an ordinary merchandise crate. The question is often asked what Cobbett wanted to do with Paine's remains. He has answered this question himself by saying: 'I have done myself the honour to disinter his bones. I have removed them from New Rochelle . . . they are now on their way to England. When I myself return, I shall cause them to speak the common sense of the great man; I shall gather together the people of Liverpool and Manchester in one assembly with those of London, and those bones will effect the reformation of England in Church and State.'

He hoped to raise money by popular subscription in England for the shrine, but his plans came to nothing. The news of his exploit was greeted with laughter. . . .

Tom Paine has passed away . . . His bones are lost. But his presence is still among us and his influence lives on.

W. E. Woodward, Tom Paine, 1946

THE LIFE OF WILLIAM COBBETT

William Cobbett was born in 1763 and died in 1835. He was born just when the forces of economic change, active for some time before, were gathering that swift momentum which in a single generation destroyed the villages of England and created the noisome factory towns. Enclosures and the rise in the cost of living were then just beginning their swift expropriation and the pauperisation of the peasantry; and the dispossessed peasants and the pauper 'apprentices' were being made the basis for the . . . modern factory proletariat. Most of the phases of this great degradation of the people passed before his own eyes. He saw the peasantry being driven from the land and the ugly towns rising in the North and Midlands. And as the peasant declined, the new rich rose to power and place. Country seats passed into the hands of bankers, stockjobbers and merchants; and when at length Reform came, it only enthroned the new lords of the people in the seats of the old. Cobbett's last years were spent in a criticism of the Reformed Parliament fully as sweeping and vigorous as any he had pronounced against the Rotten Boroughs of pre-Reform days. . . . He died before, in the Chartist Movement, the factory workers gathered up their forces for a mass protest against the new order—a last protest preceding the triumphant march of Victorian capitalism to a goal still undefined. . . .

Cobbett was born at 'The Jolly Farmer', Farnham, Surrey, in the heart of the prosperous hop country. It was an appropriate birthplace for a man who, all his life, looked and felt like the jolly farmer who is the traditional John Bull. He was 70 years old when J. S. Buckingham describes him as having 'a ruddy countenance, a small laughing eye and the figure of a respectable farmer'. . . . His earliest memories were of life and work in the fields—crow-scaring, hoeing, ploughing, gardening for the Bishop at Farnham Castle. He loved gardens and at 14 he gave a hint of his taste for adventure by running away to London in order to get a job at Kew Gardens, of whose beauty he had heard. . . . At 19 he was going to Guildford Fair and was on his way to meet 2 or 3 girls who were going with him, when he met the London coach coming up the turnpike road. In a moment he made up his mind, mounted the coach and, without a word to his friends, was off to London, arriving there with but half a crown in his pocket. He was just 20 years old. . . . He found a job in a lawyer's office but his longing for the sea returned upon him. . . . He went to Chatham and enlisted, as he thought, in the marines, only to find he had joined the infantry by mistake. He was now 21. [He became a serjeant major and served in America, visited France and then lived for eight years in the United States as a teacher of English and pamphleteer.]

Cobbett was 37 years old at the time of his return. . . . He was offered the editorship of a government newspaper but refused, and started an independent paper of his own, *The Porcupine*. Then . . . he started the weekly newspaper with which for the rest of his life his name was associated in the public mind. The first number of the *Political Register* appeared in 1802. . . .

Cobbett was no Socialist. . . . 'Liberty, Equality and Fraternity' left him cold. . . . Robert Owen's Utopian Socialism provoked only his contempt. . . . He could not abide Francis Place. . . . This disabled him from becoming the leader of the young working class Radicals who accepted the Industrial Revolution and were feeling their way towards a Socialist solution of its problems. But the very fact that he was not, was a symptom of unity with the main body of the workers. For these dispossessed peasants were no more Socialists than he. They heeded him because he felt and thought as one of themselves. . . .

Cobbett was 68 years old when he was returned to the House of Commons. . . . From the outset he made himself the leader of a small group of extreme Radicals, opening his parliamentary career by opposing the election of the Speaker, and his maiden speech with the words: 'It seems to me that since I have been sitting here I have heard a great deal of unprofitable discussion.'

On June 18th, 1835, after a few days in bed, he died peacefully. . . .
At his earnest wish he was carried round his farm the afternoon before
his death.

G. D. H. Cole, William Cobbett, 1925

COBBETT STANDS FOR PARLIAMENT

(The following passage provides a vivid picture of how an election was conducted in England before the Great Reform Act.)

[In 1806, I announced my intention to stand for the borough of Honiton.
My expressed principles were] the necessity for a strong front against
bribery; never to touch the public money either by [my] own hands, or
by those of relatives. All professions, short of this, I accounted as
nothing. . . .

Now, as to the state of this borough, who shall describe it? Who shall
describe the gulf wherein have been swallowed the fortunes of so many
ancient and respectable families? There was, the electors would tell you,
no bribery. They took a certain sum of money each, according to their
consequence; 'but this', they said, 'came in the shape of a reward after
the election, and, therefore, the oath might be safely taken'. Considered
as a question of morality, how contemptible this subterfuge was, need
hardly be noticed; but, to say the truth, they did not deceive themselves,
and I must do them the justice to say, that they were not very anxious to
deceive anybody else. They told you, flatly and plainly, that the money
which they obtained for their votes, was absolutely necessary to enable
them to live; that, without it, they could not pay their rents; and that,
from election to election, poor men ran up scores at the shops, and were
trusted by the shopkeepers, expressly upon the credit of the ensuing election; and that, thus, the whole of the inhabitants of the borough, the
whole of the persons who returned two of the members to every parliament, were bound together in an indissoluble chain of venality.

The poorest of the people made a sort of pun upon my name as
descriptive of my non-bribing principles, and moulded their sentiments
into a cry of 'Bread and Cheese and no empty Cupboard' and some of
them in a very serious and mild manner, remonstrated with me upon my
endeavour to deprive them of the profits of their vote, or, in their own
phrase, 'to take the bread out of poor people's mouths'.

In quitting this scene, looking back from one of the many hills that
surrounded the fertile and beautiful valley in which Honiton lay, with its
houses spreading down the side of an inferior eminence, crowned by its
ancient and venerable church; in surveying the fields, the crops, the cattle,

all the blessings that nature could bestow, all the sources of plenty and all the means of comfort and happiness, it was impossible to divest myself of a feeling of horror at reflecting upon the deeds which the sun witnessed upon this one of his most favoured spots.

The more I reflected upon what I had seen with my own eyes, the more firm my convictions became, that [such] was not the cause of our calamities and our dangers, and that it was not, as was vainly imagined, to be removed by laws [then] in existence. The greater fault was in those who exposed the poor and miserable to the temptation of selling their votes; [and for these something more radical was needed].

William Cobbett, *The Political Register*, 1806

COBBETT AND THE WORKING CLASSES

(The following illustrates Cobbett's attitude to the farm-labourer, in contrast to that of most farmers of his time, and also his good opinion of himself.)

[It was easy, after this, to see] in what the present Lords differed from the Lords of former times. In everything except in the shape of their bodies. It had been the business of the Lords, each one to protect his people from wrong; to see that they had fair play; they were their advocates in courts of justice. The bishops and abbots were in Parliament to take care that the poor were not plundered out of their patrimony; and thus the nobility was the 'cheap defence of the realm'. What do we behold now? A prodigious band of spongers, living upon the labour of the industrious part of the community.

For many years there existed a fashion of looking upon the working people, and particularly the labourers in husbandry, as an inferior race of human beings, and of treating them as such. . . . They are the contrary of this; they are the superior race, and they have always been so; they are content as to their station in life; they are unpresuming; they are honest; they are sincere; and he who says the contrary is a base and infamous slanderer. It has been amongst the greatest delights of my life to see them happy, and amongst my most ardent desires to contribute to their happiness. I have admired their character and their conduct ever since I was able to estimate them; and I would willingly strike dead at my feet the insolent brutes who speak contemptuously of them.

I was born and bred a farmer, or a sort of labourer; and I have never desired to have any rank, station, or name or calling, more and other than that of a farmer. [Everyone had known] that I wanted nothing for myself, but they knew that I wanted to take [away] the power of oppressing and

pillaging the order to which I belonged; admire my industry; my perseverance, my wonderful exertions; but there was at the bottom, to balance
against all these, my strong and implacable hatred of oppression, of all
sorts; and particularly the partiality of taxation; the stripping of the working people of their earnings, and the heaping of these earnings upon
idlers. This has been the constant ground of hostility to me; and I must
say, that I trust in God that I shall so conduct myself as to cause the
hostility to continue until the last hour of my life.

William Cobbett, *The Political Register*, 1830–34

SPENCE'S PLAN

Thomas Spence, the Land Nationaliser, was a typical specimen of these
political Poor Preachers. He had been a schoolmaster in Newcastle, and
had conceived of 'Spence's glorious plan' of 'parochial partnership in
land without private landlordism', while engaged in a quarrel between the
corporation and freemen of Newcastle about the rents of the Town Moor.
In 1792 he was in London, and was imprisoned for selling Paine's *Rights
of Man*. After his release he published a long series of tracts, of which the
best known was the periodical 'Pigs' Meat; or, Lessons for the Swinish
Multitude' (1793–1795). In 1801 he was again imprisoned for publishing
a tract called 'The Restorer of Society to its Natural State'. Place came
to know him in 1792 'when he kept a bookstall at the top of Chancery
Lane in Holborn. . . . He was at that time as poor as any man could well
be, and with some trifling fluctuations in his affairs he continued in this
state to the day of his death. He was a very simple, very honest, single-
minded man, querulous in his disposition and odd in his manners. . . .
His disposition was strongly marked on his countenance, which marked
him as a man soured by adverse circumstances, and at enmity with the
world. Still he loved mankind, and firmly believed that the time would
come when they would be wise, virtuous, and happy. He was perfectly
sincere, and unpractised in the ways of the world to an extent few could
imagine in a man who had been pushed about in it as he had been. . . .
A man so poor, so high in his notions of independence, so fanatically
certain of the unparalleled goodness of his system, and so easily excited,
could have no friends amongst the persons with whom he associated. . . .
Ordinary men could not be the friends of one whom they could not
appreciate; and he on his part despised such men. . . . He looked upon
them as despicable, willing slaves, who deserved no better treatment than
they met with, and he frequently told them so.' Hone afterwards described 'Spence's vehicle, like a baker's close barrow. The pamphlets

were exhibited outside, and when he sold one he took it from within, and handed and recommended others, with strong expressions of hate to the powers that were and prophecies of what would happen to the whole race of landlords.' He used to distribute copper tokens stamped with the words 'Spence's Plan', a phrase which his disciples 'chalked on every wall in London'. He died in 1814 and handed on his message to Thomas Evans, who in the year of his master's death founded the 'Society of Spencean Philanthropists'.

Graham Wallas, *Life of Francis Place*, 1897

A RADICAL PRINTER

In 1830 I became connected with the 'Unstamped Agitation', one of the most important political movements that I was ever associated with. This unstamped warfare had its commencement in the publication of the *Poor Man's Guardian* by Mr Henry Hetherington. . . . When Mr Hetherington first commenced the publication of the *Guardian* he was established in Kings-gate Street, Holborn, as a printer, with a fair run of business, which for a time was nearly ruined by the resolute course he pursued. For his name as a Radical became so obnoxious to many of his customers that they withdrew their printing from him. . . . I remember being present on one occasion when one of Mr Hetherington's customers, in a large way of business, offered to give him as much printing as he could do on his premises, provided he would give up his Radical publications; but this splendid offer (in a pecuniary sense) he very nobly refused; although, to my knowledge, his shelves were then filled with thousands of his unsold and returned publications, and all his relations and connections were loudly condemning him for his folly. Mr Hetherington however was not the kind of character to yield under such circumstances. The first time he appeared at Bow Street to answer to the charge of printing and publishing the *Guardian*, he honestly told the magistrates that he was determined to resist the efforts of a corrupt government to suppress the voice of the people. . . . Mr Henry Hetherington was imprisoned three times . . . and what adds to the monstrous injustice of this Government persecution is that fact that, after so many hundred persons had been fined and imprisoned for selling the *Poor Man's Guardian* it was finally declared before Lord Lyndhurst and a special jury, to be a *strictly legal publication*. This warfare however eventually created a public opinion sufficiently powerful to cause the Government to give up the fourpenny stamp upon newspapers and to substitute a penny stamp instead. But this triumphant change was by no means so important as the amount of good that otherwise resulted from the contest. For the unstamped publications may be said *to have originated the cheap literature of the present day*—for few publications existed before they commenced —and the beneficial effects of this cheap literature on the minds and morals of our population are beyond all calculation.

William Lovett, *Life and Struggles*, 1876

THE INDUSTRIAL REVOLUTION

What the new order did . . . was to turn the discomforts of the life of the poor into a rigid system. Hours were not shortened, the atmosphere in which they worked was not made fresher or cleaner, child labour was not abolished. In none of these respects was the early factory better than the home, in some it was worse. But to all the evils from which the domestic worker had suffered, the Industrial Revolution added discipline, and the discipline of a power driven by a competition that seemed as inhuman as the machines that thundered in factory and shed. The workman was summoned by the factory bell; his daily life was arranged by factory hours; he worked under an overseer imposing a method and precision for which the overseer had in turn to answer to some higher authority; if he broke one of a long series of minute regulations he was fined, and behind all this scheme of supervision and control there loomed the great impersonal system. Let anybody . . . enter into the feelings of a spinner at Tyldesley, near Manchester, who worked in a temperature of 80 to 84 degrees, and was subject to the following penalties:

	s	d
Any spinner found with his window open	1	0
Any spinner found washing himself	1	0
. . .		
Any spinner being five minutes after last bell rings	1	0
. . .		
Any spinner being sick and cannot find another spinner to give satisfaction must pay for steam per day	6	0

This list of fines was given by the spinners during a strike, in a pamphlet published at Manchester. The pamphlet adds: 'At Tyldesley they work fourteen hours per day, including the nominal hour for dinner; the door is locked in working hours, except half an hour at tea time; the work-people are not allowed to send for water to drink in the hot factory; and even the rain water is locked up, by the master's order, otherwise they would be happy to drink even that.' . . .

The hours at Tyldesley were exceptionally long, but the normal working day in Manchester and the neighbourhood in 1825 varied from twelve and a half to fourteen hours, and mills, like mines, sometimes worked day and night. Moreover, under the system there was a strong pressure for a longer day. A master spinner, who was a member of an association formed at Manchester in 1831 for the purpose of securing the observance of the earlier Factory Acts, gave it as his opinion that if there were no Factory Acts, the tremendous competition in the industry would make masters work their mills for the whole twenty-four hours with no relief except for meals.

J. L. and B. Hammond, *The Town Labourer, 1760–1832*, 1917

THE PROFIT MOTIVE IN THE MINES

Down to 1815 it was not the custom to hold inquests on the victims of accidents in the mines of Northumberland and Durham. That public attention was drawn to the facts was due to two men, a judge and a parson. The judge was Sir John Bayley, who made very strong representations at the Assizes at Newcastle in 1814 on the scandal of omitting all inquiry into the circumstances under which hundreds of persons had lost their lives, and the parson was John Hodgson, Vicar of Jarrow, who 'braving the displeasure of the affluent Brandlings', wrote and published an account of the accident at Felling, in which ninety-two of his parishioners had perished. Hodgson's action led to the establishment of a Society at Sunderland for preventing accidents, and it was in answer to an appeal from this Society that Sir Humphry Davy visited Newcastle and gave his mind to the problem. Unfortunately, even the alleviations of science were turned to the miner's disadvantage. The Davy lamp, for which the inventor refused to take out a patent, renouncing an income of £5000 or £10,000 a year, 'his sole object to serve the cause of humanity', was used in many cases to serve the cause of profits. Deeper and more dangerous seams were worked, and accidents actually increased in number.

J. L. and B. Hammond, *The Town Labourer, 1760–1832*, 1917

THE PROFIT MOTIVE AT SEA

If the treatment of the miners gave the new society the look of a civilisation in which human life seemed a good deal less important than the profits of capital, the same impression was made, not on the working classes only, by the behaviour of the shipowners on the Tyne and Wear. In 1815 there was a seamen's strike in the north-eastern ports, which was suppressed after a long struggle by the use of troops. The cause of the strike was the conduct of the shipowners, who made a practice of undermanning their ships and refused, in spite of the appeals of the magistrates, to bind themselves to any fixed scale. Local opinion was largely on the side of the seamen, and the behaviour of the owners was stigmatised in severe language by the general commanding the troops, by several of the magistrates, including the Vicar of Bishops Wearmouth, and by a Home Office envoy who, going down to the scene of the dispute with the strongest bias against the men, gradually learned that the seamen who had upset the entire industry of the ports, forbidding any boat to leave without their sanction and taking over the discipline of the towns, had been driven to these measures by the masters' wanton disregard of life. 'Ships from these ports', he wrote to Sidmouth [Home Secretary], 'have gone to sea shamefully deficient in strength to navigate them, and should ever the subject excite the attention of the legislature, hundreds of cases may be produced in which avarice has risked at sea a helpless insufficient crew in a crazy but highly insured ship.'

J. L. and B. Hammond, *The Town Labourer, 1760–1832*, 1917

THE STATE ALONE CAN HELP

It happened more than once in the course of agitations for better wages that the workmen were able to enlist the support and sympathy of a considerable body of masters, but sympathy and support were valueless because Parliament would not ratify their wishes. Men might work astonishing miracles in acquiring mastery and guidance over the forces of fire and water, but the industrial system itself was so contrived as to make the public spirit, or the human sympathy . . . of the best employers, dependent on the selfishness or indifference or the blind greed of the worst. A good man who built a mill gave a hostage to the man who wanted to work the longest hours at the lowest wages.

J. L. and B. Hammond, *The Town Labourer, 1760–1832*, 1917

THE MAKING OF MANCHESTER

Formerly the men and women who lived in the English town, like those who lived in Pisa or Verona, were never far from the open country: their town life was fringed with orchards and gardens. But as the Industrial Revolution advanced, a Manchester was growing up in which the work- men would find it harder and harder to escape out of the wide web of smoke and squalor that enveloped their daily lives. And as the towns grew, the spaces of common within their borders became more valuable, and they were appropriated by the powerful classes. . . . For the workman,

Manchester was a prison: he was excluded from all the amenities that other classes enjoyed. 'The commons on which the labourers indulged in healthful sports are enclosed; policemen guard the streets and keep the highways clear; high walls enclose demesnes, and even the iron palisades that surround ornamental grounds are jealously planked over to prevent the humble operative from enjoying the verdure of the foliage or the fragrance of the flowers.' 'Have we not seen the commons of our fathers enclosed by insolent cupidity—our sports converted into crimes—our holidays into fast days? The green grass and the healthful hayfield are shut out from our path. The whistling of birds is not for us—our melody is the deafening noise of the engine. The merry fiddle and the humble dance will send us to the treadmill. We eat the worst food, drink the worst drink—our raiment, our houses, our everything, bear signs of poverty, and we are gravely told that this must be our lot.' (*Pioneer or Trade Union Magazine*, 19 October 1833.)

J. L. and B. Hammond, *The Town Labourer, 1760–1832*, 1917

THE COMBINATION ACTS

(To protect themselves against exploitation by the employers, the workmen in many factories began to combine into temporary unions. To prevent this, the Combination Acts, passed in great haste in 1799, made it illegal for a workman to join with another to obtain better wages or shorter hours. He could be tried by a single magistrate, who might well be his own employer, and sentenced to three months in jail. Until the repeal of the Acts in 1824 there was no hope of any worthwhile Trade Union being formed. It is noteworthy that the employers, whose constant demand had been that the state should 'give free enterprise a chance' and not interfere in their industries, were quite willing that it should intervene on their behalf against their workmen. In time the working class realized that their best protection was to capture the machinery of state for themselves, and began the long agitation for political power and representatives of their own which culminated in the formation of the Labour Party. The leader of the agitation against the Combination Acts was the Radical tailor Francis Place.)

The Combination Laws lasted for a quarter of a century, and during that time the workpeople were at the mercy of their masters. A great deal can be learnt about the effects and working of the Laws from the evidence taken by the Committee on Artisans and Machinery over which Hume presided in 1824. Francis Place collected enough facts to fill eight volumes. He showed that under cover of these laws magistrates had threatened workmen with imprisonment or service in the fleet as the alternative to accepting the wages their masters chose to offer them. 'Could an accurate account be given of proceedings, of hearings before magistrates, trials at sessions and in the Court of King's Bench, the gross injustice, the foul invective, and terrible punishments inflicted would not, after a few years have passed away, be credited on any but the best evidence.' ...

John Alexander, a journeyman bootmaker, described how Mr Algar of Lombard Street halved his pay, and then, when his six or seven men refused to work for it, summoned them before the Lord Mayor for combination. They were imprisoned for fourteen days with hard labour. The Lord Mayor remarked that it was a hard case, and gave them the choice of this sentence or two months without hard labour.

J. L. and B. Hammond, *The Town Labourer*, *1760–1832*, 1917

THE FIRST FACTORY ACT

(Under the influence of certain humanitarians, Parliament was at last persuaded to use its powers to protect the child labourer as well as the employers. The first Factory Act, however, applied only to apprentices—i.e. children 'farmed out' by some parish on the manufacturers—and only to textile mills. It was largely ignored by the employers, most of whom bitterly opposed its enactment.)

The original Bill was 'for the better preservation of the Health and Morals of Apprentices and others employed in cotton mills and cotton manufactories'. ... There were several debates on the Bill. ... Lord Belgrave declaring with vehemence that 'Wealth was pursued in this country, with an eagerness to which every other consideration was sacrificed, and with excesses calculated to call down the vengeance of Heaven, if the Legislature did not put a stop to them'. ...

The Act prescribed that all cotton or woollen mills or factories where three or more apprentices or twenty or more other persons worked, must be kept clean and airy. Most of the provisions applied only to apprentices. These children were not to work more than twelve hours a day, exclusive of meal times, and these twelve hours must be taken between 6 a.m. and 9 p.m. Night work was prohibited after June 1803, except in the case of the bigger mills. Part of the working day was to be given up to instruction in reading, writing, and arithmetic; each apprentice was to have one new suit of clothing every year, and boys and girls were to sleep in separate rooms and not more than two in a bed. ... The Justices of the Peace at their Quarter Sessions were to appoint two visitors, unconnected with the mills, one a magistrate, the other a clergyman, who should have full power to inspect the mills and enforce the Act.

It is interesting to notice the welcome given by the employers to this, the first Factory Act. . . . One of these papers consists of Observations on the Act, drawn up by the proprietors of some mills at Burley, near Otley. They point out that the cotton trade cannot go on unless about a sixth of the apprentices can be worked at night. 'Free labourers cannot be obtained to perform the night work, but upon very disadvantageous terms to the manufacturers.' . . . As for the clause about the education of the children in working hours . . . to take an hour or two from the twelve working hours 'would amount to a surrender of all the profits of the establishment'. The severest strictures are reserved for the clause which gives the two visitors power to inspect the mill. . . . 'What effects will be produced in such establishments by the introduction of visitors (whom the children will regard as invested with a controlling power over their masters) it is easy to foresee. All subordination will be at an end . . . the Mills and Factories will become a scene either of idleness and disorder, or of open rebellion; or the masters, harassed and tired out by the incessant complaints of their apprentices, and the perpetual interference of the visitors, will be obliged to give up their works; and some of them, after being involved in difficulties (resulting from the operation of the Act) may perhaps become bankrupts, or be obliged to remove to a foreign country, leaving their apprentices a grievous load upon the parish where they were employed.'

J. L. and B. Hammond, *The Town Labourer, 1760–1832*, 1917

THE UNPROTECTED CHILDREN

(Free-labour children, sent to the factories by their parents, who frequently could not live without their earnings, were not protected by the 1802 Act. An Act of 1819 in theory limited the hours of work of children between nine and sixteen to thirteen and a half each day, but was not enforced. The first effective Act was passed by the reformed Parliament in 1833.)

The fourteen or fifteen hours' confinement for six days a week were the 'regular' hours; in busy times hours were elastic and sometimes stretched to a length that seems almost incredible. Work from 3 a.m. to 10 p.m. was not unknown; in Mr Varley's mill, all through the summer, they worked from 3.30 a.m. to 9.30 p.m. At the mill, aptly called 'Hell Bay', for two months at a time, they not only worked regularly from 5 a.m. to 9 p.m., but for two nights each week worked all through the night as well. The more humane employers contented themselves when busy with a spell of sixteen hours (5 a.m. to 9 p.m.).

It was physically impossible to keep such a system working at all except by the driving power of terror. . . . The punishments for arriving late in the morning had to be made cruel enough to overcome the temptation to tired children to take more than three or four hours in bed. One witness before Sadler's Committee [1832] had known a child, who had reached home at eleven o'clock one night, get up at two o'clock next morning in panic and limp to the mill gate. In some mills scarcely an hour passed in the long day without the sound of beating and cries of pain. Fathers beat their own children to save them from a worse beating by other overseers. In the afternoon the strain grew so severe that the heavy iron stick known as the billy-roller was in constant use and, even then, it happened not infrequently that a small child, as he dozed, tumbled into the machine beside him to be mangled for life, or, if he were fortunate, to find a longer Lethe than his stolen sleep.

J. L. and B. Hammond, *The Town Labourer, 1760–1832,* 1917

CHILDREN IN THE MINES

At that time [1842] boys were employed everywhere, girls in certain districts, Lancashire, Cheshire, the West Riding and South Wales, besides Scotland. In some of the districts where girls were employed, they were apparently employed as often as boys. Children were employed as trappers, that is to open and shut the doors that guided the draught of air through the mine; as fillers, that is to fill the skips and carriages when the men had hewn the coal; and as pushers, or hurriers, that is to push the trucks along from the workers to the foot of the shaft. But in some mines these trucks were drawn instead of being pushed. 'A girdle is put round the naked waist, to which a chain from the carriage is hooked and passed between the legs, and the boys crawl on their hands and knees drawing the carriage after them.' (Children's Employment Commission, First Report, Mines, 1842.)

J. L. and B. Hammond, *The Town Labourer, 1760–1832,* 1917

THE NEED FOR INCENTIVES

On this view of life it seemed specially important to avoid discouraging private industry and effort by removing the pressure of want. Society ought to do nothing for its members that the prudent man would do for himself, otherwise the motive to prudence would disappear, and men instead of acquiring property by self-denial would live on the public funds. Perhaps the most notable illustration of this spirit is the speech in which Brougham defended the new Poor Law [1834] in the House of Lords: a speech in which social imagination touches its lowest temperature. Applying this canon of the prudent man, Brougham argued that the only evils against which society should protect people were those the prudent man could not foresee; he could foresee old age, illness, unemployment: against these he should make provision. On the other hand, society might help him in the case of accidents and violent diseases. It is difficult, when one reads this speech, to remember that the prudent man who happened to be a hand-loom weaver in Lancashire (one of the largest classes of workpeople in the country) was earning a good deal less than ten shillings a week. It is perhaps still stranger to remember that no small proportion of the class that thought all this wisdom . . . were living on the public funds.

The idea of the State as an association for mutual aid had almost vanished from the mind of a generation that believed the degradation of the working classes had begun with the Speenhamland system [1795], and would cease with the austerity of the new Poor Law. Paine, who had presented a programme of old age pensions, maternity benefits, and free and compulsory education, seemed a crude and mischievous politician to statesmen who thought that the great secret that the State had to learn was to leave mankind to the steam engine and the railways.

J. L. and B. Hammond, *The Town Labourer, 1760–1832*, 1917

THE VILLAGE IN DISTRESS

(The condition of the rural working class became desperate between 1790 and 1830. The main cause was the Speenhamland system, introduced in 1795, by which the parish made up to the barest subsistence level the inadequate wages paid by the farmer to his labourers. The farmer ceased to make even the pretence of paying adequate wages, and the worker became resigned to poverty and pauperism. The policy of Protection, beloved of the inefficient farmer and the Tory landlord, prevented the importation of cheaper food from abroad. The 'charming, happy, united village' in which squire and labourers loved each other is a fiction of sentimental novelists. The countryside was populated by a class of illiterate, ill-housed, underfed labourers, always discontented and often openly rebellious. Traditionally stupid, they were slower than the factory workers of the towns to realize that only in combination and by political action could their wrongs be righted. It was not until 1884 that they received the vote.)

The agricultural labourers whose fathers had eaten meat, bacon, cheese, and vegetables were living on bread and potatoes. They had lost their gardens, they had ceased to brew their beer in their cottages. In their work they had no sense of ownership or common interest. They no longer 'sauntered after cattle' on the open common, and at twilight they no longer 'played down the setting sun'; the games had almost disappeared from the English village, their wives and children were starving before their eyes, their homes were more squalid, and the philosophy of the hour taught the upper classes that to mend a window or to put in a brick to shield the cottage from damp or wind was to increase the ultimate miseries of the poor. . . . there were English villages in which it was the practice of the overseer to harness men and women to the parish cart, and the sight of an idiot woman between the shafts was not unknown within a hundred miles of London. Men and women were living on roots and sorrel; in the summer of the year 1830 four harvest labourers were found under a hedge dead of starvation, and Lord Winchilsea, who mentioned the fact in the House of Lords, said that this was not an exceptional case. The labourer was worse fed and worse housed than the prisoner, and he would not have been able to keep body and soul together if he had not found in poaching or in thieving or smuggling the means of eking out his doles and wages.

J. L. and B. Hammond, *The Village Labourer,* *1760–1832,* 1911

THE VILLAGE IN REVOLT

(Risings took place during the winter of 1830 in all the counties of southern England, when the labourers forced local farmers and magistrates to agree to lower prices for food and higher wages. The risings were all remarkably orderly and little blood was shed, but as soon as the labourers had dispersed the government proceeded to execute and transport many of those involved; transportation at this time was equivalent to a prolonged death-sentence and meant at best a life-long exile from England. Some improvement in the labourers' condition resulted from the New Poor Law of 1834, introduced by the Reformed Parliament, but as the later extracts from Charles Kingsley's novel show, it was slow and inadequate.)

At Ringmer in Susesx the proceedings were marked by moderation and order. Lord Gage, the principal landowner of the neighbourhood, knowing that disturbances were imminent, met the labourers by appointment on the village green. There were about one hundred and fifty persons present. By this time magistrates in many places had taken to arresting arbitrarily the ringleaders of the men, and hence when Lord Gage, who probably had no such intention, asked for the leader or captain nobody came forward, but a letter was thrown into the ring with a general shout. The letter which Lord Gage picked up and took to the Vestry for consideration read as follows: 'We the labourers of Ringmer and surrounding villages, having for a long period suffered the greatest privations and endured the most debasing treatment with the greatest resignation and forbearance, in the hope that time and circumstances would bring about an amelioration of our condition, till, worn out by hope deferred and disappointed in our fond expectations, we have taken this method of assembling ourselves in one general body, for the purpose of making known our grievances, and in a peaceable, quiet, and orderly manner, to ask redress; and we would rather appeal to the good sense of the magistracy, instead of inflaming the passions of our fellow labourers, and ask those gentlemen who have done us the favour of meeting us this day whether 7d. a day is sufficient for a working man, hale and hearty, to keep up the strength necessary to the execution of the labour he has to do? We ask also, is 9s. a week sufficient for a married man with a family, to provide the common necessaries of life? Have we no reason to complain that we have been obliged for so long a period to go to our daily toil with only potatoes in our satchels, and the only beverage to assuage our thirst the cold spring; and on retiring to our cottages to be welcomed by the meagre and half-famished offspring of our toilworn bodies? All we ask, then, is that our wages may be advanced to such a degree as will enable us to provide for ourselves and families without being driven to the overseer, who, by the bye, is a stranger amongst us, and as in most instances where permanent overseers are appointed, are men callous to the ties of nature, lost to every feeling of humanity, and deaf to the voice of reason. We say we want wages sufficient to support us, without being driven to the overseer to experience his petty tyranny and dictation. We therefore ask for married men 2s. 3d. per day to the first of March, and from that period to the first of October 2s. 6d. a day: for single men 1s. 9d. a day to the first of March, and 2s. from that time to the first of October. We also request that the permanent overseers of the neighbouring parishes may be directly discharged, particularly Finch, the governor of Ringmer poorhouse and overseer of the parish, that in case we are obliged, through misfortune or affliction, to seek parochial relief, we may apply to one of our neighbouring farmers or tradesmen, who would naturally feel some sympathy for our situation, and who would be much better acquainted with our characters and claims. This is what we ask at your hands—this is what we expect, and we sincerely trust this is what we shall not be under the painful necessity of demanding.'

While the vestry deliberated the labourers remained quietly in the yard of the poorhouse. One of them, a veteran from the Peninsular War who had lost a limb, contrasted his situation on 9d a day with that of the Duke of Wellington whose 'skin was whole' and whose pension was £60,000 a year. After they had waited some time, they were informed that their demands were granted, and they dispersed to their homes with huzzas and tears of joy, and as a sign of the new and auspicious era they broke up the parish grindstone, a memory of the evil past.

... At Abingdon ... one young labourer, Richard Kempster by name, who was found guilty of breaking a threshing machine, had carried a black-and-red flag in the mob, and when arrested had exclaimed, 'be damned if I don't wish it was a revolution, and that all was afire together'.

J. L. and B. Hammond, *The Village Labourer, 1760–1832*, 1911

THE TOLPUDDLE MARTYRS

The story of the trial and transportation of the Dorchester labourers is the best-known episode of early Trade Union history. The agricultural labourers of the southern counties, oppressed by the tacit combinations of the farmers and by the operation of the Corn Laws, as well as exceptionally demoralised by the Old Poor Law, had long been in a state of sullen despair. The specially hard times of 1829 had resulted in outbursts of machine-breaking, rick-burning, and hunger riots, which had been put down in 1830 by the movement of troops through the disturbed districts, and the appointment of a Special Commission of Assize to try over 1000 prisoners. ... With the improvement of trade a general movement for higher wages seems to have been set on foot. In 1832 we find the Duke of Wellington, as Lord-Lieutenant of Hampshire, reporting to Lord Melbourne that more than half the labourers in his county were contributing a penny per week to a network of local societies affiliated, as he thought, to some National Union. 'The labourers said that they had received directions from the Union not to take less than ten shillings, and that the Union would stand by them.' These societies, whatever may have been their constitution, had apparently the effect of raising wages not only in Hampshire, but also in the neighbouring counties. In the village of Tolpuddle, in Dorsetshire ... an agreement was made between the farmers and the men, in the presence of the village parson, that the wages should be those paid in other districts. This involved a rise to ten shillings a week. In the following year the farmers repented of their decision, and successively reduced wages shilling by shilling until they were paying only seven shillings a week. In this strait the men made inquiries about 'the Trades Union', and two delegates from the Grand National visited the village. Upon their information the Lovelesses established 'the Friendly Society of Agricultural Labourers', having its 'Grand Lodge' at Tolpuddle. . . . The farmers took alarm, and induced the local magistrates, on February 21, 1834, to issue placards warning the labourers that any one joining the Union would be sentenced to seven years' transportation. This was no idle threat. Within three days of the publication of the notice the Lovelesses and four other members were arrested and lodged in gaol.

The trial of these unfortunate labourers was a scandalous perversion of the law. The Lovelesses and their friends seem to have been simple-minded Methodists, two of them being itinerant preachers. No accusation was made, and no evidence preferred against them, of anything worse than the playing with oaths, which . . . formed a part of the initiation ceremony of the Grand National. . . . Not only were they guiltless of any intimidation or outrage, but they had not even struck or presented any application for higher wages. Yet the judge, who had only recently been raised to the bench, charged the grand jury on the case at portentous length, as if the prisoners had committed murder or treason, and inflicted on them, after the briefest of trials, the monstrous sentence of seven years' transportation. . . .

The Case was tried on March 18, 1834; before the 30th the prisoners were in the hulks; and by the 15th of the next month Lord Howick was able to say in the House of Commons that their ship had already sailed for Botany Bay.

Sidney and Beatrice Webb, *The History of Trade Unionism*, 1894

KNOWLEDGE IS POWER

As our period closes [1832] a battle began for a cheap Press . . . a whole army of working men defied the law and published journals without a stamp. In October 1830 Henry Hetherington began to publish the *Penny Papers for the People*. The battle was won in 1836, when the stamp was reduced from 4d to 1d, but in the five years 500 persons had been sent to prison. . . .

But the main burden of . . . giving to classes that seemed to exist only for other people's ends a value and purpose of their own, of making wider and deeper the range and play of imagination and sympathy . . . fell in the main on the nameless working classes themselves. They had to overcome all the obstacles that were put in their way by a class holding the power that law, custom, education, and wealth can bestow. Of all

the documents in the Home Office papers, none illustrates better the difficulties of that struggle than a confiscated copy-book, seized by an active
magistrate and sent to the Home Office in a time of panic as a dangerous
piece of sedition, in which a working man, secretary of a little society of
working-men Reformers, had been practising his elementary powers of
writing and spelling. Reform, education, combination wore a very different look to the rich and the poor. To the working classes they were
ladders from a prison: to their rulers they were ladders whereby the prole-
tariate might one day take the State by storm.

J. L. and B. Hammond, *The Town Labourer, 1760–1832,* 1917

THE COMING OF THE CHAPELS

On this population, partly neglected, partly dragooned by the Church,
there descended a religion that happened to supply almost everything
that it wanted. The Church offered no function to the poor man: his
place was on a rude bench or a mat, listening to sermons on the importance
of the subordination of the lower classes to the grand family worshipping
amid the spacious cushions of the squire's pew. The Chapel invited him
to take a hand in the management of the affairs of his religious society;
perhaps to help in choosing a minister, to feel that he had a share in its
life, responsibility for its risks and undertakings, pride in its successes and
reputation. As a mere exercise in self-government and social life, the
Chapel occupied a central place in the affections and the thoughts of
people who had very little to do with the government of anything else. . . .

What was the effect of this religion on the mind of the working classes?
Many magistrates wrote to the Home Office that it helped to make them
discontented and to strengthen the forces of working-class organisation.
Thus the Vicar of Sandal near Wakefield, writing in 1819, asserted that
the greater part of the people called Methodists were united with the
Radicals, that under the pretence of religious worship they met in private
houses . . . and formed plans for advancing wages. . . .

The official attitude of the Methodist leaders seems to have been quite
clearly conservative in the years of crisis, 1817 and 1819. In 1817 the
Reformers appealed to them . . . but they seem to have replied by warning their congregations to keep away from Reform meetings. . . .

. . . The devotees who preached in the early Primitive Methodist
camps, and the leaders of the Conferences that laid down the essential
hostility of their religion to the spirit of democracy, were alien or hostile
influences, but there must have been many in the Methodist world who
were neither enthusiasts nor conservatives. A religion does not affect

everybody in the same way, or with the same power, or for the same time. This religion which drew men and women out of their immediate and visible surroundings would not necessarily draw them all, or keep them all, under the spell of its quieting harmonies. Men and women might put their social indignation to sleep for years in this atmosphere and yet emerge ardent for reform and agitation. For Methodism was in a very real sense a school, and when men and women go to school they may learn more lessons than those taught on the blackboard. Moreover, the early Methodists had the credit of introducing the teaching of writing in the Sunday-schools. . . . The teaching of writing was an enormous boon to the working classes. And there were other important arts that might be acquired in this school. The upper class could learn to speak at Eton: the working class in the little Bethel. The Methodist Sunday-schools would attract men and women with the gifts of oratory, leadership, organisation; they gave scope, experience, and training. It is significant that it is more than once mentioned that speakers at miners' meetings were Methodists, and Lloyd of Stockport complained that the Reformers cap- tured one of the Sunday-schools in that town, holding meetings partly religious, partly political, in which they quoted the Bible on the subject of the possessions of the rich.

J. L. and B. Hammond, *The Town Labourer, 1760–1832*, 1917

IN UNION, STRENGTH

The first important effort to consolidate the working-class forces seems to have been made in August 1818. In the closing hours of the great spinners' strike of that year, a General Union of Trades was suggested as a last desperate manœuvre. Rumours of this new and dangerous development were sent up to the Home Office at the beginning of August, but the first definite news is contained in a letter, dated August 5th, from Mr Norris, the stipendiary magistrate of Manchester, enclosing a hand- bill. This handbill is addressed 'To the Labourers of Manchester and its Vicinity'. . . .

'The road is not long to that respectable walk in society in which the Labourer ought to tread; tho' in the present state of things, I must con- fess, it is rather rugged; yet unless you not only make the attempt to regain that respectable walk; but also be determined to recover it, you may depend upon it, that both you and your children will be trodden into the earth by your interested and hard hearted Employers. The first thing necessary to be done is to take your Master's conduct for a model. They call their meetings, at which every one who has a labourer to oppress, most scrupulously attends; at which meetings whatever mode of oppression is agreed upon, it is as coldly, and as religiously fulfilled, as though they were doing that which was pleasing their Maker. Every branch of labourers, namely Husbandmen, Weavers of all classes, Dyers, Fustian Cutters, Calico Printers, Spinners of all classes, Hatters of all classes, Machine makers, Joiners, Bricklayers, Masons, Shoe Makers, Tailors &C. &C, in short every branch of Labourers necessary in every well regulated society, ought immediately to call district meetings, and appoint *delegates* to meet at some convenient central place, to establish such a connexion as shall be deemed necessary for the good of the whole, and also they should be empowered to agree to the following or similar resolutions:

'1. That Labour being the Corner-stone upon which civilized society is built, no able, active Labourer ought to be offered less for his labour, than will support the family of a sober and orderly man in decency and credit.

'2. That whatever trade or employment will not leave profit sufficient to reward the Labourer, so as to enable him to live in credit, and respect, provided he be an able, active and sober man, the loss of such a trade is a public benefit.'

J. L. and B. Hammond, *The Town Labourer, 1760–1832*, 1917

THE LIFE OF FRANCIS PLACE

(Francis Place, who was born in 1771 and died in 1854, was one of the men who did most to make the working-class movement in the first half of the nineteenth century. He was acquainted with philosophers, such as James Mill and Jeremy Bentham, as well as with all the Radical leaders of the time.)

Francis Place was a Londoner; he was born on November 3, 1771, in a 'sponging house' or private debtors' prison, in Vinegar Yard, near Drury Lane, kept by his father, Simon Place, who was at that time a bailiff to the Marshalsea Court. . . .

When Francis was nearly nine years old the sponging house was given up, and Simon Place took a tavern with the savings which he had made by legalised blackmail. . . .

Some months before Francis was fourteen years old his father announced that he should be apprenticed to a conveyancer. The boy flatly refused to be 'made a lawyer', and declared that he would prefer anything else if it were a trade. 'This', he says, 'was in the evening, and my father went immediately into his parlour and offered me to any one who would take me. A little man named France said he would, and I was sent the very next morning on liking for a month to learn the art and mystery of leather-breeches making.' . . .

In July 1789, before he was yet eighteen years old, his indentures were given up, and he became an independent journeyman breeches-maker. . . .

It is one of the most astonishing signs of Place's resolution and courage that throughout his 'out of work' months, while constantly faced with hunger and apprehension, he devoted a great part of his undesired leisure to severe intellectual work. . . . During the first year of his married life he had lodged with an old woman who took charge of chambers in the Temple, and lent him books borrowed from the rooms which she cleaned. . . .

After a few months his employer sent less and less work, and soon he was again discharged. He then reorganised the Breeches-Makers' Union, early in 1794, under the guise of a Sick Club, became its secretary in the spring of 1795 with a salary of £10 per annum and obtained in the spring of 1795, without a strike, the advance which had been vainly asked for in 1793. . . .

But no young man could have lived as he did in London throughout the five years which followed the French Revolution, organising Trade Unions and suffering himself personally from the effects of unjust laws, without being profoundly influenced by the great message which the French Republic was proclaiming to the world. And indeed when 'at the request of my landlord', he joined the London Corresponding Society in June 1794, it is evident that this step was the result not of a casual impulse, but of a steady intellectual development. . . .

The Corresponding Society formed the working-class wing of the Democratic movement of the time. The societies of 'The Friends of the People' and 'Constitutional Information' were already in existence, and engaged in spreading the ideas of the French Revolution. But their annual subscriptions of five guineas and two guineas and a half respectively excluded working-men from membership. Hardy [founder of the Society] therefore fixed his subscription at a penny per week, with a shilling entrance fee. The political programme of the Society consisted of the 'Plan of Radical Reform'—universal suffrage, annual parliaments, payment of members—which Major Cartwright had advocated in 1776, and which was to reappear more than forty years later as 'The People's Charter' . . .

[On 8 April 1801 Place opened a tailor's shop] on his own account at No. 16 Charing Cross. . . . For the first five years after taking the Charing Cross shop . . . he had withdrawn himself entirely from public life. . . . On the day of the [Westminster] election [in 1806] the Duke of Northumberland, the façade of whose house was only a few doors from Place's shop, distributed bread and cheese and beer from his steps. Place describes the scene and his own feelings. 'My indignation was greatly increased when I saw the servants of the Duke of Northumberland, in their showy dress liveries, throwing lumps of bread and cheese among the dense crowd of vagabonds they had collected together. To see these vagabonds catching the lumps, shouting, swearing, fighting, and black-guarding in every possible way, women as well as men, all the vile wretches from the courts and alleys in St Giles and Westminster, . . . and other miserable places; to see these people representing, as it was said, the electors of Westminster, was certainly the lowest possible step of degradation, except, indeed, if it be possible, to hear it said, as it was said, that "the electors of Westminster had been treated by the bounty of the Duke". Some who mingled in the mob were ashamed of the proceedings, and as the mob pressed round the butts which contained the beer, suggested that the best way would be to knock in the heads as they stood up on end. This was done immediately. The heads were beaten in, and the coal-heavers ladled the beer out with their long-tailed, broad-brimmed hats; but the mob pressing on, the butts were upset, and the beer flowed along the gutters, from whence some made efforts to obtain it. It may be possible to imagine something like the disgraceful scene, but it is not possible either to describe it or to excite in the reader the almost uncontrollable feelings of a spectator. I was not the only one who felt indignation. Almost every man I knew was much offended with the whole of the proceedings and with all who were concerned in them.'

Graham Wallas, *Life of Francis Place*, 1897

THE EDUCATED TRADESMAN

Later on as his books accumulated he had to be more and more careful that none of his ordinary customers should be allowed to go into the library at the back of the shop, or to 'know anything of me except as a tailor'. He complains that on several occasions he lost good customers owing to their learning something of his habits of study, and being per-haps quick enough to guess at the biting scorn which underlay his guarded politeness. 'Had these persons been told that I had never read a book, that I was ignorant of everything but my business, that I sotted in a public-house, they would not have made the least objection to me. I should have been a "fellow" beneath them, and they would have patron-ised me; but . . . to accumulate books and to be supposed to know some-

thing of their contents, to seek for friends, too, among literary and scientific men, was putting myself on an equality with themselves if not, indeed
assuming a superiority; it was an abominable offence in a tailor, if not a
crime, which deserved punishment. Had it been known to all my
customers that in the few years from 1810 to 1817 I had accumulated a
considerable library, in which I spent all the leisure time I could spare
had the many things which I was engaged in during this period, and the
men with whom I associated been known, half of them at the least would
have left me, and these, too, by far the most valuable customers individually.' And ten years later he recurred to the same subject, and noted
the very little change which had taken place in this respect. 'The nearer
a common tradesman approximates in information and manners to a footman,' he says, 'the more certainly will he please his well-bred customers
the less he knows beyond his business, the more certain, in general, will
be his success.'

In spite of this the business rapidly and regularly increased. In 1816
when it reached its maximum, the net profits for the year were considerably over three thousand pounds. At the same time, Place's family
grew rapidly, and in 1817, when he retired from business, and handed the
shop over to his eldest son, he had ten children living out of fifteen who
had been born to him.

Graham Wallas, *Life of Francis Place*, 1897

THE CHARING CROSS LIBRARY

(Although never a Member of Parliament himself, Francis Place,
by the information and advice he supplied to the Radical M.P.s,
exerted an enormous influence on the reform movement, in particular
in securing the repeal of the Combination Laws. His work may be
compared to that of the Webbs, fifty years later.)

There is an old gentleman still alive and active, who can remember being
taken as a boy, about the year 1820, up into a big room lined with books
at the back of Place's shop, and being told in a reverential voice that this
was the headquarters of English Radicalism. Place had been a collector of
books ever since his school-days, and continued to collect nearly to the end
of his life. From the first the library was especially rich in Parliamentary
papers, catalogued by subjects, and in pamphlets and newspaper cuttings,
bound and lettered with his own hand. Everything was arranged with
that scrupulous 'method and tidiness and comfort' to which Place's
correspondents often refer.

This was the 'Civic Palace, Charing Cross', where the 'Arch Radical' sat all day long on a high stool at his desk, as before his retirement from business he had sat all day long in the adjoining shop. Every member of Parliament who lived, as most members then did, in Bloomsbury or the City, would pass Charing Cross twice a day. In any case, the House of Commons and Downing Street were both within a few minutes' walk.

'My library', says Place, 'was a sort of gossiping shop for such persons as were in any way engaged in public matters having the benefit of the people for their object. . . . No one who knew me would hesitate to consult with me on any subject on which I could either give or procure information.' And again, 'When I lived at Charing Cross my library was frequented very much in the manner of a common coffee-house room. It was open to a considerable number of persons, many of them members of Parliament.' In times of excitement the room became crowded.

A very good description of Place and his daily life about this time was given in the *Northern Liberator*. 'Francis Place . . . is in the sixty-fifth year of his age. He is about five feet seven inches high . . . and is of a stout, stalwart frame. A walk of twenty or thirty miles a day is one of his favourite amusements; but his time, from six in the morning to eleven at night, is generally spent in his library, where he is surrounded with books, pamphlets, journals, and memoranda of every kind—political, philological, physiological, and every other "cal" which can be imagined, all arranged in such perfect order that he can put his hand on any book or paper he may want in a moment. The bump of order is in him very prominent indeed.'

Graham Wallas, *Life of Francis Place*, 1897

ORATOR HUNT

The distress throughout 1817 and 1818 had been very great . . . and the working classes, as usual, were the first to feel the effects of the deep commercial depression. They were taught to look upon misgovernment as the cause of their misery and they attributed that misgovernment to the grossly defective state of the representation. They saw Manchester, Salford, Bolton, Blackburn, Rochdale, Bury, Ashton under Lyme, Oldham and Stockport without members whilst Old Sarum—a mound of earth without inhabitants—a host of villages, decayed and rotten, each sent two. It was not to be wondered at that they complained—not to be wondered at that they crowded round those who appealed to their sympathies, gave articulate utterance to their complaints and offered to aid them in obtaining redress of their grievances. . . . A fresh campaign was vigorously commenced with the commencement of the year 1819. Henry Hunt had come forward as the champion of the people's rights and he was well fitted to appeal with effect to the excited passions of the multitude. His portrait is thus drawn by Samuel Bamford: 'He was gentlemanly in his manner and attire, six feet and better in height, and extremely well formed. He was dressed in a blue lapelled coat, light waistcoat and kerseys and topped boots; his leg and foot were about the firmest and neatest I ever saw. He wore his own hair; it was in moderate quantity and a little grey. His features were regular, and there was a kind of youthful blandness about them which, in amicable discussion, gave his face a most agreeable expression. His lips were delicately thin, and receding; but there was a dumb utterance about them which in all the portraits I have seen of him was never truly copied. His eyes were blue or light grey—not very clear, nor quick but rather heavy, except—as I afterwards had opportunities for observing—when he was excited in speaking, at which times they seemed to distend and protrude; and if he worked himself furious, as he sometimes would, they became blood-streaked and almost started from their sockets.'

A. Prentice, *Historical Sketches and Personal Recollections of Manchester*, 1851

DRINK AND THE CITIZEN

On the 21st of June 1819 another meeting was held in St Peter's Fields, Manchester, and resolutions were passed appointing district delegates from a general national union to reform the government. Meetings took place about the same time at Oldham, Stockport, Leeds and other towns, all unrepresented in parliament, and, says, Mr Wheeler, 'with a view to embarrass the government, a pledge was generally entered into by the people attending the usual place of rendezvous to abstain from the use of any exciseable article not absolutely necessary to support existence'. Hunt, to supply the place of coffee, recommended his own roasted corn, which was found to be a very unpalatable substitute, and sloe leaves did not produce so pleasant a beverage as tea. The main stress was laid on abstinence from spirits and ale; and the good old loyalists were shocked at the iniquity of soberness from such a motive. A placard, signed 'Bob Short' was stuck on all the walls and distributed from house to house, denouncing all as enemies to the working people who would persuade them to renounce the use of the good old English drinks and urging the readers to return to their good old drunken habits, to prove their attachment to king and church and constitution, endangered by the conspiracy to promote sobriety. The expense of this precious production was defrayed from the *church-rates*.

A. Prentice, *Historical Sketches and Personal Recollections of Manchester*, 1851

THE MANCHESTER MASSACRE

(Although reform meetings were frequently attacked during the great period of repression from 1815 to 1830 it was the suppression of a peaceful gathering at Manchester in 1819 with much unnecessary bloodshed and violence which first caught the public imagination.)

The morning of 16th August came and soon after 9 o'clock the people began to assemble. From the windows of Mr Baxter's house in Morley Street, I saw the main body proceeding towards St Peter's Field, and never saw a gayer spectacle. There were haggard-looking men certainly, but the majority were young persons in their best Sunday suits, and the light coloured dresses of the cheerful tidy-looking women relieved the effect of the dark fustians worn by the men. The 'marching order' of which so much was said afterwards, was what we often see now in the processions of Sunday school children and temperance societies. To our eyes the numerous flags seemed to have been brought to add to the picturesque effect of the pageant. Our company laughed at the fears of the magistrates and the remark was that, if the men intended mischief, they would not have brought their wives, their sisters or their children with them. . . . I saw Hunt arrive and heard the shouts of the 60,000 persons by whom he was enthusiastically welcomed, as the carriage in which he stood made its way, through the dense crowd, to the hustings. I proceeded to my dwelling house in Salford, intending to return in about an hour or so to witness in what manner so large a meeting would separate. I had not been at home more than a quarter of an hour when a wailing sound was heard from the main street and, rushing out, I saw people running in the direction of Pendleton, their faces pale as death and some with blood trickling down their cheeks. It was with difficulty I could get anyone to stop and tell me what had happened. The unarmed multitude, men, women and children, had been attacked with murderous results by the military.

The magistrates had resolved, at the last moment, that Hunt and the friends who accompanied him to the hustings, should be apprehended in the face of the meeting. It was a great assemblage and, no doubt, they thought the capture of the ringleaders in the presence of 60,000 persons would produce a salutary effect. . . . Near to the field, ready the moment

C

their services were required, were 6 troops of the 15th Hussars, a troop of horse artillery, with two guns, the greater part of the 31st regiment of infantry, some companies of the 88th regiment, the Cheshire yeomanry, of between 300 and 400 men, and the Manchester Yeomanry of about forty, the latter hot-headed young men who had volunteered into that service from their intense hatred of radicalism. With such a force at command, the warrant might have been executed without the slightest tumult. . . . Hunt had addressed the dense multitude, now hushed into a deep silence intensely listening to the opening of his speech, when suddenly at a quick trot past the corner of a wall which bounded Brown's cottage, appeared the Manchester yeomanry, and drew up in front of the house in which the magistrates were met. The crowd received them, as Bamford says, with a shout of good will, as the aggressors said, with a shout of defiance, when, as suddenly as they had appeared at the outskirts of the meeting, they drew their swords, waved them round their heads and dashed into the crowd! Nadin [deputy constable] had said that he was afraid to serve the warrant and this was the way it was to be served. As the yeomanry neared the hustings, the inert resistance of those who could not move out of the way increased, and the troops were separated, each man striving to open out his own way, some with pale faces and firmly-closed eyes, striking with their sabres as if they were insane. . . . The hussars in their turn, and with resistless force, dashed into the crowd. . . .

Bamford says: 'On the breaking of the crowd, the yeomanry wheeled; and dashing wherever there was an opening, they followed, pressing and wounding. Many females appeared as the crowd opened and striplings and mere youths were also found. Their cries were piteous and heart-rending; and would, one might have supposed, have disarmed any human resentment; but their appeals were vain. Women, white-vested maids and tender youths, were indiscriminately sabred or trampled on. . . . In ten minutes from the commencement of the havoc, the field was an open and almost deserted space. The sun looked down through a sultry and motionless air; the curtains and blinds of the windows within view were all closed. A gentleman or two might occasionally be seen looking out from some houses . . . near the door of which a group of persons (special constables) were collected, and apparently in conversation; others were assisting the wounded or carrying off the dead. The hustings remained, with a few broken and hewed flag-staves erect, and a torn or gashed banner or two drooping, whilst over the whole field were strewn bonnets, hats, shawls and shoes, and other parts of male and female dress, trampled, torn and bloody. The yeomanry had dismounted; some were easing their horses' girths, others adjusting their accoutrements, and some were wiping their sabres. Several mounds of human beings still remained where they had fallen, crushed down, and smothered, some of them were still groaning, and others, with staring eyes, were gasping for breath; and others would never breathe again. All were silent save those low sounds, and the occasional snorting and pawing of steeds. Persons might sometimes be noticed peeping from attics, and over the tall ridging of houses, but they quickly withdrew, as if fearful of being observed, or unable to sustain the full gaze of a scene so hideous and abhorrent.' . . .

The subscription [for the victims] was for a double purpose—to relieve the sufferings of those who, being wounded or bruised, had been deprived of the means of obtaining bread—and to protect and defend the persons who had been arrested. . . . The amount of the subscription proved that a deep sympathy for the oppressed and injured reformers prevailed amongst the middle classes. . . . It was a healthful sign of the times, which should not be passed over in silence; for sympathy with reformers gave the promise of co-operation in the work of reform; and from this period may be dated a marked and favourable change in the current of public opinion.

A. Prentice, *Historical Sketches and Personal Recollections of Manchester*, 1851

(Eleven people were killed and 600 injured in the Massacre. Hunt received two and a half years' imprisonment and Bamford one year.)

ONE MAN'S REACTION

Place when he heard the news of 'Peterloo' wrote to Hobhouse: 'These Manchester yeomen and magistrates are a greater set of brutes than you form a conception of. They have always treated the working people in a most abominable manner. I know one of these fellows who swears: "Damn his eyes, seven shillings a week is plenty for them"; that when he goes round to see how much work his weavers have in their looms, he takes a well-fed dog with him, almost, if not entirely, for the purpose of insulting them by the contrast. He said some time ago that "The sons of bitches had eaten up all the stinging nettles for ten miles round Manchester, and now they had no greens to their broth". Upon my expressing indignation, he said, "Damn their eyes, what need you care about them? How could I sell you goods so cheap if I cared anything about them?" I showed him the door, and never purchased any of his goods afterwards. Another of these fellows, a manufacturer and yeoman, said yesterday, we in London did not know what a set of damned villains the fellows at Manchester were. They must be kept quiet by the sword. He was told to take care of himself; he laughed and said "Ah, you know nothing of the weight of a sabre; that's the argument!" What but what has happened could be expected from these fellows when let loose? They never for a moment thought of consequences. They cut down and trampled down people; and then it was to end, just as cutting and trampling the furze bushes on a common would end.' . . .

. . . On August 21 the Regent sent a letter to the Lord-Lieutenants of Lancashire and Cheshire, requesting them to convey to the magistrates and yeomanry of those counties 'the great satisfaction derived by his Royal Highness the Prince Regent for their prompt, decisive, and efficient measures for the preservation of the public tranquillity'.

Graham Wallas, Life of Francis Place, 1897

A PETITION TO VICTORIA

(William Lovett, who was born in 1800 and died in 1877, helped to draft the People's Charter and suffered imprisonment for his beliefs. He was a fanatical believer in the power of education to enable the masses to gain political power and to train them to exercise it wisely when gained.)

When Queen Victoria ascended the throne our association . . . prepared what we believed to be a loyal and outspoken address to her. Having appointed a deputation for the purpose of presenting it, I sent the following letter to the Secretary of the Home Department:

Working Men's Association,
6 Upper North Place,
Gray's Inn Road.
Sept. 1st, 1837.

My Lord: The Working Men's Association of London having prepared an address to her Majesty, they are desirous of having it presented to her personally by a deputation of six persons, whom they have selected for that purpose. They have therefore requested me to ascertain from your Lordship when it will please her Majesty that they shall wait on her with the address?

The answer received to this was the following.

Whitehall.
Sept. 6th, 1837.

Sir, I am directed by Lord John Russell to inform you in reply to your letter of the 1st inst. that the address of the Working Men's Association cannot be presented, till her Majesty holds a levee, when the deputation must attend in *court dress*. No time for a levee is yet fixed, but it will be publicly announced in the Gazette.

To this we sent the following reply, accompanied with the address:

My Lord: According to your answer of the 6th inst., we find that we are precluded by those forms which Gothic ignorance has imposed, and custom sanctified, from personally presenting our address; for with every respect for those forms which make personal cleanliness and respectful behaviour necessary qualifications to approach her Majesty, we have neither the means nor the inclination to indulge in such absurdities as dress-swords, coats and wigs. We beg, therefore, to request that your lordship, in your official capacity, will at the earliest opportunity present our address to her Majesty, in hopes she may chance to read the sentiments of a portion of her *working-class population*, which the necessity of appearing in court dress excludes from her presence. We hope, my Lord, that day is not far distant when some better means will be devised for letting the sovereign hear of the addresses and petitions of the people.

'To the Queen of the United Kingdom of Great Britain and Ireland and its Dependencies.

'Madam: While we approach your Majesty in the spirit of plain men, seeking their political and social rights, apart from mere names, forms and useless ceremonies, we yield to none in the just fulfilment of our duties, or in the ardent wish that our country may be made to advance to the highest point of prosperity and happiness. . . .

'The country over which your Majesty has been called on to preside has by the powers and industry of its inhabitants been made to teem with abundance, and were all its resources *wisely developed and justly distributed*, would impart ample means of happiness to *all its inhabitants*

'But by many monstrous anomalies springing out of the constitution of society, the *corruptions* of government, and *the defective education of mankind*, we find the bulk of the nation toiling slaves from birth to death —thousands wanting food, or subsisting on the scantiest pittance, having neither time nor means to obtain instruction, much less cultivating the higher faculties and brightest affections, but forced by their situation to engender enmity, jealousy, and contention and too often to become the victims of intemperance and crime.

'We find the majority of the middling classes equally the toiling and by far too many of them the avaricious pursuers of wealth—often following that which eludes their grasp, or if attained, fails of imparting happiness —racked with the cares of business, distrust and suspicion, and often filled with apprehensions of bankruptcy and insolvency which few in the present state of things are secure from.

'And even among the exclusive few who possess the chief fruits of all this toil and anxiety; to nurture whom in idleness and pamper in luxury, all this sacrifice is made by the other classes of society, but a trifling portion can be found free from the diseases of sloth, the cares of idleness and debauchery, and of apprehensions and alarms lest the indignation of the multitude summon them to justice, despite of their wealth, powers and possessions. . . .

'We respectfully submit to your Majesty, that *it is not just*, that out of a population of *twenty-five millions of people*, only *eight hundred thousand* should have the power of electing what is called the Commons House of Parliament; since so small a number, divided as it is, subjects by far the greater portion to be *bribed* or *intimidated* by the wealthy and the powerful; but that in accordance with justice those who by their industry support and defend their country have *the first claim* to political rights. . . .

'That the poverty and ignorance which pervade numerous districts of the kingdom justly call for investigation and immediate redress; which can only be effected by a Parliament selected from the wise and good of every class, to consult all interest and to protect all just rights. . . .

'We entreat your Majesty that, whoever may be in your councils, you will instruct them, as a first and essential measure of reform, to prepare a Bill for extending the Right of Suffrage *to all the adult population of the kingdom* . . . together with such other essential details as shall enable all men to exercise their political rights unmolested.'

William Lovett, *Life and Struggles*, 1876

The petition produced no results; universal suffrage was not achieved until 1928.)

THE ORIGIN OF CHARTISM

(The disappointment of the working classes at the failure of the Reform Act of 1832, for which they had struggled, under the leadership of Cobbett and Francis Place, to give them the vote, led to the great agitation for the 'People's Charter'—a six-point programme of electoral reform. After the fiasco of 1848, described in the following extracts, the movement died away and its supporters in due time provided recruits for the groups of Socialists which now began to be formed. These possessed not merely the desire to gain the vote but a much clearer idea than the Chartists of the programme to be realized once power was obtained.)

The Working Men's Association was formally established on June 26, 1836, when a prospectus and rules were submitted and agreed to. The prospectus began as follows:

'Among the causes that most contribute to the perpetuation of abuses and corruption in every department of the State, and the indifference manifested towards the interest of the millions, none have been more pregnant with evil than the divisions and dissensions among the working classes themselves.' . . . The Association, it would appear, was to concentrate on the industrial salvation of the working classes. Members were to belong to the 'industrious classes'; others might be elected, but they were to be mere honorary members. . . . William Lovett was the first secretary, Henry Hetherington the first treasurer. . . .

At the end of February [1837] the Working Men's Association held a meeting at the Crown and Anchor Tavern, in order to submit a petition for presentation to Parliament demanding Equal Representation (200 electoral districts of equal size), Universal Suffrage (males over the age of twenty-one), residential qualification (six months), Annual Parliaments (general election every June 24), No Property Qualification (but 200 supporters required to nominate), Vote by Ballot (to take place in the Church buildings), and Payment of Members (£400 a year). This petition was submitted to a public meeting at the Crown and Anchor, in the Strand, on February 28, 1837, and approved. This was the 'nucleus of the far-famed *People's Charter*, which may be said to have had its origin at this meeting' [William Lovett].

Julius West, *A History of the Chartist Movement*, 1920

. . . AND ITS END

At last the 10th [of April, 1848—when the Charter was to be presented to Parliament after a great demonstration in London] dawned upon the waiting world. Prodigious preparations had been made by the authorities. Four thousand policemen guarded the bridges, Palace Yard, and Trafalgar Square; 1,500 Chelsea pensioners had been fetched out from their retirement and entrusted with the defence of Battersea and Vauxhall. Eight thousand soldiers were distributed over various strategic points along the Embankment between the Tower and Millbank. Twelve guns were in readiness at the Royal Mews. Three steamboats had been procured in order to move soldiers about from point to point should occasion arise for their services. The clerks at the General Post Office had been equipped with rifles. And, finally, over one hundred and fifty thousand special constables had been sworn in to protect property behind the firing line. . . . The late Sir Spencer Ponsonby-Fane, then a junior clerk in the Foreign Office, has described the internal defences of his Department on the great day. 'The ground-floor windows of the office were all blocked up with the huge bound volumes of the *Times* newspaper, which it was supposed would resist bullets.' . . . At eight o'clock the Convention [of Chartist leaders] met. . . . At ten o'clock a car drawn by six horses arrived, . . . and the delegates mounted and were driven to Kennington Common. . . . Within the next hour a number of other processions from various parts of London had congregated. What was the total number of Chartists present? . . . According to *The Northern Star* [the Chartist newspaper], 250,000. There is no reason to doubt the correctness of the official estimate of '15,000 to 20,000'. . . . About 2 p.m. the meeting dispersed. The Petition was packed into three cabs and . . . was driven off to the House of Commons. They were refused a safe-conduct over Westminster Bridge, and had ignominiously to reach Westminster through back streets and over Blackfriars Bridge. . . .

The fate of the Petition was even more ignominious than that of the projected procession. Even before its presentation voices had been heard to suggest that the alleged total number of signatures—5,706,000 according to O'Connor's most frequent estimate—was largely inflated. . . . The Government worked on the line suggested by these doubters. The Petition was immediately on its arrival handed over to a staff of clerks, who counted up the signatures and found that there were no more than 1,975,496. On April 13 the Committee on Public Petitions presented its report. It stated that large numbers of signatures on consecutive sheets were in the same handwriting; and that a large number of distinguished individuals whose allegiance to Chartism had been completely unsuspected had put their names to the Petition. Among these, the Committee grieved to find Victoria Rex [*sic*], April 1, the Duke of Wellington, Sir Robert Peel, and Colonel Sibthorp. [Col. Sibthorp was the most notorious and violent reactionary of his day and won fame by bitterly opposing the holding of the Great Exhibition of 1851.] Another class of signatures was represented by a few specimens such as No Cheese, Pugnose, Flatnose, Punch. . . . The Committee did not even give O'Connor's estimate of the weight of the Petition the benefit of the doubt. He had declared it weighed five tons; the Committee, after trial, reduced the estimate to five hundredweight three-quarters.

Julius West, *A History of the Chartist Movement*, 1920

THE NEED FOR CO-OPERATION

In Rochdale, as elsewhere, Co-operation was born out of distress. Holyoake, in his 'History of the Rochdale Pioneers', relates as follows the conditions in Rochdale in the early '40s: 'The condition in Rochdale would be incredible, did it not rest upon authority. Sharman Crawford, the member for the borough, declared in the House of Commons in the debate, September 20th, 1841, that in Rochdale there were 136 persons living on 6d a week, 200 on 10d per week, 508 on 1s per week, 855 on 1s 6d per week, and 1,500 were living on 1s 10d per week. Five-sixths of those he spoke of had scarcely any blankets, 85 families had no blankets, 46 families had only chaff beds with no covering at all.' We can agree with Holyoake that the facts would be incredible without authority for them; what makes the facts about blankets seem worse and the conditions less necessary is that Rochdale was, and is, in a woollen-weaving district, and that many weavers were at the time out of work. . . .

F. Hall and W. P. Watkins, *Co-operation*, 1937

. . . AND THE ANSWER

Stories about the Rochdale Pioneers are legion. Many of them are apocryphal. Yet the facts of achievement speak louder and more romantically than the words of all the imaginative historians.

Their number, it is said, comprised 28 weavers whose capital of £28 was raised in weekly subscriptions of a few coppers. Their first stock, housed in a humble shop at Toad Lane, consisted of flour, oatmeal, sugar, butter and candles. The bare shelves excited as much derision as the informal opening ceremony on December 21st, 1844; for then the bold adventurers suffered so much from stage fright that it was left to a woman to pull down the shutters and reveal to the waiting crowd how poor were the resources with which the Pioneers hoped to emancipate consumers from the evils inherent in the Industrial Revolution. Fortunately, in their rules, their statement of objectives, and their method of trading, the men of Rochdale showed common sense well calculated to attract wide support.

The Rochdale Society of Equitable Pioneers was registered under the Friendly Societies Act on October 24th, 1844. Included in its book of rules was this seven-point programme:

(1) The objects of this Society are to form arrangements for the pecuniary benefit and improvement of the social and domestic condition of its members, by raising a sufficient amount of capital in shares of one pound each, to bring into operation the following plans and arrangements.

(2) The establishment of a store for the sale of provisions, clothing, etc.

(3) The building, purchasing, or erecting of a number of houses, in which those members desiring to assist each other in improving their domestic and social conditions may reside.

(4) To commence the manufacture of such articles as the Society may determine upon, for the employment of such members as may be without employment, or who may be suffering in consequence of repeated reduction in their wages.

(5) As a further benefit and security to the members of this Society, the Society shall purchase or rent an estate or estates of land, which shall be cultivated by the members who may be out of employment or whose labour may be badly remunerated.

(6) That as soon as practicable, this Society shall proceed to arrange the powers of production, distribution, education and government; or in other words to establish a self-supporting home colony of united interest, or assist other societies in establishing such colonies.

(7) That for the promotion of sobriety a Temperance Hotel be opened in one of the Society's houses as soon as convenient.

. . . Point seven, it is recorded, was incorporated following a discussion held in 'The Weavers' Arms'. . . . Co-operators in Rochdale had discovered the secret of taking profit out of price. No longer were they to labour and wait for the benefits of a distant millennium. The rewards of purchasing locally were to be immediate and tangible; pure food, full weight, and a dividend every six months, of a few shillings or pounds, which they could convert into clothing or furniture, or allow to accumulate in the funds of the Society. . . . Rochdale's pioneers were possessed of high courage. They fostered the idea that the welfare of their association stood above every personal interest, fostered it so sedulously that members gave gladly of their time to act as voluntary shop assistants. . . . The Christian Socialists scattered broadsheets among the working men of England during Chartist times. "Many of you are wronged, and many besides yourself know it', they told the people, but 'you want more than Acts of Parliament can give'. This 'something more', whether provided by Trade Unionism or Co-operation, had to be protected by Acts of Parliament. . . . The Christian Socialists formulated and forced through Parliament the Industrial and Provident Societies Act of 1852— the first dim outline of a new commercial code—which gave legal sanction to co-operative shopkeeping. . . .

In 1913 retail societies numbered 1390. Their three million members held £46,000,000 in share and loan capital and reserve funds. . . . If laisser-faire was in eclipse, Co-operation was at least preparing to greet a new dawn.

S. R. Elliott, *England, Cradle of Co-operation*, 1937

KEIR HARDIE'S CHILDHOOD, 1866

I sometimes think if the ministers of our Churches and those who profess to be workers for Christ only realised all that is meant to be poor under our present system, they would bestir themselves to find out and remove the cause. Without any egotism, let me recall this incident from my own boyhood:

The year 1866 was nearing its close. Owing to a lock-out in the ship-building yards on the Clyde, my father had been out of employment for nearly six months. The funds of the Union were so exhausted that the benefits were reduced to 1/6 and 2/- a week. I was the only breadwinner, being employed by a high-class baker in Lancefield Street, Glasgow, for 3/6 a week. My hours were from 7 a.m. to 7.30 p.m., 12½ each day. I was the eldest of a family of three, and the brother next to me was down with fever, from which he never recovered, though his life dragged on for two years thereafter. As most of the neighbourhood had children, they feared coming into the house because of the danger of contagion, and my mother, who was very near her confinement, was in delicate health.

It was the last week in the year. Father had been away for two or three days in search of work. Towards the end of the week, having been up most of the night, I got to the shop fifteen minutes late, and was told by the young lady in charge that if that occurred again I would be 'punished'. I made no reply. I couldn't. I felt like crying. Next morning the same thing happened—I could tell why, but that is neither here nor there. It was a very wet morning and when I reached the shop I was drenched to the skin, barefooted and hungry. There had not been a crust of bread in the house that morning.

But that was pay-day, and I was filled with hope. 'You are wanted upstairs by the master,' said the girl behind the counter, and my heart almost stopped beating. Outside the dining-room door a servant bade me wait till 'master had finished prayers'—he was much noted for his piety. At length the girl opened the door and the sight of that room is fresh in my memory even as I write, nearly fifty years after. Round a great mahogany table sat the members of the family, with the father at the top. In front of him was a very wonderful-looking coffee boiler, in the great glass bowl of which coffee was bubbling. The table was loaded with dainties. My master looked at me over his glasses, and said, in quite a pleasant tone of voice, 'Boy, this is the second morning you have been late. . . . I therefore dismiss you, and, to make you more careful in the future, I have decided to fine you a week's wages. And now you may go.'

I wanted to speak and explain about my home, and I muttered ou
something to explain why I was late, but the servant girl took me by th
arm and led me downstairs. As I passed through the shop the girl i
charge gave me a roll and said a kind word. I knew my mother was waiting for my wages. As the afternoon was drawing to a close I venturec
home, and told her what had happened. It seemed to be the last blow.
The roll was still under my vest, but soaked with rain. That night the
baby was born, and the sun rose on the first of January 1867 over a home
in which there was neither fire nor food . . . the memory of those early
days abides with me and makes me doubt the sincerity of those who
make pretence in their prayers. For such things still abound in our midst.

Keir Hardie, 1915

HARDIE AS A LABOUR CANDIDATE

You are now in the position of men called upon to decide your own fate.
Your lot in life hitherto has been hard and bitter. The commercial
classes are now feeling keenly the effects of the poverty which has been
yours so long. Why is it that in the richest nation in the world those
who produce the wealth should alone be poor? What help can you
expect from those who believe they can only be kept rich in proportion
as you are poor?

. . . I ask you therefore to return to Parliament a man of yourselves
who, being poor, can feel for the poor, and whose whole interest lies in
the direction of securing for you a better and a happier lot. You have
the power to return whom you will to Parliament; I only ask you to use
that power as a means of securing justice to yourselves, by which you
will do injustice to no man.

Keir Hardie, address to the electors of Mid-Lanark at the
by-election of 1888

'TO THE GALLANT SIX HUNDRED'

Men: In my own name, and that of the poor and needy everywhere, I
thank you for your votes. You have shown that there are still a remnant
left of those whose hearts beat true to humanity's cause. . . .

In days to come the great Liberal victory in Mid-Lanark will be remembered only in connection with the stand you made.

Your vote marks a turning-point in history. You have raised the
'conditions of the people' question to a first place.

The meaningless drivel of the ordinary politician must now give place

to the burning words of earnest men, whose hearts are on fire with love
to their kind, men who believe in the Fatherhood of God, the brotherhood of man. . . .

Perfect your organisation; educate your fellows; look to the register;
spread the light—and the future is yours.

> Keir Hardie, address to the 617 men who voted for him,
> 1888 (He came at the bottom of the poll)

VICTORY AT LAST

. . . As land is a prime necessity, not only to living but as to the production of all that goes to support life, it should—so far as practicable—be
common property. It is not proposed to parcel out the land in equal
shares, but to secure to the nation at large that value which the operation
of natural laws, aided by the industry of man, has given to the soil, and
which is at present claimed by a small section of the community who have
done nothing towards producing it. Further, it is now being recognised
that monopoly in land is the parent of all other monopolies, and that
many of the industrial evils from which we suffer have their roots in our
land system. . . .

I have no sympathy whatever with a system which robs the nation of
its wealth, acts as a drag on industry, and cheats labour of its own.

What is known as the Labour Movement has taken firm hold in this
country. It is the outcome of a quickening of the public conscience
towards the condition of the toiling millions, and of the extremes of
wealth and poverty which at present exist. . . . The Government, or
Local Councils, might also with advantage own and manage all Mines,
Banks, Railways, Docks, Waterways, and Tramways. These, and similar
measures designed to lighten and sweeten the cheerless lot of the workers,
would find in me a willing advocate, while I would cordially support all
forms of legislation which would rid honest industry of the useless idler,
whether personified in the absentee landlord, the sweating shareholder,
or the gambling and swindling stockbroker.

> Keir Hardie, address to the electors of South West Ham, who
> in 1891 returned him with a majority of 1,232

HOW HARDIE WENT TO WESTMINSTER

The dockers of West Ham had decided that I should go to Parliament
in a 'coach', like other M.P.s, and had actually raised money for the purpose. When, however, I declined their offer, they resolved to have a

'beano' on their own. Whereupon they hired a large-sized waggonette to drive to Westminster in, from which to give me a cheer as I entered the gates, and, good honest souls, invited me to a seat therein. Only a churl could have said them nay. The cornet-player 'did himself proud' on the way up from Canning Town, and the occupants of the brake cheered lustily as I was crossing Palace Yard. The cornet may also have been used, though that I cannot now for certain recall. The incident was no scheme of mine—in fact, I knew nothing about the arrangements until asked to occupy a seat. It was the outcome of the . . . warm-hearted enthusiasm of my supporters, for which I honoured them then, even as I do now.

Keir Hardie, the first Labour M.P., 1892

HARDIE'S MAIDEN SPEECH

I am told my amendment, if it should pass, will be a vote of censure on the Government. It is meant for a vote of censure; any Government that can ignore this question of the unemployed, and that yet claims to represent and guard the interests of every class of the community, is unworthy the confidence of this House and of the nation.

Keir Hardie, on an amendment to an address to the throne, 1893

THE LIFE OF JOSEPH ARCH

I was born at Barford in Warwickshire on 10 November 1826. . . . Three generations of Arches sleep the sleep of the just in Barford Churchyard. . . . Within a stone's throw of the graveyard and nearly opposite the parish church, with its fifteenth-century tower, stands the homely cottage in which I first saw the light. It had been in the possession of the Arch family for a good 150 years. . . . The open chimney and the black beams of the living room show its true age plainly enough; so do the black beams of the gable at the back which overlooks my workshop and my half acre of garden. . . . My mother was shrewd, strong-willed and self reliant. In personal appearance she was a fine, big, stout, healthy-looking woman, and I am as like her as two peas. . . . In our village we had a most despotic parson's wife, a kind of would be lady pope, and one day she took it into her head to issue a decree. She gave out that all the girls attending school were to have their hair cut round like a basin more like prison girls than anything else. My mother put her foot down and said she would never allow her daughters to have their hair cut in such an unsightly way. When she heard this the parson's wife became very nasty. . . . She proceeded to make things very uncomfortable for my mother; but she had met her match and more in the agricultural labourer's wife. My mother fought it out inch by inch and though she had a tough fight of it she won in the end. My father, if he had been left to himself, would have given in at once, for the sake of peace and quietness—he was against offending the 'powers that be' in a general way—but my mother pulled too hard for him. She went out and did battle, but from that time my parents never received a farthing's worth of charity in the way of soup, coals or the like, which were given regularly and as a matter of course from the rectory to nearly every poor person in the village.

Though this was a real hardship with wages at nine shillings or at most twelve shillings a week, my mother would not let it trouble her. Numbers of people used to go to the rectory for soup but not a drop of it did we touch. I have stood at our door with my mother and I have seen her in fact look sad as she watched the little children toddle past, carrying the tin cans, and their toes coming out of their boots. . . .

I was a youngster of nine when I began to earn money. My first job was crow-scaring and for this I received fourpence a day. . . . Had I been a miner's son I might have been in those days slaving my wretched little life away in the depths of a coal mine, breathing foul air, herding with other children of my own age or younger still, dragging load after load of coal up ladders, or sitting behind a door in the pitch dark for 14 hours at a stretch. . . . I must admit however that if this sort of thing did not prove harmful to robust boys with a sound constitution, like myself, it played havoc with the weakly ones and set loose all too soon the sleeping dogs of disease, the fell dogs of consumption and bronchitis and rheumatism, which devoured them wholesale when they should have been in their manhood's prime. . . .

From crow-scarer to ploughboy was my next step, with an accompanying increase in wage of twopence a day. . . . I went into different English counties and also into Wales, hedge-cutting, and I kept my eyes and ears wide open, while going my hedge-cutting and mowing rounds. I saw there was a smouldering discontent among the different classes of agricultural labourers, but they lacked the energy to better themselves. The fact was, very few of them could write a letter, so the majority were afraid to go from home. . . . Practically, they were voiceless and voteless and hopeless . . .

It was early in the forties when I made my way back like a homing pigeon to the old Arch roof tree. . . . By this time I had formed my political opinions. When I was only about 18 years of age I made up my mind to be a Liberal, and I have stuck to the party ever since. I expect the Tory

barley bread I had to feed on got into my bones and made me a Liberal.
. . . As a lad, every time I earned a penny, by doing odd jobs or running
an errand, I would buy some old papers . . . I would read Gladstone and
Bright's speeches and from them I formed my opinions. . . . There was
only one remedy and that was *combination*. . . . I saw the time coming when
as one man they would waken to the fact that 'Union makes Strength'. . . .
In 1872 that time came and found me ready.

Joseph Arch, *The Story of His Life, by Himself*, 1898

THE CALL TO ACTION

The day was 7 February 1872. It was a very wet morning and I was busy
at home on a carpentering job. I was making a box. My wife came in to
me and said, 'Joe, here's three men come to see you. What for, I don't
know.' But *I* knew fast enough. In walked the three, they turned out to
be labourers from over Wellesbourne way. I stopped work and we had a
talk. They said they had come to ask me to hold a meeting at Wellesbourne that evening. They wanted to get the men together and start a
Union directly. I told them, if they did form a Union, they would have
to fight hard for it and they would have to suffer a good deal; both they
and their families. They said the labourers were prepared both to fight
and suffer. Things could not be worse; wages were so low and provisions
were so dear, that nothing but downright starvation lay before them
unless the farmers could be made to raise their wages. Asking was of no
use; it was nothing but waste of breath; so they must join together and
strike and hold out till the employers gave in. . . .

I remember that evening as if it were but yesterday. When I set out
I was dressed in a pair of cord trousers, and cord vest and an old flannel
jacket. . . . The off chance of failure was present with me as I trudged
forward through the slush that chill February evening. . . . When I
reached Wellesbourne lo and behold it was as lively as a swarm of bees
in June. We settled that I should address the meeting under the old
chestnut tree and I expected to find some 30 or 40 of the principal men
there. What then was my surprise to see not a few tens but many hundreds of labourers; there were nearly 2,000 of them. The news that I was
going to speak that night had been spread about; and so the men had come
in from all the villages round within a radius of 10 miles. Wellesbourne
village was there, every man in it; and they had come from Marston and
Cocksley and Charlecote and Hampton Lucy and from Barford to hear
what I had to say to them. By this time the night had fallen pitch dark;
but the men got bean poles and hung lanterns on them and we could see
well enough. It was an extraordinary sight and I shall never forget it, no

not to my dying day. I mounted an old pig-stool and in the flickering light of the lanterns I saw the earnest, upturned faces of these poor brothers of mine—faces gaunt with hunger and pinched with want, all looking towards me and ready to listen to the words that would fall from my lips. These white slaves of England stood there with the darkness all about them, like the Children of Israel waiting for some one to lead them out of the land of Egypt. I determined that, if they made a mistake and took the wrong turning it would not be my fault and so I stood on my pig-stool and spoke out straight and strong for Union. My speech lasted nearly an hour I believe, but I was not measuring my minutes then. By the end of it the men were properly roused and they pressed in and crowded up asking questions; they regularly pelted me with them; it was a perfect hailstorm. We passed a resolution to form a Union then and there, and the names of the men could not be taken down fast enough; we enrolled between 200 and 300 that night. It was a brave start, and before we parted, it was arranged that there should be another meeting at the same place in a fortnight's time. I knew now that a fire had been kindled which would catch on, and spread and run abroad like sparks in the stubble; and I felt certain that this night we had set light to a beacon, which would prove a rallying point for the agricultural labourers throughout the country. . . .

A small committee was got together, a secretary appointed, and we set actively to work. Notices were served upon the farmers asking for sixteen shillings a week, with a week's notice if they refused. . . . In a very short time there were a hundred men out in Wellesbourne alone. . . . The movement spread on and on into no less than 8 counties. The men of Oxfordshire, Herefordshire, Leicestershire, Somersetshire, Norfolkshire, Northamptonshire, Essex and Worcestershire rose to their feet in their valley of dry bones and stood up for Union. Then the whole country was aroused and was ringing with the news. All the leading papers took note of the strange thing; they could no longer ignore that a great moral and intellectual awakening was in progress among the downtrodden peasantry of England.

Joseph Arch, *The Story of His Life, by Himself*, 1898

(Joseph Arch eventually became a Liberal M.P., after leading a campaign for the granting of the vote to farm labourers.)

FOUNDATION OF THE FABIAN SOCIETY

In 1883 we were content with nothing less than the prompt 'reconstruction of society in accordance with the highest moral possibilities'. . . . The Fabian Society was warlike in origin: it came into existence through a schism in an earlier society for the peaceful regeneration of the race by the cultivation of perfection of individual character. Certain members of that circle, modestly feeling that the revolution would have to wait an unreasonably long time if postponed until they personally had attained perfection, set up the banner of Socialism militant; seceded from the Regenerators; and established themselves independently as the Fabian Society. That was how the Fabian began; and although exactly the same practical vein which had led its founders to insist on an active policy afterwards made them the most resolute opponents of Insurrectionism, the Constitutionalism which now distinguishes us was as unheard of at the Fabian meetings in 1884 and 1885 as at the demonstrations of the Social Democratic Federation, or the Socialist League. . . .

. . . It will at once be asked why, in that case, we did not join them instead of forming a separate society. Well, the apparent reason was that we were then middle class all through, rank and file as well as leaders, whereas the League and Federation were quite proletarian in their rank and file. But whatever weight this sort of consideration may have had with our members in general, it had none with our leaders, most of whom, indeed, were active members of the Federation as well. It undoubtedly prevented working men from joining the Fabian whilst we were holding our meetings in one another's drawing rooms; but it did not prevent any Fabian worth counting from joining the working-class organisations. The true cause of the separation lay deeper. Differences, which afterwards became explicit and definite, were latent from the first in the temperament and character of the Fabians. When I myself, on the point of joining the Social Democratic Federation, changed my mind and joined the Fabian instead, I was guided by no discoverable difference in programme or principles, but solely by an instinctive feeling that the Fabian and not the Federation would attract the men of my own bias and intellectual habits who were then ripening for the work that lay before us. . . . Our preference for practical suggestions and criticisms, and our impatience of all general expressions of sympathy with working-class aspirations, not to mention our way of chaffing our opponents in preference to denouncing them as enemies of the human race, repelled from us some warm-hearted and eloquent Socialists, to whom it seemed callous and cynical to be even commonly self-possessed in the presence of the sufferings upon which Socialists make war. But there was far too much equality and personal intimacy among the Fabians to allow of any member presuming to get up and preach at the rest in the fashion which the working classes still tolerate submissively from their leaders. We knew that a certain sort of oratory was useful for 'stoking up' public meetings; but we needed no stoking up, and, when any orator tried the process on us, soon made him understand that he was wasting his time and ours. I, for one, should be very sorry to lower the intellectual standard of the Fabian by making the atmosphere of its public discussions the least bit more congenial to stale declamation than it is at present. If our debates are to be kept whole-some, they cannot be too irreverent or too critical. And the irreverence, which has become traditional with us, comes down from those early days when we often talked such nonsense that we could not help laughing at ourselves.

Bernard Shaw, *Essays in Fabian Socialism*, 1889

A SOCIALIST MEETING IN HAMMERSMITH, 1890

The Sunday morning of my visit . . . he [William Morris] was scheduled as one of the speakers at Hammersmith Bridge, the favourite Sunday morning pitch of the branch. . . . Shortly after 10 o'clock one or two other members called in, in order to take with them the literature and the banner for the meeting . . . and we sallied forth. The banner of the branch was a handsome ensign and Morris bore it furled on its pole over his shoulder. . . .

It was a glorious morning and the propaganda strength of the branch was well represented at the bridge. . . . At least 5 or 6 of us spoke [and] the meeting was prolonged beyond the usual hour—1 p.m.—with the result that three quarters of the audience had melted away into the neigh-bouring public houses before a collection could be taken or a proper opportunity afforded for questions.

The audience at the bridge consisted for the most part of working men, who were accustomed to spend an hour or so on Sunday morning lounging on the bridge before dinner—or public-house time. The majority of them seemed quite amicably disposed towards the Socialist meeting, but did not trouble themselves much about politics. . . . There was not wanting, however, a sufficient spice of opposition on the part of one or two habitués, men from the Tory Democratic camp, who inter-jected questions and occasionally insisted on stating their views. One of these—the most harassing of them in fact—eventually declared himself a convert to Socialism and joined the branch—an acquisition which proved a misfortune in disguise. As an interrupter and opponent the individual excited interest at the meetings, and gave easy points to our speakers; but as an evangelist of Socialism he did not shine. He was so blundering in his arguments and so obviously disreputable in his boozing habits that the branch prayed audibly for his reconversion to his old anti-Socialist principles and his return to the Tory fold.

R. B. Glasier, *William Morris*, 1929

COMPETITION AT THE DOCKS

(Henry Mayhew's work on the condition of the poorer classes in London, like that of Charles Booth later in the same century, was important in that it helped to show the need for social reform—a need which most Victorians refused to believe existed.)

In the scenes I have lately witnessed, the want has been positively tragic and the struggle for life partaking of the sublime. . . . He who wishes to behold one of the most extraordinary and least-known scenes of this metropolis, should wend his way to the London Dock gates at half-past seven in the morning. There he will see congregated within the principal entrance masses of men of all grades, looks and kinds. Some in half fashioned surtouts burst at the elbows, with the dirty shirts showing through. Others in greasy sporting jackets with red pimpled faces. Others in the rags of their half-slang gentility, with the velvet collars of their patelots worn through to the canvas. Some in rusty black, with their waistcoats fastened tight up to the throat. Others, again, with the knowing thieves' curl on each side of the jaunty cap; whilst here and there you may see a big-whiskered Pole, with his hands in the pockets of his plaited French trousers. Some loll outside the gates, smoking the pipe which is forbidden within; but these are mostly Irish.

Presently you know, by the stream pouring through the gates and the rush towards particular spots, that the 'calling foremen' have made their appearance. Then begins the scuffling and scrambling forth of countless hands high in the air, to catch the eye of him whose voice may give them work. As the foreman calls from a book the names, some men jump on the backs of the others, so as to lift themselves high above the rest, and attract the notice of him who hires them. All are shouting. Some cry aloud his surname, some his christian name, others call out their own names, to remind him that they are there. Now the appeal is made in Irish blarney—now in broken English. Indeed, it is a sight to sadden the most callous, to see thousands of men struggling for only one day's hire; the scuffle being made the fiercer by the knowledge that hundreds out of the number there assembled must be left to idle the day out in want. To look in the faces of that hungry crowd is to see a sight that must be ever remembered. Some are smiling to the foreman to coax him into remembrance of them; others, with their protruding eyes, eager to snatch at the hoped-for pass. For weeks many have gone there, and gone through the same struggle—the same cries; and have gone away, after all, without the work they had screamed for. . . . The scenes witnessed at the London Dock were of so painful a description, the struggle for one day's work—the scramble for twenty-four hours' extra-subsistence and extra-life were of so tragic a character that I was anxious to ascertain if possible the exact number of individuals in and around the metropolis who live by dock labour. . . . Until I came to investigate the condition of the dock-labourer I could not have believed it possible that near upon 2,000 souls in one place alone live, chameleon-like, upon the air, or that an easterly wind . . . could deprive so many of bread. . . . That the sustenance of thousands of families should be as fickle as the very breeze itself; that the weathercock should be the index of daily want or daily ease to such a vast number of men, women and children, was a climax of misery and wretchedness that I could not have imagined to exist; and since that I have witnessed such scenes of squalor, and crime and suffering as oppress the mind even to a feeling of awe. . . . Many come to see the riches, but few the poverty, abounding in absolute masses round the far-famed port of London. . . . By the labourers themselves I am assured that, taking one week with another, they do not gain 5 shillings weekly throughout the year.

Henry Mayhew, *London Labour and the London Poor*, 1861

THE FIRST GREAT VICTORY

From the Dock Strike of 1889, the present-day organisation of the wage-earners took its rise. It marked the beginning of that close alliance in thought and purpose between the Trade Union Movement and the Socialist Movement which produced in due time the Labour Party. . . . I am also on historically firm ground in saying that the regeneration of the Trade Union Movement dates from this great social event. Trade Unionism among the general workers, let me repeat, was an absolute weakling, regarded as an illegitimate offspring, and treated like one by the well-established and respectable Trade Unionism of the skilled crafts and trades. To set our Union on its feet and to win the respect of the craft Unions, we had to demonstrate the strength of our purpose, the soundness of our strategy, and the skill of our generalship in actual warfare with the employers. The Dock Strike was a test, not only of intelligence and will on our part, but of the ability to seize opportunities as they arose, to evoke and to make use of public sympathy as one of the weapons of our warfare and to transform militant enthusiasm and hectic excitement into Trade Union loyalty and sober realism. . . .

Even so, our battle with the Dock Company seemed to my imagination to resemble the duel of David and Goliath. This comparison I made when I went to see, in his office in Leadenhall Street, the Chairman of the Directors of the Dock Company, Mr Norwood. He was a man of Herculean proportions, six feet high and weighing twenty stone. He glowered with wrath at my Lilliputian presence. I was David to his Goliath. He fired at me in thunderous tones the question: 'Do you think you can manage the Docks?' My audacity was challenged and the opening having been given to me, I hurled back my answer like the pebble from David's sling: 'If I could not manage better than you muddlers, I would cut my throat.' . . .

From Leadenhall Street to Tower Hill is but a small distance as the motor bus rolls. It was on Tower Hill that the fight was really fought. . . . Here, where Wat Tyler once pitched his camp when he led the peasants of Norfolk and Suffolk, Cambridge and Hertfordshire, Sussex and Surrey, and the men of Kent, on London, our ragged battalions assembled, day after day, and every day, for more than a month, in sunshine and in rain. . . . Our daily processions, it must be understood, were not only demonstrations and advertisements for our cause, but in the nature of relief expeditions. In our marches we collected contributions in pennies, sixpences and shillings, from the clerks and City workers, who were touched perhaps to the point of sacrifice by the emblem of poverty and starvation carried in our procession—the 'dockers' dinner', a herring and dry bread, which the strikers found a sardonic pleasure in displaying, particularly in the business centres of the city, and before the eyes of the Dock officials gathered at the windows of Dock House when the procession, with bands playing, went by. . . .

From the first the Cardinal [Cardinal Manning, chairman of the self-appointed arbitration committee] showed himself to be the dockers' friend, though he had family connections in the shipping interests, represented on the other side. Our demands were too reasonable, too moderate to be set aside by an intelligence so fine, a spirit so lofty, as that which animated the frail, tall figure with its saintly, emaciated face and the strangely compelling eyes.

On our side there was no margin for concession. We had made no extravagant demands. The Cardinal's diplomacy, suave, subtle, ineffably courteous to all parties concerned, yet exercised with that suggestion of authority which seems to attach to the priestly office only when it is exercised by Roman Catholics, was devoted to giving the Employers'

Committee an avenue for retreat. Not all the mediators entered into the negotiations in this spirit. Some of them felt that it would be dangerous for the dockers to win. I have met that spirit since. It is the fatal delusion of the small group of class-proud, stiff-necked, arrogant people, possessing all the defects of an aristocracy, with none of its virtues, who think they are placed by Providence in a position to command and rule, and think that the common masses must merely submit. . . .

Nobody more human, more diplomatic, more skilled in dealing with the human heart and mind, could have been found: patient, persuasive, but very, very firm in handling the injured feelings of the Lord Mayor, and the harsh and unsympathetic attitude of the Bishop [Temple, Bishop of London and later Archbishop of Canterbury], no less than the thrusting aggressiveness of John Burns. . . . Alone among my colleagues I opposed his compromise. How could I resist this gentle old man, bowed with the weight of years, who bent his tall, stooping figure over the school desk and talked to us about the sufferings which the Strike inflicted on the workers' families, commending the settlement he had secured, as a business arrangement which gave us all he had demanded, or nearly all, to become effective in six weeks' time. . . .

I have refrained for many years from saying these things, and I still hope to live many years longer, but in my moments of despair, of heartache and apparent failure, I have remembered the martyrdom of the pioneers. I carry in my memory the inspiring words of Cardinal Manning, 'Whatever is worth doing, is worth doing well, whether you succeed or not; to wear a crown you must bear a cross'.

Ben Tillett, Memories and Reflections, 1931

A SOCIALIST ROMANCE

It was, I think, in the spring of 1888 that my friend J. J. Dent, at that time General Secretary of the [Working Men's] Club and Institute Union, talked to me, in tones of mingled admiration and suspicion, about a group of clever young men who, with astonishing energy and audacity, were haranguing the London Radical clubs; contributing innumerable articles and paragraphs, signed or unsigned, to the *Star* and the *Daily Chronicle*, and distributing, far and wide, 'Facts for Socialists', and other subversively plausible pamphlets. One result of these activities was a stream of resolutions to Liberal Headquarters and Liberal leaders, passed by Radical clubs and Trade Union branches, in favour of the legal eight hours day; of municipal ownership and administration of water, gas, tramways and docks for the profit of the ratepayers; of an unlimited extension of free educational and health services; and, in order to meet the cost, of stiff taxation of wealth by increased and steeply graduated income taxes and death duties. 'There are among them', said he, 'some very clever speakers, but the man who organises the whole business, drafts the resolutions and writes the tracts, is Sidney Webb.' . . .

Hence when, in October 1889, a friend forwarded to me the recently published *Fabian Essays* as the true gospel of distinctively British social-ism, I read this daintily-turned-out volume from cover to cover. In passing it on to J. C. Gray of the Co-operative Union, I find that I inci-dentally remarked . . . that 'by far the most significant and interesting essay is the one by Sidney Webb; *he has the historic sense*'. Those interested in tracing 'affinities' may find amusement if not instruction in the fact that, in an appreciative review of Charles Booth's first volume published in the *Star* in the preceding spring . . . [Webb] had observed that 'the only contributor with any literary talent is Miss Beatrice Potter'! . . .

The reason for our meeting in the first days of January 1890 was in itself a presage of our future comradeship in work. The critical phase of my father's illness having once again passed away, my sister Kate begged me to return with her husband to London for a week's rest and recreation, a welcome opportunity to get material I urgently needed for the first chapter of my forthcoming book. For whilst planning out my analysis of the Co-operative Movement of that day, I became aware that I lacked historical background. . . . 'Sidney Webb, one of the Fabian Essayists, is your man,' casually remarked a friendly woman journalist. 'He knows everything; when you go out for a walk with him he literally pours out information.' An interview was arranged during my short stay in Lon-don. A list of sources, accessible at the British Museum, including the then little known Place manuscripts, various State trials, old Chartist periodicals, and autobiographies of working-class agitators, was swiftly drafted, then and there, in a faultless handwriting, and handed to me. A few days later brought the first token of personal regard in the shape of a newly published pamphlet by the Fabian on the Rate of Interest, thus opening up a regular correspondence.

I give a few from many entries from the manuscript diary revealing the new ferment at work. . . .

I feel exiled from the world of thought and action of other men and women. London is in a ferment: strikes are the order of the day; the new Trade Unionism, with its magnificent conquest of the docks, is striding along with an arrogance rousing employers to a keen sense of danger, and to a determination to strike against strikes. The socialists, led by a small set of able young men (Fabian Society), are manipulating London radicals, ready, at the first checkmate of Trade Unionism, to voice a growing desire for state action; and I, from the peculiarity of my social position, should be in the midst of all parties, sympathetic with all, allied with none, in a true vantage ground for impartial observation of the forces at work. Burnett and the older Trade Unionists on the one side; Tom Mann, Tillett and Burns on the other; round about me co-operators of all schools, together with new acquaintances among the leading socialists. And as a background, all those respectable and highly successful men, my brothers-in-law, typical of the old reign of private property and self-interested action. . . . And then I turn from the luxurious homes of these picked men of the individualist system, and struggle through an East End crowd of the wrecks, the waifs and strays of this civilisation; or I enter a debating society of working men, and listen to the ever-increasing cry of active brains, doomed to the treadmill of manual labour, for a career in which intellectual initiative tells: the bitter cry of the nineteenth-century working man and the nineteenth-century woman. And the whole seems a whirl of contending actions, aspirations and aims, out of which I dimly see the tendency towards a socialist community, in which there will be individual freedom and public property, instead of class slavery and private possession of the means of subsistence of the whole people. [1 February 1890.]

Sidney Webb, the socialist, dined here [Devonshire House Hotel] to meet the Booths. A remarkable little man with a huge head and a tiny body, a breadth of forehead quite sufficient to account for the encyclopædic character of his knowledge. A Jewish nose, prominent eyes and mouth, black hair, somewhat unkempt, spectacles and a most bourgeois black coat shiny with wear. But I like the man. There is a directness of speech, an open-mindedness, an imaginative warm-heartedness which will carry him far. He has the self-assurance of one who is always thinking faster than his neighbours; who is untroubled by doubts, and to whom the acquisition of facts is as easy as the grasping of things; but he has no vanity and is totally unself-conscious. Hence his absence of consciousness as to treading on his neighbours' corns. Above all, he is utterly disinterested and is, I believe, genuine in his faith that collective control and collective administration will diminish, if not abolish, poverty. [14 February 1890.] . . .

Glasgow Co-operative Congress. Exquisite Whitsun weather. A long journey up in third-class saloon, I, on one of the two comfortable seats of the carriage, with S.W. squatted on a portmanteau by my side, and relays of working-men friends lying at my feet, discussing earnestly Trade Unionism, co-operation and socialism. . . .

In the evening S.W. and I wandered through the Glasgow streets. A critical twenty-four hours, followed by another long walk by glorious sunset through the crowded streets, knocking up against drunken Scots. With glory in the sky and hideous bestiality on the earth, two socialists came to a working compact. [Whitsun, 1890.]

A day out in Epping Forest. . . . We talked economics, politics, the possibility of inspiring socialism with faith leading to works. He read me poetry, as we lay in the Forest, Keats and Rossetti, and we parted. [27 July 1890.]

Throughout the remaining months of 1890 we saw little of each other. When not in attendance on my father, I was staying in Glasgow, Manchester, Leeds, Leicester and other big industrial centres, completing the cooperative enquiry and starting the investigation into Trade Unionism. But letters in the faultless handwriting followed me wherever I went, suggesting new sources of information, or telling me of the doings of the Fabians. Occasionally he would forget the 'inevitability of gradualness' and there would be a hitch. But he was soon forgiven after due penitence! In the spring of 1891 I sent my newly-found counsellor proofs of my forthcoming book on the Co-operative Movement. 'I am disappointed', he wrote with commendable sincerity; 'this book ought to have taken six weeks to write, not seven months. Why not let me help you in the investigation into Trade Unionism? Whilst you interview officials and attend Trade Union meetings, I can rush through reports and manuscript minutes at the Union offices.' . . .

The Lincoln Co-operative Congress of 1891 found us journeying down together. 'I cannot tell how things will settle themselves', I write in my diary; 'I think probably in his way. His resolute, patient affection, his constant care for my welfare—helping and correcting me—a growing distrust of a self-absorbed life and the egotism of successful work, done on easy terms and reaping more admiration than it deserves—all these feelings are making for our eventual union.' . . .

We are both of us [I write in my diary, July 7] second-rate minds; but we are curiously combined. I am the investigator and he the executant; between us we have a wide and varied experience of men and affairs. We have also an unearned salary. These are unique circumstances. A considerable work should be the result if we use our combined talents with a deliberate and persistent purpose. . . .

On the first of January 1892 my father died; and six months later we were married.

Here ends 'My apprenticeship' and opens 'Our Partnership'; a working comradeship founded in a common faith and made perfect by marriage; perhaps the most exquisite, certainly the most enduring, of all the varieties of happiness.

Beatrice Webb, *My Apprenticeship*, 1926

(The honeymoon was spent in Ireland, combining pleasure with an investigation into Trade Societies in Dublin.)

THE WORK OF THE WEBBS

Not the smallest part of their contribution has been the visual fact of two Socialists for whom Socialism is not a vague, occasional aspiration towards a hazy, distant ideal, but a robustly practical rule of present existence, and of happy existence. Their action helped—the simplicity, nay austerity of their personal lives and habits. For years, Mrs Webb on 'best' occasions wore the same crimson velvet dress—and very becoming it was. In it, with her tall slender darkness, her vivid flashing eyes, and her agitated dark hair, in which two wings of grey were beginning to appear, she could look very handsome, though she had an inveterate habit of tying herself into knots as she sat on her favourite stool. Sidney was, invariably, in neat blue serge. They eschewed evening dress, as they did the sort of parties at which it was obligatory. . . . For some they talked too much; he softly, she shrilly: but their talk helped, notably in their constant habit of presenting the Socialist point of view as the one that really had got to be taken by any rational, informed intelligence. This enraged some people; enraged them the more that they saw them making Socialism respectable—intellectually and also economically and morally respectable. Not by toning it down, but by treating it as obvious, once you began to use your head. The combination of tolerance with serene conviction, based on knowledge, and on an experience incapable of knowing the taint of envy or jealousy, made them very hard people indeed to argue against. No captain of industry, no banker, no economist, no representative of that governing order which derives its easy authority from command over, and indubitable familiarity with the world as it is, could 'down' them. They always, he from one angle, she from another, knew more about it; the interlocutor could never get across his sense that their views were odd; they suggested to him that his were; that he in fact, could not defend them.

Mary Agnes Hamilton, *Sidney and Beatrice Webb*, 1932

THE GREAT DOCK STRIKE

(Neither Sidney nor Beatrice Webb ever became a 'popular' writer; their work was too scholarly, too factual. The most important of their books, which made clear the benefits that unity had brought to the workers in the past and pointed to the possibilities of greater benefits in the future, was their *History of Trade Unionism*. The following passage can be compared with Ben Tillett's account of the same events.)

The success of such unorganised and unskilled workers as the Matchmakers and the Gas-stokers led to renewed efforts to bring the great army of Dock-labourers into the ranks of Trade Unionism. For two years past the prominent London Socialists had journeyed to the dock gates in the early hours of the morning to preach organised revolt to the crowds of casuals struggling for work. Meanwhile Mr Benjamin Tillett, then working as a labourer in the tea warehouses, was spending his strength in the apparently hopeless task of constituting the Tea-workers and General Labourers' Union. The Membership of this society fluctuated between 300 and 2,500 members; it had practically no funds; and its very existence seemed precarious. Suddenly the organisation received a new impulse. An insignificant dispute on the 12th of August 1889 as to the amount of 'plus' (or bonus earned over and above the fivepence per hour) on a certain cargo, brought on an impulsive strike of the labourers at the South-West India Dock. The men demanded sixpence an hour, the abolition of sub-contract and piecework, extra pay for overtime, and a minimum engagement of four hours. Mr Tillett called to his aid his friends Tom Mann and John Burns, and appealed to the whole body of dock labourers to take up the fight. The strike spread rapidly to all the docks north of the Thames. Within three days ten thousand labourers had, with one accord, left the precarious and ill-paid work to get which they had, morning after morning, fought at the dock gates. The two powerful Unions of Stevedores (the better-paid, trained workmen who load ships for export) cast in their lot with the dockers, and in the course of the next week practically all the river-side labour had joined the strike. Under the magnetic influence and superb generalship of Mr John Burns, . . . the traffic of the world's greatest port was, for over four weeks, completely paralysed. An electric spark of sympathy with the poor dockers fired the enthusiasm of all classes of the community. Public disapproval hindered the dock companies from obtaining, even for their unskilled labour, sufficient blacklegs to take the strikers' place. A public subscription of £48,736 allowed Mr Burns to organise an elaborate system of strike-pay, which not only maintained the honest docker, but also bribed every East End loafer to withhold his labour; and finally the concentrated pressure of editors, clergymen, shareholders, ship-owners, and merchants enabled Cardinal Manning and Mr Sydney Buxton, M.P., as self-appointed mediators, to compel the Dock Directors to concede practically the whole of the men's demands.

Sidney and Beatrice Webb, *The History of Trade Unionism*, 1894

PROGRESS FROM POVERTY

(In 1884, as the following extract points out, one of the periodic slumps of capitalism produced widespread unemployment and distress in Jarrow. Fifty years later, as the passages from *The Town that was Murdered* show, the same events were repeated, not merely in the same trade, but even in the same place. For the whole of this period, under both Liberal and Conservative Governments, booms and slumps continued to alternate. It was only with the election of a Labour Government in 1945 that the remedy proposed by the Socialists as early as 1884 was at last adopted—the planning of national resources for the benefit of the nation and not for private profit.)

Laisser faire, then, was the political and social creed of the Trade Union leaders of this time. Up to 1885 they undoubtedly represented the views current among the rank and file. Ten years ago all observers were agreed that the Trade Unions of Great Britain would furnish an impenetrable barrier against Socialistic projects. Today we find the whole Trade Union world permeated with Collectivist ideas, and . . . the Socialist party supreme in the Trade Union Congress. This revolution in opinion is the chief event of recent Trade Union history. . . .

If we had to assign to any one event the starting of the new current of thought, we should name the wide circulation in Great Britain of Mr Henry George's *Progress and Poverty* during the years 1880–82. The optimist and aggressive tone of the book, in marked contrast with the complacent quietism into which the English working-class movement had sunk . . . sounded the domination note alike of the 'New Unionism' and of the English Socialist Movement of today. Mr George made, it is true, no contribution to the problems of industrial organisation; nor had he, outside of the 'Single Tax' on land values, any intention of promoting a general Collectivist movement. But he succeeded, where previous writers had failed, in widely diffusing among all classes a vivid appreciation of the nature and results of the landlord's appropriation of economic rent. . . .

But if Mr Henry George gave the starting push, it was the propaganda of the Socialists that got the new movement under way. The Socialist party, which became reorganised in London between 1881 and 1883, after practically a generation of quiescence, merged the project of Land Nationalisation in the wider conception of an organised Democratic community in which the collective power and the collective income should be consciously directed to the common benefit of all. . . .

The economic circumstances of the time supplied the Socialist lec
turers with dramatic illustrations of their theory. The acute depressio
of 1878–79 had been succeeded by only a brief and partial expansio
during 1881–83. A period of prolonged though not exceptional contrac
tion followed, during which certain staple trades experienced the mos
sudden and excessive fluctuations. In the great industry of shipbuilding
for instance, the bad times of 1879 were succeeded by a period durin
which trade expanded by leaps and bounds, more than twice the tonnag
being built in 1883 than in 1879. In the very next year this enormou
production came suddenly to an end, many shipbuilding yards bein
closed and whole towns on the north-east coast finding their occupatio
for the moment destroyed. The total tonnage built fell from 1,250,00
in 1883 to 750,000 in 1884, 540,000 in 1885, and to the still lower total o
473,000 in 1886. Thousands of the most highly skilled and best organise
mechanics, who had been brought to Jarrow or Sunderland the yea
before, found themselves reduced to absolute destitution, not from any
failure of their industry, but merely because the exigencies of competitiv
profit-making had led to the concentration in one year of the norma
production of two. 'In every shipbuilding port', says Mr Robert Knigh
in the Boilermakers' Annual Report for 1886, 'there are to be seer
thousands of idle men vainly seeking for an honest day's work. The
privation that has been endured by them, their wives and children, is
terrible to contemplate. Sickness has been very prevalent, whilst the
hundreds of pinched and hungry faces have told a tale of suffering and
privation which no optimism could minimise or conceal. Hide it—cover
it up as we may, there is a depth of grief and trouble the full revelations
of which, we believe, cannot be indefinitely postponed. The workman
may be ignorant of science and the arts, and the sum of his exact knowledge may be only that which he has gained in his closely circumscribed
daily toil; but he is not blind, and his thoughts do not take the shape of
daily and hourly thanksgiving that his condition is not worse than it is;
he does not imitate the example of the pious shepherd of Salisbury Plain,
who derived supreme contentment from the fact that a kind Providence
had vouchsafed him salt to eat with his potatoes. He sees the lavish display
of wealth in which he has no part. He sees a large and growing class enjoying inherited abundance. He sees miles of costly residences, each occupied
by fewer people than are crowded into single rooms of the tenement in
which he lives. He cannot fail to reason that there must be something
wrong in a system which effects such unequal distribution of the wealth
created by labour.'

. . . We see the same spirit spreading even to the most conservative

nd exclusive trades. 'To our minds', writes the Central Secretary of the
powerful Union of Flint Glass Makers, 'it is very hard for employers to
attempt to force men into systems by which they cannot earn an honourable living. ... Why, for example, should Lord Dudley inherit coal-mines
and land producing £1000 a day while his colliers have to slave all the
week and cannot get a living?'

Sidney and Beatrice Webb, *The History of Trade Unionism*, 1894

OUR GREATEST ALLY—FACT

(Charles Booth was not a Socialist, but the vast sixteen-volume
survey of the condition of the people of London which he prepared
during the eighteen-nineties converted many to the cause. His work
revealed both that talk of poverty was not merely the propaganda of
wild agitators, and also that only in state action could improvement
be sought. The young Beatrice Potter was one of the investigators
who collected material for the first volume.)

East London lay hidden from view behind a curtain on which were
painted terrible pictures ... starving children, suffering women, overworked men; horrors of drunkenness and vice; monsters and demons of
inhumanity; giants of disease and despair. Did these pictures truly represent what lay behind, or did they bear to the facts a relation similar to
that which the pictures outside a booth at some country fair bear to the
performance on show within? This curtain we have tried to lift. ...

EAST LONDON

Grouping the classes together, A, B, C, and D are the classes in poverty
or even in want and add up to 314,000 or 35% of the population; while
E, F, G, and H are the classes in comfort ... and add up to 577,000 or
65% of the population.

Separating East London from Hackney the same system of grouping
gives us for East London 370,000 or 38% in poverty, against 440,000
or 62% in comfort, and for Hackney by itself, 43,000 or 24% in poverty
against 140,000 or 76% in comfort. ...

NO. 40 RUPERT PLACE

Occupied by Duckenfield, a man about 30 ... who is now working for a
bricklayer. He has been very uncertain [i.e. often unemployed]. Was out
of work 4 or 5 months and pawned everything. The wife does mangling,
but is much too delicate to keep it up, so does anything she can get. She
works for the Boys' Home. There are 5 children; the eldest, a boy, at

work, who earns 4 shillings a week. Mrs Duckenfield is very ill now; she starves herself for her children. When her husband is in work they pull up arrears. For lodgers, they have in the front room (rent 4 shillings) Maitland, a 'coachman' who 'does anything he can in stables'. Mrs Maitland says they are in a terrible state of poverty. They are quite old people, 60 and 62 respectively. They sold a table and looking glass the other day for 12/6 to get food and pay rent. In the back room (3/6) lives Grindley, who is in consumption; dying. His wife does charring and has 3 days a week at the hospital at 1/6 a day. The man was a butcher and afterwards potman in a public house. Has come down through drink. He is only 30, his wife is 42. She is very good to him. . . .

The state of things which I describe in these pages, though not so appalling as sensational writers would have us believe, is still bad enough to make us feel that we ought not to tolerate it in our midst if we can think of any feasible remedy. To effectually deal with the whole of Class B (very poor but not criminal), for the State to nurse the helpless and incompetent as we in our own families nurse the old, the young, and the sick and provide for those who are not competent to provide for themselves,—may seem an impossible undertaking, but nothing less than this will enable self-respecting labour to obtain its full remuneration and the nation its raised standard of life. . . .

To bring Class B under State regulation would be to control the springs of pauperism; hence what I have to propose may be considered as an extension of the Poor Law. What is the Poor Law system? It is a limited form of Socialism. . . .

Charles Booth, *Life and Labour of the People in London,*
Volumes I and II, 1892

HOW IT ALL BEGAN

Let me next speak of the men and women who made and led the Socialist party through the years of hard labour and adversity. The public could not cotton to the idea of a third party. They had been bred and born in the 2 party tradition. The Tories they knew and the Liberals they knew, but an independent party which took orders from neither of the old parties, but opposed them both, they could not believe in. These Socialists and I.L.P. men must be the dupes or jackals of the Tories, bribed to break the Liberal ranks. Or, if that were not the explanation, they were mere demagogues with some kind of illicit axe to grind. So they wrote and spoke of us scornfully as 'paid agitators'. There was not much pay for these stalwart pioneers and there was not, to all seeing, any chance of kudos or promotion. Hard work, hard knocks and hard fare were their portion. No woman or man inspired by mercenary motives would have worked in the movement for half a year. They were suspected and reviled on every hand, defeated in every battle. When they began with an almost heroic temerity to set up municipal or parliamentary candidates the monotonous results of the polls would have broken any but the stoutest hearts. How often did we open our papers to read:

Eatanswill Election

Sir George Speakeasy (Conservative)	13,450
Mr Athanisis Blowhard (Liberal)	12,201
John Smith (Socialist)	195

But the movement moved. The party grew. The Socialists had one great advantage over the old parties. Their propaganda was continuous. The Tories and Liberals only took their coats off a short time before an election. The Socialists never ceased working. Their meetings went on all the year round, year after year. Their members and their leaders never slackened, never went to sleep. They had active helpers by tens of thousands. They had something more vital and inspiring than a party; they had a cause. They had a definite aim. They knew what they wanted and that if they were to get it they must work for it. So the party increased in numbers and their candidates learned to turn defeat into victory. They won seats on town and city councils, even seats in Parliament, and they gained in confidence and experience. Tory gold does not explain that progress.[1] The new party was better trained and better led than the old. It was like Cromwell's Army 'an army of men of religion'. ... The rank and file understood as well as their commanders what they were fighting for, and were as able and eager to win. I will say for all the Socialist and Labour leaders I met that they were absolutely honest and sincere and that they did not know when they were beaten.

Robert Blatchford, My Eighty Years, 1931

HOW *MERRIE ENGLAND* WAS WRITTEN

We started the *Clarion* on a capital of £400. My brother put in £50 A. M. Thompson and I mortgaged our insurance policies and put in £350 between us. ... And so in the winter of 1891 we buckled to and began to hoe our barren and toilsome row. ...

[1] The charge that Labour candidates were financed by the Conservatives was constantly made at this time but never substantiated. Except in the case of two S.D.F. candidates in 1885, who were repudiated by other Socialists, the charges were without foundation.

D

With a circulation of about 40,000 we plodded on. Then in 1894 I had a brain-wave. We had published a series of my articles in book form with the title *Merrie England* and had sold some 20,000 at a shilling. I suggested an edition at a penny. We found that we could do it at a slight loss if we could sell 100,000. My partners were doubtful. They asked who was going to buy such numbers. I pressed the scheme and the edition was put in hand and advertised in the *Clarion*. The result was startling. Before the 100,000 copies were printed 200,000 were ordered. In less than a year we had printed and sold three quarters of a million copies and the *Clarion* circulation had gone up to 60,000. This success was due to the Socialist and Labour rank and file. If they did not see the use of Labour papers they did see the use of *Merrie England*.

Merrie England was published soon after the formation of the I.L.P., when things were beginning to hum. It came out at the right time. Enthusiasts bought the book by the thousand. It was sold in the streets in Scotland and the North. In Glasgow the scouts went out with a cargo on a lorry. I was offered copies again and again by amateur hawkers who did not know me. I saw one scout in Glasgow sell a copy to a constable on point duty. One day in Manchester, as I was standing by the train ready to start for London, the engine driver came to me and said 'I've got them with me. Six of 'em.' He showed me a copy of the penny *Merrie England* and slapped his chest where others were concealed. Another time I was waiting in the office of Messrs Lewis and Lewis . . . when a grave clerk stepped into the room and, pulling a copy of 'it' out of his pocket, whispered: 'Got it, you see. Always carry one.' The vogue of the book was a surprise to me. I suppose it was the right thing at the right time.

Robert Blatchford, My Eighty Years, 1931

THE EFFECT OF *MERRIE ENGLAND*

There issued from our little room in Corporation Street, Manchester, a million copies of *Merrie England*. There were possibly as many more pirated copies sold in America, and countless thousands more through Welsh, Dutch, German, Scandinavian and Spanish editions. We made no profit out of the sale, but we secured our object by making converts. A year before its issue there were not 500 Socialists in Lancashire; 12 months after there were 50,000. A census taken at the time in a North of England Labour Club showed that 49 members out of 50 had been 'converted' by *Merrie England*. As the *Manchester Guardian* lately said:

'For every convert made by *Das Kapital* there were a hundred made by *Merrie England*.'

> A. M. Thompson, in a preface to *My Eighty Years*, by Robert Blatchford, 1931

A COCKNEY PIONEER

Hawker, stableman, cab-washer, window-cleaner and general handyman, he typified in his wage earning sorrows and his unemployed intervals the 'proletariat' of the Western world. Street corner orator and prisoner for free speech in the street, Williams was an extraordinary example of energetic faith and service to the Socialist cause. Sometimes he strayed into middle class and aristocratic 'Social Welfare' or 'Missionary' assemblies. The staunch old trade unionist tailor, James Macdonald (not Ramsay) had known him many years, and related [in *Justice* on 15 November 1917] how Williams dropped into a drawing room meeting which was discussing methods of bringing the heathen into the Christian fold:

'The chair was occupied by an elderly lady, who waxed eloquent on the necessity of spreading a network of missionaries from some coast-line right into the interior of some benighted place, where the people were heathens of a very low type. Jack spoke, protesting against the sending of missionaries out to foreign parts, when people at their very doorsteps were crying for food and living under conditions that were certainly as bad as those of any heathen. The lady of the chair rose in the most dignified manner and, pointing with her fan to Jack said if that person was invited here, it must have been a mistake. Jack rose slowly from his chair, with a particular look on his face, that I had always noted in him when going to say something nasty, looked round the room, at the floor, at the ceiling, at the walls, at the audience. Then, raising his forefinger and rubbing his ear, his gaze fell slowly on the lady, and he began at his best cockney style: "It's like this 'ere, mum; you don't ask the heathen if they want your missionaries. They go whether they are invited or not. So, as I regard you as heathens, and of a very vicious type, I came to missionise you!" A few suppressed giggles were all the reply that Jack heard as he leisurely left the room.'

> E. J. Gould, *Hyndman, Prophet of Socialism*, 1928

SOCIALISM IN THE CITY

The S.D.F. marched merrily on. In the first week of 1885, Hyndman was lecturing on a possible revolution in 1889, only 4 years ahead—as a joyful centenary of the French crisis of 1789. A few days later, when the S.D.F. discussed the Morris secession [William Morris and nine others had just left the S.D.F.], John Burns of Battersea rose up in the midst of the brethren and affirmed that Hyndman deserved a loyal following, for he had addressed, in the Socialist cause, 66 street corner meetings on 66 successive Sundays. And history tells how Burns himself contributed a hearty share in the agitation of that Winter. Henry George and his friends assembled one day on the steps of the Royal Exchange, and the apostle of the Single Tax [on land] ironically remarked that while a Bible text over the Exchange claimed the earth and its fullness as the Lord's, the actual ownership fell to the landlords. But this was not, after all, adequate Socialism. Jack Williams and John Burns appeared on the scene and drew away part of the audience. Williams demanded the right to work. Burns declared the meeting, held in the centre of profit-making, would become historical by giving three cheers for the social revolution. The cheers were raised.

E. J. Gould, *Hyndman, Prophet of Socialism*, 1928

SOCIALISM IN TRAFALGAR SQUARE

'For Heaven's sake, Burns, keep control of this meeting, for we can't,' said a police inspector to John Burns.

These words were spoken on February 8th, 1886, in Trafalgar Square, where a Fair Trade League demonstration had assembled to demand protectionist tariffs on British products and where the S.D.F. had drawn a crowd to protest that Socialism was the only remedy for unemployment and poverty. From the Northern balustrade of the Square, speeches were delivered by Burns, Champion, Jack Williams, Hyndman . . . and 20 or 30,000 voices shouted in favour of the Social Revolution. Burns, carrying a red flag and riding on men's shoulders, led his multitude past Hyde Park and past aristocratic clubs. Not long before this exciting day, he had been turned out of the New University Club for addressing a crowd of unemployed in a fiery tongue. Clubland temper was combustious on this day and jeering members gathered at club-windows, and missiles, more insulting than hurtful, were flung upon the noisy mob who symbolised the misery and poverty of British millions. At the Achilles statue in Hyde Park, the S.D.F. leaders rallied their comrades, and Burns, Champion, Williams and Hyndman advised a peaceful dispersal. The next day, alarmed tradesmen barricaded their shop-windows. A singular uprush of conscience swelled the Mansion House Relief Fund for the unemployed, to more than £70,000 in 48 hours. . . . An Old Bailey jury, on April 10th, acquitted Burns, Champion, Williams and Hyndman on the charge of seditious conspiracy. In the course of his address to the jury, Hyndman had strikingly referred to his travels round the world and declared that having seen many communities, he judged the condition of the poor classes in Britain and the Continent to be worse than that of the worst savages.

E. J. Gould, *Hyndman, Prophet of Socialism*, 1928

BLOODY SUNDAY

The closing phase of the year was darkened by 'Bloody Sunday', November 13th, 1887, in Trafalgar Square. The authorities had decided to close the Square to the crowds who gave all-too-threatening voice to discontent. Radicals and Socialists resolved to meet and condemn coercion in Ireland. Police stood four deep on all sides of the open Square. Rushes, batonings and blood, supported by the appearance of Grenadier and Life Guards, ended the attempt. John Burns and Cunningham Grahame flung themselves against policemen and suffered 6 weeks' imprisonment in consequence. A young man named Linnell had his thigh broken by a policeman's horse in the scrimmage and he died a few weeks later. His funeral procession from Mid-London to the East End and Bow Cemetery, moved slowly to the moving sound of the 'Dead March', and a burial service, read by the light of a lantern amid December gloom, was followed by speeches by Quelch and William Morris. . . . Morris' poem, prompted by the sadness of Linnell's grave, scorned the reactionary minds that darkened the hopes of a new day and its refrain ran:

> Not one, not one, nor thousands must they slay,
> But one and all if they would dusk the day.

Herbert Burrows composed, for the Bishop of London, a Christmas sermon. In this remarkable sermon, which, though never preached, produced acute impressions, the priest was supposed to say: 'Too long have I neglected the miserable social effects of our so-called Christian civilisation. . . . Today I lay down my robes, I give up my bishopric, my palace and my income. I resign my seat in the House of Lords . . . I give up the pleasures of society and of the world and at last take my place as a man amongst men. . . . The reward of a good conscience and of noble work well done is better far than a palace and £10,000 a year.'

E. J. Gould, *Hyndman, Prophet of Socialism*, 1928

OUR MARTYRED DEAD

(From William Morris's speech over Alfred Linnell's grave.)

Our friend who lies here has had a hard life and met with a hard death, and if society had been differently constituted his life might have been a delightful, a beautiful and a happy one. It is our business to begin to organise for the purpose of seeing that such things shall not happen; to try and make this earth a beautiful and happy place.

William Morris, 1887

SELLING *JUSTICE* ON FOOT

Those were the days [1884] when none of us were above doing anything. We distributed bills, took collections, bawled ourselves hoarse at street-corners and sold *Justice* down Fleet Street and the Strand. This last was really a most extraordinary venture.

It was a curious scene. Morris in his soft hat and blue suit, Champion, Frost and Joynes in the morning garments of the well-to-do, several working men comrades and I myself, wearing the new frock-coat in which Shaw said I was born, with a tall hat and good gloves, all earnestly engaged in selling a penny Socialist paper during the busiest time of day in London's busiest thoroughfare.

H. M. Hyndman, *The Record of an Adventurous Life*, 1911

. . . AND *CLARION* BY BICYCLE

I am an ardent cyclist and have long desired to organise a 'Clarion Cycling Club' in this city. . . . I write to ask whether you will be good enough to mention the subject in the *Clarion* requesting all Clarionettes in Newcastle who are cyclists . . . to communicate with me. . . .

The principal objects of the club will be to visit outlying districts and scatter *Clarions* and Socialistic literature amongst the mining and agricultural population; and, if we have any good speakers among us, deliver addresses on Labour and social questions.

In conclusion, allow me to thank you and the other members of your staff for the glorious revolution the *Clarion* has effected in me. I now have a purpose in life, and my heart yearns to relieve and mitigate the intense poverty and misery existing around me. . . . Before reading your paper I was a rank Tory.

From a letter in the *Clarion*, 28 July 1894

A PAINTER HAS DOUBTS

c. 1895. I asked [William Morris] if Burne-Jones were getting at all inclined towards Socialism. He shrugged his shoulders. 'The Trafalgar Square riots terrified him at the outset,' he said. 'If only we could guarantee that the Social Revolution would not burn down the National Gallery he might almost be persuaded to join us, I think.'

R. B. Glasier, *William Morris*, 1929

A PROPHECY ABOUT THE LIBERALS

'Which of the parties—Liberal or Tory—is it that is bound to get crushed out in the struggle between Commercialism and Socialism?' My reply is, The Liberal Party. Conservatives, by being opposed to change in political affairs and being the defenders of all existing things, are recognised as the natural defenders of property, and it is towards Toryism that men of property are drifting. Liberalism does not attack property, but it is supposed by the Tory to be dangerous to the rights of property. . . . Liberalism as a creed is opposed to any legal inequality save as between rich and poor. There it draws the line harshly, and will allow no interference any more than—nay, probably much less than—the most crusted old Toryism. Liberalism, therefore, is the political bulwark behind which Toryism and all the monopolies of commercialism lie entrenched. Between the militant Socialist and the moribund Tory lies the body of a mass of jellyfish Liberalism which would fain claim kindred with both sides, but dare not proclaim itself the friend of either.

Keir Hardie, 1896

A LABOUR MEETING IN WALES, 1898

The meetings which I addressed revealed how eagerly the people will drink in the teachings of Socialism, when placed before them in language which they can understand. At Peny-daren and Troedyrhiw the muster was very large. At the latter place the villagers had decorated the outside of the houses with coloured bunting, streamers were stretched across from window to window, and the place had the appearance which it might have presented in time of peace on the occasion of a royal visit. Five bands of music turned out, and played the men up from Plymouth . . . and the surrounding districts generally. A platform had been erected in the stone-yard, with a flagpole, from which the Union Jack proudly floated. . . . The rain came down in torrents, and whilst the meeting was going

on a veritable deluge lasted, but not a soul budged. Patiently the thousands stood and listened, and, as one could see from their eager faces,
longed for the good time coming when industrial strife would only be a
hateful memory of the past, and when poverty . . . would have passed
from their midst. A male voice choir sang a grand old psalm tune
'Aberystwyth', and the soul-stirring anthem, 'The Crusaders'. . . .

House after house we visited, and found starvation—literal starvation
—in every one. In several we saw baskets of crusts which the children
had been to beg.

                                                    Keir Hardie, 1898

THE TRADE UNIONS TAKE COURAGE

(The following is the text of the resolution passed by the Trades
Union Congress, by 546,000 votes to 434,000, in September 1899, in
favour of summoning a special conference on Labour representation.)

That this Congress, having regard to its decisions in former years, and
with a view to securing a better representation of the interests of Labour
in the House of Commons, hereby instructs the Parliamentary Committee
to invite the co-operation of all the co-operative, socialistic, trade-union,
and other working class organisations, to jointly co-operate on lines
mutually agreed upon, in convening a special congress of representatives
from such of the above-named organisations as may be willing to take
part to devise ways and means for securing the return of an increased
number of Labour members in the next Parliament.

. . . THE CONFERENCE TAKES ACTION

(The following resolution replaced one designed to restrict the
choice of Labour Members of Parliament to actual members of the
working classes. It was carried by 102 votes to 3. This was the occasion on which John Burns told the delegates that they were prisoners
of class prejudice and remarked: 'I am getting tired of working-class
boots, working-class brains, working-class houses and working-class
margarine.')

That this Conference is in favour of working-class opinion being represented in the House of Commons by men sympathetic with the aims and
demands of the Labour movements and whose candidatures are promoted
by one or other of the organised movements represented at this Conference.

. . . AND THE LABOUR PARTY IS BORN

(The following resolution brought about the creation of the
Labour Representation Committee, which later took the name of the
Labour Party. The date was Tuesday, 27 February 1900.)

That this Conference is in favour of establishing a distinct Labour Group
in Parliament, who shall have their own whips and agree upon their
policy, which must embrace a readiness to co-operate with any party
which, for the time being, may be engaged in promoting legislation in the
direct interest of labour, and be equally ready to associate themselves
with any party in opposing measures having an opposite tendency; and,
further, members of the Labour Group shall not oppose any candidate
whose nomination is being promoted in terms of Resolution 1.

THE FIRST SOCIALIST RESOLUTION IN PARLIAMENT,
23 APRIL 1901

That, considering the increased burden which the private ownership of
land and capital is imposing upon the industrious and useful classes of the
community, the poverty and destitution and general moral and physical
deterioration resulting from a competitive system of wealth production
which aims primarily at profit-making, the alarming growth of trusts
and syndicates able by reason of their great wealth to influence Governments and plunge peaceful nations into war to serve their interests, this
House is of opinion that such a condition of affairs constitutes a menace
to the well being of the realm, and calls for legislation designed to remedy
the same by inaugurating a Socialist Commonwealth founded upon the
common ownership of land and capital, production for use and not for
profit, and equality of opportunity for every citizen.

WHY THE S.D.F. HAS FAILED

For twenty-one years the S.D.F. has based its propaganda on the class-
war theory, and the result is dismal failure. How could it be otherwise?
Mankind in the mass is not moved by hatred, but by love of what is
right. If we could have Socialism on S.D.F. lines, nothing would be
changed—save for the worse. . . . The economic side of the Movement,
like the political, is merely a means to an end, the end being Socialism.
The common ownership of land and capital and production for use and
not for profit are indispensable to the realisation of Socialism, but they
are not Socialism. They are but the Socialist method of wealth produc-

tion—the economic expression of the spirit of Socialism. But the sam
fraternal spirit which insists upon economic equality and common owner
ship in the means of life also implies fraternity all round, and that ca
never grow out of a propaganda of class hatred. Life is already barre
enough without our voluntarily adding to its bitterness.

Keir Hardie, 190

UNITED AT LAST

Behind the Labour Party stands in solid array the intellect and will, anc
the sense of every section of Socialist and Labour thought and feeling
The men and women of our movement are not fretful children. Tha
which they laboured so long and hard to create they will amend anc
improve, but not destroy. I am not to be taken as saying that the Labou
Party is faultless; no human institution is. Its shortcomings are many
and manifold. . . . I think the Parliamentary pace might be quickened witl
advantage. Probably many people think the same. But a great chasm
yawns between that saying and the disruption of the movement. It may
be that we have slipped into the habit of making the path of the Government too smooth. I like not that save when the pathway makes for ou
goal. The imagination of the people requires to be appealed to, as wel
as their reason. When there is no vision the people perish.

Keir Hardie, 1908

THE I.L.P. COMES OF AGE—1914

I shall not weary you by repeating the tale of how public opinion has
changed during these twenty-one years. But, as an example, I may recall
the fact that in those days and for many years thereafter, it was tenaciously
upheld by the public authorities, here and elsewhere, that it was an offence
against the laws of nature and ruinous to the State for public authorities
to provide food for starving children, or independent aid for the aged
poor. Even safety regulations in mines and factories were taboo. They
interfered with the 'freedom of the individual'. As for such proposals
as an eight-hour day, a minimum wage, the right to work, and municipal
houses, any serious mention of such classed a man as a fool. . . .

And if to-day there is a kindlier social atmosphere it is mainly because
of the twenty-one years' work of the I.L.P.

Keir Hardie, 1914

THE PARTY IN 1914

. . . a Labour Party has been formed, which proclaims itself, and which is,
independent of either the Liberal or the Conservative Parties. Men and

women belonging to all ranks and stations in life are giving their adhesion to its principles and policy in daily increasing numbers. . . .

The aim of the new party is to realise Socialism by constitutional means. It sets out from the assumption that the collective ownership of land and industrial capital is essential to the salvation of the community. That poverty with all its attendant evils is as removable as any other form of disease; that the causes have only to be sought and removed, and poverty dies out. That charity in its multifarious forms is but an attempt to plaster over the sore—to hide it from the public gaze without removing it.

Keir Hardie, 1914

HOW THEY DEALT WITH THE SOCIALIST VAN

(Robert Tressall was a Socialist house-painter who left behind him at his death the manuscript of a novel, which has become one of the best-known works of political propaganda. He called it *The Ragged Trousered Philanthropists*, as a just description of the working men of his time, who threw away their own prospects of happiness by continuing to support a system from which they could expect, at best, hardship, at worst, actual starvation.)

One Sunday morning towards the end of July, a band of about twenty-five men and women on bicycles invaded the town. Two of them, who rode a few yards in front of the others, had affixed to their handle bars a slender upright standard from the top of one of which fluttered a small flag of crimson silk with 'International Brotherhood and Peace' in gold letters. The other standard was similar in size and colour, but with a different legend: 'One for all and All for one.'

As they rode along they gave leaflets to the people in the streets, and whenever they came to a place where there were many people they dismounted and walked about, distributing leaflets. They made several long halts during their progress along the Grand Parade, where there was a considerable crowd, and then they rode over the hill to Windley, which they reached just before opening time. There were little crowds waiting outside the several public-houses, and a number of people passing through the streets on their way home from church and chapel. To all who would take them the strangers distributed leaflets, and they also went through the side streets putting them under the doors and in the letter boxes. When they had exhausted their stock they remounted and rode back the way they came.

Meanwhile the news of their arrival had spread, and as they returned through the town they were greeted with jeers and booing. Presently someone threw a stone, and as there happened to be plenty of stones just there, several others followed suit and began running after the retreating cyclists, throwing stones, hooting and cursing.

The leaflet which had given rise to all this fury read as follows:

WHAT IS SOCIALISM?

At present the workers with hand and brain produce continually food, clothing and all useful and beautiful things in great abundance,

BUT THEY LABOUR IN VAIN

for they are mostly poor and often in want. They find it a hard struggle to live.

Their women and children suffer, and their old age is branded with pauperism.

Socialism is a plan by which poverty will be abolished and all will be enabled to live in plenty and comfort, with leisure and opportunity for ampler life.

If you wish to hear more of this plan, come to the field at the Cross Roads on the hill at Windley, on Tuesday evening next at 8 p.m., and

LOOK OUT FOR THE SOCIALIST VAN.

The cyclists rode away amid showers of stones without sustaining much damage. One had his hand cut and another, who happened to look round, was struck on the forehead, but these were the only casualties.

On the following Tuesday evening, long before the appointed time, a large crowd assembled at the cross roads on the hill at Windley, evidently prepared to give the Socialists a warm reception. There was only one policeman in uniform but several plain-clothes were amongst the crowd. . . .

As it was quite evident that the crowd meant mischief—many of them had their pockets filled with stones, and were armed with sticks—several of the local Socialists . . . were in favour of going to meet the van to endeavour to persuade those in charge from coming further, and with that object they went down the road in the direction from which the van was expected. They had not gone very far, however, before the people, divining their intention, began to follow them, and while they were hesitating what course to pursue, the Socialist Van, escorted by five or six men on bicycles, appeared round the corner at the bottom of the hill.

As soon as the crowd saw the van they gave an exultant cheer, or rather, yell, and began running down the hill, and in a few minutes it was surrounded by a howling mob. The van was drawn by two horses; there was a door and a small platform at the back and over this was a

sign with white letters on a red ground: 'Socialism, the only hope of the
workers.'

The driver pulled up, and another man on the platform at the rear,
attempted to address the crowd, but his voice was inaudible in the din of
howls, catcalls, hooting and obscene curses. After about an hour of this,
as the crowd began pushing against the van and trying to overturn it, the
terrified horses became restive and uncontrollable and the man on the box
attempted to drive up the hill. This seemed still further to infuriate the
horde of savages who surrounded the van. Numbers of them clutched
the wheels and turned them the reverse way, screaming that it must go
back to where it came from; and several of them accordingly seized the
horses' heads and, amid cheers, turned them round.

The man on the platform was still trying to make himself heard, but
without success. The strangers who had come with the van and the little
group of local Socialists, who had forced their way close to the platform
in front of the would-be speaker, only increased the din by their shouts of
appeal to the crowd to 'give the man a fair chance'. This little body-guard
closed round the van as it began to move slowly downhill, but it was completely outnumbered, and the mob, being dissatisfied with the rate at
which the van was proceeding, began to shout: 'Run it away!' 'Take
the brake off!' and several savage rushes were made with the intention
of putting these suggestions into execution.

Some of the defenders were hampered by their bicycles, but by tremendous efforts they succeeded in keeping the crowd off until the foot of the
hill was reached, and then someone threw the first stone, which by a
strange chance happened to strike one of the cyclists, whose head was
already bandaged. It was the same man who had been hit on the Sunday.
This stone was soon followed by others, and the man on the platform was
the next to be struck. He got it right on the mouth, and as he put up
his handkerchief to staunch the blood another stone struck him on the
forehead just above the temple, and he dropped forward on his face onto
the platform as if he had been shot. As the speed of the vehicle increased,
a regular hail of stones fell upon the roof and against the sides of the van,
and whizzed past the retreating cyclists, while the crowd followed close
behind, cheering, shrieking out volleys of obscene curses, and howling
like wolves.

'We'll give the swines Socialism!' shouted Crass, who was literally
foaming at the mouth.

'We'll teach 'em to come 'ere trying to undermine our bloody
morality,' howled Dick Wantley, as he hurled a lump of granite at one of
the cyclists.

After pursuing the van until it was out of range the mob bethought themselves of the local Socialists; but these were nowhere to be seen, having prudently withdrawn as soon as the van had got clear. The victory gained, the upholders of the present system returned to the piece of waste ground on the top of the hill, where a gentleman in a silk hat and frock coat stood up on a little hillock and made a speech. He said nothing about the Distress Committee or the Soup Kitchen or the children who went to school without proper clothes or food, and made no reference to what was to be done next winter when nearly everybody would be out of work. But he said a great deal about the Glorious Empire and the Flag, and his remarks were received with rapturous applause; and at the conclusion of his address the crowd sang the National Anthem with great enthusiasm and dispersed, congratulating themselves that they had shown, to the best of their ability, what Mugsborough thought of Socialism.

Robert Tressall, *The Ragged Trousered Philanthropists*, 1914

A LIBERAL SPEAKS ON SOCIALISM

Sweater had carefully rehearsed his speech and he delivered it very effectively. Some of those Socialists, he said, were well-meaning but mistaken people, who did not realise the harm that would result if their extraordinary ideas were ever put into practice. He lowered his voice to a bloodcurdling stage whisper as he asked:

'What is this Socialism that we hear so much about, but which so few understand? What is it, and what does it mean?'

Then, raising his voice till it rang through the air and fell upon the ears of the assembled multitude like the clanging of a funeral bell, he continued:

'It is Madness! Chaos! Anarchy! It means Ruin! Black Ruin for the rich, and consequently, of course, Blacker Ruin still for the poor!'

As Sweater paused, a thrill of horror ran through the meeting. Men wearing broken boots and with patches upon the seats and knees, and ragged fringes round the bottoms of the legs of their trousers, grew pale and glanced apprehensively at each other. If ever Socialism did come to pass they evidently thought it very probable that they would have to go without any trousers or boots at all.

Toil-worn women, most of them dressed in other women's shabby cast off clothing, weary tired-looking mothers who fed their children for the most part on adulterated tea, tinned skimmed milk, bread and margarine, grew furious as they thought of the wicked Socialists who were trying to bring Ruin upon them.

The awful silence that had fallen on the panic-stricken crowd was presently broken by a ragged trousered philanthropist, who shouted out:

'We knows wot they are, sir. Most of 'em is chaps wot's got tired of workin' for their livin', so they wants us to keep 'em.'

Encouraged by numerous expressions of approval from the other philanthropists, the man continued:

'But we ain't such fools as they thinks, and so they'll find out next Monday. Most of 'em wants 'anging, and I wouldn't mind lendin' a 'and with the rope myself.'

Robert Tressall, *The Ragged Trousered Philanthropists*, 1914

A SOCIALIST CHRISTMAS PARTY

Bert White had not only accepted the invitation to the Christmas party but had promised to bring his home made 'Pandoramer' with him to entertain the other guests. . . . The idea of constructing this machine had been suggested to Bert by a panorama entertainment he had been to see some time before. . . . He lit the candles at the back and desired the audience to take their seats. When they had all done so, he requested Owen to put out the lamp and the candles on the Christmas tree, and then he made a speech, imitating the manner of the lecturer at the panorama entertainment: . . .

'We finds ourselves back once more in Merry Hingland, where we see the inside of a blacksmith's shop with a lot of half-starved women making iron chains. They work seventy hours a week for seven shillings. Our next scene is hintitled "The Hook and Eye Carders". 'Ere we see the inside of a room in Slumtown, with a mother and three children and the old grandmother sewin' hooks and eyes on cards to be sold in drapers' shops. It ses underneath the pitcher that 384 hooks and 384 eyes has to be joined together and sewed on cards for one penny. . . .

'Our next picture is called "An Englishman's Home". 'Ere we see inside of another room in Slumtown, with the father and mother and four children sitting down to dinner—bread and drippin' and tea. It ses underneath the pitcher that there's thirteen millions of people in England always on the verge of starvation. These people that you see in the pitcher might be able to get a better dinner than this if it wasn't that most of the money wot the bloke earns 'as to go to pay the rent. Again we turns the 'andle and presently we comes to another very beautiful scene, "Early Morning in Trafalgar Square". 'Ere we see a lot of Englishmen who have been sleepin' out all night because they ain't got no 'omes to go to. . . .

'Next we 'ave a view of the dining hall at the Topside Hotel in London, where we see the tables set for a millionaire's banquet. The forks and spoons is made of solid gold and the plates is made of silver. The flowers that you see on the tables and 'angin' down from the ceiling and on the walls is worth £2000, and it cost the bloke wot give the supper over £30,000 for this one beano. A few more turns of the 'andle shows us another glorious banquet—the king of Rhineland being entertained by the people of England. Next we finds ourselves looking on at the Lord Mayor's supper at the Mansion House. All the fat men that you see sittin' at the tables is Liberal and Tory members of Parlimint. . . .

'Here we see another unemployed procession,' continued Bert, as he rolled another picture into sight; 'two thousand able-bodied men who are not allowed to work. Next we see the hinterior of a Hindustrial 'Ome— blind children and cripples working for their living. Our next scene is called "Cheap Labour". 'Ere we see a lot of small boys about twelve and thirteen years old bein' served out with their Labour Stifficats, which gives 'em the right to go to work and earn money to help their unemployed fathers to pay the Slumrent.

'Once more we turns the 'andle and brings on one of our finest scenes. This lovely pitcher is hintitled "The Hangel of Charity" and shows us the beautiful Lady Slumrent seated at the table in a cosy corner of 'er charmin' boodore, writin' out a little cheque for the relief of the poor of Slumtown.

'Our next scene is called "The Rival Candidates", or "A Scene during the General Election". On the left you will observe, standin' up in a motor car, a swell bloke with a eye-glass stuck in one eye, and a overcoat with a big fur collar and cuffs, addressing the crowd: this is the Honourable Augustus Slumrent, the Conservative candidate. On the other side of the road we see another motor car and another swell bloke with a round pane of glass in one eye and a overcoat with a big fur collar and cuffs, standin' up in the car and addressin' the crowd: this is Mr Mandriver, the Liberal. The crowds of shabby-lookin' chaps standin' around the motor cars wavin' their 'ats and cheerin' is workin' men. Both the candidates is tellin' 'em the same old story, and each of 'em is askin' the workin' men to elect 'im to Parlimint, and promisin' to do something or hother to make things better for the lower horders. . . .

''Ere we 'ave another election scene. At each side we see the two candidates the same as in the last pitcher. In the middle of the road we see a man lying on the ground, covered with blood, with a lot of Liberal and Tory working men kickin' 'im, jumpin' on 'im, and stampin' on 'is face with their 'obnailed boots. The bloke on the ground is a Socialist, and the reason why they're kickin' 'is face in is because 'e said that the only difference between Slumrent and Mandriver was that they was both alike.'

Robert Tressall, The Ragged Trousered Philanthropists, 1914

IN THIS FAITH WE LIVE

(The pre-Great War Labour Party had no declared objective other than 'to organize and maintain in Parliament and in the country a political Labour Party'. In February 1918 a new constitution was adopted, and is still in force, under which the Labour Party is declared to be Socialist in its aims. The key words are given below.)

To secure for the producers by hand and by brain the full fruits of their industry and the most equitable distribution thereof that may be possible, upon the basis of the common ownership of the means of production and the best obtainable system of popular administration and control of each industry and service.

THE GENERAL STRIKE

(The General Strike of 1926, which terrified the governing classes but ended in their complete victory, failed owing to the feebleness and incompetence of the Trade Union leaders. Although the victorious Conservatives passed the Trade Disputes Act, which made alliance between the Labour Party and the Unions more difficult, the final effect of the strike was to turn the aspirations of the working class away from industrial and towards political action. This change of attitude was in the best tradition of British Socialism, which has always been an essentially constitutional movement.)

After the temporary prosperity of 1924 a steady decline had set in. The Chancellor, Winston Churchill, with the approval of the City and the Treasury, had put British currency back on the gold standard, at the pre-War level. This was equivalent to an automatic tax on every export. Markets shrank and profits fell; with them wages. . . . Large reserves of coal were piled up. An elaborate organisation was set up, divided into ten areas, under Civil Commissioners . . . who would be entitled to 'give decisions on behalf of the government'. Ex-viceroys and ex-admirals were put at the head of a voluntary strike-breaking organisation, called the Organisation for the Maintenance of Supplies, which was to provide these divisional generals with troops. All the machinery was ready by April 1926, to move on receipt of the one telegraphed word 'Action'.

On the Labour side a mixture of inopportune pacifism and over-confidence had produced an exactly opposite result. No organisation, local or national, to carry out a General Strike was countenanced, let alone started. . . . The Council [of the Trades Union Congress] indeed, re-affirmed its support of the miners, but many of its members had reached the conclusion that a fall in wages was inevitable. The knowledge of this had a grave effect upon the miners' executive; they voted when the crisis was obviously near at hand [in April 1926], not as before to put their case in the hands of the Council unreservedly, but only subject to 'consultation' with themselves, modified later to the more exact condition that the miners' slogan of 'not a penny off the pay, not a minute on the day' should be agreed to—a condition which was never formally accepted.

Despite all the omens, the Labour leaders were surprised when the conflict actually came. The subsidy [to the coal-owners from the Government] ended, the owners demanded their wage-cuts, the Government refused assistance. The Labour leaders, in Thomas's words, 'begged and pleaded . . . almost grovelling'. But the Government had decided, and behind Baldwin were Winston Churchill . . . and Lord Birkenhead, spoiling for a fight. On Friday, the last day of April 1926, the lock-out notices went into effect. On Saturday, the most sensational of all May Days, the Council reported the facts to a specially summoned conference of Trade Union executives and asked for a mandate to call a general strike. The answer was given by roll-call, Union by Union, and the final figures were: Against, 49,911; Awaiting instructions, 319,000; For, 3,653,529. A wave of enthusiasm swept round the conference and out into the world beyond. Ernest Bevin spoke of the 'magnificent generation' that had 'placed its all upon the altar'; . . . Ramsay MacDonald joined in tumultuous singing of the 'Red Flag'. . . .

When the bells rang at midnight on Monday [May 3, 1926] over the silent cities, they announced the beginning of a stillness which nobody had ever known before in English history. The Council had said that all activities should cease, in the trades that it named, and cease they did. There were no trains, no bus services, no trams, no papers, no building, no power. In a strike 100 per cent is an unobtainable figure, generally . . . but even this ideal 100 per cent was frequently achieved. Unions like the Railway Clerks' Association—black-coated, of recent date and doubtful spirit—in most cases came out as loyally as modern fighting Unions like the National Union of Railwaymen or ancient and obstinate craft societies like the London Compositors. Whatever plans there may have been for mining, railway or other services by the famed 'Organisation' under the Commissioners broke down at once; the Commissioners had to do the best they could either by negotiation with the strikers, or by a scratch service of middle class volunteer drivers.

The T.U.C. permitted foodstuffs to pass, and others to move by 'permit from the T.U.C.', brightly placarded in black on yellow. But no effective direction was given to local strike committees from head-quarters, no scheme of organisation for councils of action or strike committees sent out, no clear instructions issued even on how to deal with the Co-ops. Too few of the General Council were of an age or resolution to cope with the immense problem they had set themselves: the work fell on a small handful of men who were soon overworked and exhausted. Initiative returned to the localities and the local Trade Union and Labour officers rose splendidly to the occasion. It was for many a dazzling revelation of the workers' real power. As lapsed members and 'nons' joined up, drawn at last by the sight of real action by the Unions, employers were more and more forced to come to the strike headquarters as real centres of authority, 'begging for permission to do certain things. . . . "Please can I move a quantity a coal from such and such a place?" or "Please can my transport workers move certain foodstuffs in this or that direction?"' 'I thought', wrote an Ashton committeeman, 'of the many occasions when I had been turned empty away from the door of some workshop in a weary struggle to get the means to purchase the essentials of life for self and dependants. I thought of the many occasions I had been called upon to meet these people in the never-ending struggle to obtain decent conditions for those around me, and its consequent result in my joining the ranks of the unemployed. . . . The only tactic practised by some of them was bullying, and that was no use in a situation such as this; some tried persuasion, referring to us as "Mr Chairman and Gentlemen", but only a rigid examination of the stern facts of the case moved our actions. The cap-in-hand position reversed.' . . .

As far as can be judged (reports are fallible) there is no reasonable doubt that the efficiency and the effectiveness of the strike were steadily increasing up to the very end. . . . [But] the enthusiasm of the rank and file had no reflection at headquarters. Muddle and fear reigned there. Fear among many Council members who dreaded the strike weapon they had chosen and wanted only to lay it down; muddle between the miners and the Council itself. The two mining members, incredible though it may seem, absented themselves throughout the whole period. . . . It is certain that when the news of the calling off came it was received with universal anger, as from an army which felt itself to be victorious. . . .

The miners fought on, and in November had to accept defeat. Nothing whatever had been secured by the greatest effort the British workers had ever made.

G. D. H. Cole and R. Postgate, The Common People, 1938

RAMSAY MACDONALD

Ramsay MacDonald fascinated me. His head was a thing of beauty. Black hair waved and rolled over a fine brow, one curl almost touching his straight, strong eyebrows, from under which his eyes glowed. His voice was rugged, but soft, and as he spoke there came into it a throb. It was the natural instrument of an orator. Standing upright he was a splendid figure of a man, and his appearance of height and strength was increased by his habit of rising on his toes and throwing back his head. . . . He told me once that a certain nobleman had chaffed him about his association with our Movement and had added: 'You know, you are really one of us.' He was not displeased by the remark. He is of that mould.

David Kirkwood, My Life of Revolt, 1935

NO SURRENDER!

> (Arnold Ryerson is replying to suggestions from Hamer Shawcross that he should support the 'National' Government which the latter is joining. Although *Fame is the Spur* is a work of fiction, the parallel with the events of 1931 is obvious.)

'The Labour Party will break down, anyway,' said Hamer. 'The Labour Party, Arnold, is finished. At least for a long time to come.'

Arnold looked at him dumbfounded. 'No Labour Party! Then what in hell are we going to live for, Hamer—you and I? Why, good God lad, we made it. It's been the breath of our beings. . . . Before I'd sign myself "National Labour" or whatever fancy name you invent, I'd cut my throat. And I'd think that a better action than to cut the throat of my life-long principles. . . . Such wits as God gave me made me believe t'Labour Party were t'reight party for me. If the earth were crumblin' Ah'd still think as our Party were best to stop t'rot. Maybe tha's been converted, lad. But, wi' me, Ah wouldn't be a convert. Ah'd be a renegade.'

Arnold Ryerson in Howard Spring's novel, Fame is the Spur, 1940

THE DAY THEY STOPPED THE DOLE

(The existence of mass, long-term unemployment between the two wars has been the subject of many factual reports, which describe its corrupting effect upon both the health and spirit of the workless and their dependants. It was however a novel which first brought home the gravity of the problem to many people, and the inadequacy of attempts by capitalist economists, whether Liberal, Conservative or 'National Labour', to solve it. *Love on the Dole* is thus of first importance as an historical document and may well have contributed to the Labour victory of 1945, which finally banished unemployment from Britain. The author is here describing the effect on a group of unemployed of the first of the 'National' Government's economy measures—the refusal, or reduction of the unemployment benefit to those requiring it.)

Harry Hardcastle was staggered: 'Y' what . . . ? What did y' say?' he asked, staring, incredulously, at the unemployment exchange clerk on the other side of the counter.

'A' y' deaf?' retorted the clerk, pettishly: he added, snappily: 'There's nowt for y'. They've knocked y' off dole. Sign on of a Tuesday for future if y' want y' health insurance stamp. Who's next?'

The man behind Harry shouldered him away. Dream-like, he turned and paused, holding the dog-eared, yellow unemployment card in his hand. This was catastrophic: the clerk was joking, surely; a mistake must have been made. He hadn't asked the clerk the reason why they had stopped paying him his unemployment benefit: 'Gor blimey' he muttered: 'Hell, what am Ah gonna do?' He remembered Helen instantly. . . . He licked his lips, and, dazed, turned to the counter once again in time to hear his unspoken question answered indirectly. The man who had succeeded him was angrily demanding an explanation of the clerk; those in the queue behind and those on either side listened attentively. That which passed concerned them all.

Hearing the man's indignant expostulations, a policeman, on duty at the door, came nearer, silently. The man, grey-haired, middle aged, a stocky fellow in corduroys, clay-muddied blucher boots and with 'yorks' strapped about his knees, exclaimed 'Wha'd'y'mean? Nowt for me. Ah'm out o' collar ain't Ah?'

The clerk put aside his pen and sighed, wearily: 'Doan argue wi' me,' he appealed: 'Taint my fault. If y' want t' know why, go'n see manager. Blimey, you blokes 're bloody well drivin' me barmy this mornin','

'Manager, eh?' the man snapped: 'You bet Ah'll see the manager. Where is 'e?' The clerk jerked his thumb towards the far end of the counter. 'Ask at "Enquiries",' he said. 'Who's next?'

Harry followed the man.

The manager ordered a clerk to look up the man's particulars; the clerk handed over some documents after a search in a filing cabinet. His superior, after perusing some notes written upon the forms, looked at the applicant and said: 'You've a couple of sons living with you who are working, haven't you?'

'Aye,' the man answered: 'One's earnin' twenty-five bob an' t'other a couple of quid, when they work a full week. An' the eldest . . .'

'In view of this fact,' the manager interrupted, 'the Public Assistance Committee have ruled your household's aggregate income sufficient for your needs; therefore, your claim for transitional benefit is disallowed.' He turned from the man to glance interrogatively at Harry.

The man flushed: 'The swine,' he shouted: 'The' eldest lad's getting wed . . . 'as 'e t' keep me an' the old woman?' Raising his fist: 'Ah'll . . .' But the attendant policeman collared him and propelled him outside, roughly, ignoring his loud protestations.

Harry learnt that, in the opinion of the Public Assistance Committee, his father's dole and Sally's wages were sufficient to keep him. No more dole would be forthcoming. And when he asked whether he could re-state his case the manager informed him that there was no appeal. He didn't argue; went outside, dazed.

A quite different atmosphere from the usual, enlivened the adjacent streets. Police were conspicuous. Knots of men barred pavements and roadways listening and interjecting, as various spokesmen voiced heated criticisms of this, the latest economy move on the part of the National Government. Occasionally, the spokesmen's words would be lost in rowdy, jumbled torrents of cursings and abusive oaths. From the labour exchange there came a continuous trickle of men wearing appropriate expressions as became their individual dispositions. Men of Harry's kind dazed, mystified, staring at the ground, more spirited individuals, flushed with anger, lips trembling, eyes burning with resentment. They joined the groups, finding a sorry sort of relief in the knowledge that all here assembled were similarly affected. Most of those more fortunate ones whose benefits had remained untouched cleared off home jealously hugging their good fortune and telling themselves that what was passing was no concern of theirs.

Walter Greenwood, *Love on the Dole*, 1933

DECLINE OF THE MIDDLE CLASSES, 1933

(Although a work of fiction, Winifred Holtby's *South Riding* provides a dramatic and accurate picture of conditions in one county of England during the nineteen-thirties and of the extent to which local authorities could help to remedy them.)

In the motor-bus, grinding along the softened tarry highway, Joe Astell rode to the Public Assistance Committee for the Cold Harbour Division of South Riding.

For him it was a journey without satisfaction. Because his heart was tender and his imagination keen, the details of individual need and suffering hurt him. He would fight the battle for humanity in terms of an extra two shillings a week, a grocery order or a sack of coals. He would attempt to soften the inquisitional harshness of men and women who enjoyed, he thought, this business of hunting down the miseries of defeat, the shameful expedients of poverty. They got their money's worth out of the joys of interference.

But Astell found no joy even in victory. The grudging ameliorations of a system which kept the defeated alive, so that they might not rise in their despair and seize for themselves and for their children those things they need, gave mild solicitude for bare existence. He should be up, away, fighting to change the system, not content to render first aid to its victims. The picturesque streets of Yarrold closed in upon him. He saw not the lovely shades of the old brick walls, soft rose, warm purple, the patchwork of rough tiled roofs, the rambler roses frothing and showering round the small closed windows; he saw poverty and disease, stunted rickety children, the monotony of women's battle against dirt, cold and inconvenience. The insecurity and loneliness of old age. . . . He climbed from the bus, a sad dispirited man. . . .

Before each member of the committee lay a small pile of papers. Each recorded a story of individual defeat. Here were the men and women who had fallen a little lower even than those on transitional benefit, the disallowed, the uninsured, the destitute. The Means Test was no new humiliation to them. Since the days of Queen Elizabeth those who had become dependent on their neighbours, had to submit to inquiry and suggestion. What was new, was the type of person who came to ask for outdoor relief. The middle-class worker fallen on evil times, the professional man, the ruined investment holder.

Astell was not moved by the special pity for these which distressed his colleagues. If their plight marked the failure of capitalism, so much the better—so much the sooner would end this evil anarchy, with its injustice, its confusion, its waste, its class divisions. So much the sooner would come the transformation to the classless planned community. But he was not happy. His ruthless theory guided uneasily his tender heart. . . .

Astell disliked these families who had seen better days. . . . He did his duty. In his harsh, unsympathetic voice he retailed the details of the Mitchells' case. He knew what arguments appealed to the committee. He despised himself for displaying them.

Thompson opened the door and called:

'Mr Mitchell.'

Mitchell entered.

Everything about him signified the black-coated worker—his hair neatly sleeked with water, his well-pressed, shiny, pin-striped suit, his white collar, his jaunty yet humiliated manner.

'You were in the Diamond Insurance, Mr Mitchell?'

These were the representatives of society—the solid family men—income-tax payers, before whom Fred Mitchell had laid the well-worn arguments for security. Have you thought of your wife's future? Your little daughter, what is she worth to you?

His familiar slogans now returned to mock him. They ran round and round his brain. He fidgeted with his tie.

The chairman repeated his question.

Mitchell started. His mouth contracted with dumb effort. He saw Astell's face, stern with dislike and forced benevolence.

He croaked out his confession: 'I had a book.'

He had reached the bottomless pit of humiliation. A pauper. On the rates, begging for food tickets. He remembered his office in Kingsport where he had had two clerks and a boy under him. He had been going to buy a car.

He could not speak. This was a nightmare in which his feet were chained so that he could not flee from horror.

May I put a little scheme before you?

O God, how are we going to live?

A choked groan, half a sob, shook his body. . . .

He withdrew from the dreaded inquisition, comforted. The temporary order for groceries which Thompson had given, had been confirmed; in addition there was to be milk for Peggy, oil for the lamp and stove and a cash grant of fifteen shillings. Little enough, God knows, but they would manage. The committee, Colonel Whitelaw had explained, had to work within strict legal limitations; they could not go beyond their powers. . . .

It was half-past one when the committee adjourned for lunch. Astell went off through the crooked street, shimmering in the hot sun, for his meal—a glass of milk and a sandwich at the baker's. Three men marched in single file beside the pavement, playing a drum and two mouth organs. 'Genuine Welsh Miners' proclaimed a notice on their collecting box.

Suddenly Astell's patience failed.

I'm through, he said. I'm off. This is no place for me. These local committees. You can't fight on them. You can't alter things here. Once the laws have been passed, we only can administer them. He saw his work here as something worse than useless. Why struggle to get another Labour man on to the U.D.C.? Why lecture on 'Imperialism or War' to twenty bored old women of the Co-operative Guild in Unity Hall? Futile, futile, futile. Why should he do it, when he might be back, fighting not to mitigate but to change the system? To save his life? What did his life matter?

He turned and dropped sixpence into the miners' collecting-box, despising his weak-kneed bourgeois philanthropy.

It was his lunch money.

Winifred Holtby, South Riding, 1936

WHAT FREE ENTERPRISE DID FOR JARROW

At Middlesbrough [my own constituency] I had thought that I had known what poverty could mean. But in that town some industry was going on, some people had work. Compared to Jarrow, things on Tees-side were moving. Jarrow in that year, 1932–33, was utterly stagnant. There was no work. No one had a job, except a few railwaymen, officials, the workers in the co-operative stores, and the few clerks and craftsmen who went out of the town to their job each day. The unemployment rate was over 80%. 'Six thousand are on the dole, and 23,000 on relief out of a total population of 35,000', was the estimate given at the time by the Medical Officer of Health.

Ellen Wilkinson, The Town that was Murdered, 1939

A DEPUTATION CALLS ON MACDONALD

At the house . . . where the Premier was staying, eight of the leaders and myself were invited in. . . . Mr MacDonald came into the room, the first time we had met since the election [of 1931]. It was always difficult to resist MacDonald when he himself had determined to be charming. . . . I tried to be hard, unimpressed, to remember what this man had done to the movement that alone could help these men and women. But the whole atmosphere under J.R.M.'s skilful handling became like one of those 'socialist firesides' which had formed the perorations of his best speeches in times past. . . . We stood up to take our leave. Mr MacDonald put his hand on my shoulder: 'Ellen, why don't you go out and preach Socialism, which is the only remedy for all this?' Which priceless remark from the Premier of a predominantly Conservative government jerked me back to reality . . . the sham, by the soft firelight, of that warm but oh so easy sympathy. . . . Yet I am sure that at that moment MacDonald was as sincere as he had ever been. The tragedy was that he knew the real cure for the evils of which we told him, but had run away at the moment of the trial that he had himself forecast so accurately years before.

Ellen Wilkinson, *The Town that was Murdered*, 1939

WHY JARROW MARCHED TO LONDON

In the months that followed the march to Easington [to see MacDonald] things in Jarrow got steadily blacker. . . . The final closing of Palmer's by National Shipbuilders' Security Ltd, came as a terrible shock. Deputation after deputation from the town . . . went to see Mr Walter Runciman, the President of the Board of Trade, himself a member of a great shipowning family. . . .

Then came the crash of the steelworks' scheme; the realization that the Government were backing the steel combine, and that Walter Runciman would 'do nothing' to prevent the steel masters from strangling the Jarrow scheme at birth. To the Town Council deputation which met him at the moment when the Cartel proposals were being forced through the House of Commons . . . Mr Runciman coldly told them that the Government could do nothing for Jarrow. 'Jarrow', he said, 'must work out its own salvation.'

That phrase kindled the town. All the respectable deputations had got nowhere. At a great demonstration of the unemployed, Councillor David Riley, as chairman, suggested that the unemployed of Jarrow should march to London and tell the people of England on their way down of the treatment they had received. That was in July 1936. . . . The Mayor decided that if there were to be a march it must be a town's march, with the backing of the whole of the citizens from bishop to business man. . . .

That was ambitious, . . . but it was this idea which more than anything gave the march its kudos. Hunger marches of desperate men from the distressed areas there had been in plenty. The comfortable had dismissed these efforts as 'Communist demonstrations' as though that accounted for everything. But the fact that the Town Council sanctioned the

march, practically unanimously, meant that appeals for support were sent
out over the signature of the Mayor. . . .

A large number of men volunteered to go, but we could not take an
army. Finally 200 men were selected, every one of them vetted by the
borough medical officer. . . . Prayers were said for the marchers that
Sunday of October 4th, 1936, in every church and chapel in Jarrow. On
Monday morning the men lined up for a final review by the Mayor outside the Town Hall. The men had done their best to look smart on the
little they had. Faces carefully shaved—but so thin. Broken boots
mended and polished. Shabby clothes brushed and mended by their
wives. The waterproof cape rolled over the shoulder, bandolier fashion.
We marched to Christ Church for a short service, which the men's wives
and the Mayor and Corporation attended. The words of that grave and
saintly man, Bishop Gordon of Jarrow, as he pronounced the blessing
and bade us Godspeed gave to the men and their wives a sense of high
purpose in their Crusade.

Ellen Wilkinson, The Town that was Murdered, 1939

FROM EACH ACCORDING TO HIS ABILITY

The March Committee had realized from the first the possibilities of
strain on men who had been underfed. The Inter-Hospital Socialist
Society came to our rescue. At their own suggestion, they supplied relays
of two students a week, with a car and medical equipment . . . [and] impro-
vised a clinic in a corner of whatever chapel or drill hall or casual ward
the men were to sleep in. Often they shared the hard boards with them.
These medical students soon diagnosed the complaints that ill-fed and
wrongly fed men had been suffering from for years. . . . What a blessing
this medical care was I only understood to the full when, the Jarrow
men having returned home, I went to help the men who had marched
from Durham without such skilled assistance. I had to cut socks that had
become embedded in broken blisters and bandage the feet of men who
must have walked in agony. Yet these men too had kept the road and
were not far behind our schedule. . . .

When we had taken all this care it was a little hard to be lectured by
the Press for 'exposing the miseries of the men on the road' especially
as these comments were in newspapers that had never so much as mentioned the hunger and misery of these men when they had stayed at
home. . . .

At that moment, in October 1936, the time was set for *action* regard-
ing the distressed areas. Their neglect of this grim problem was the weak

spot of the National Government. The Cabinet were pouring out gifts to their own class in the form of subsidies, tariffs and quotas, which were substantial presents to the big industrialists. . . . For the Special Areas just nothing had been done at all. . . . And the Special Areas were not isolated phenomena. At that time, 47% of the industrial population of the country were living in areas either scheduled as 'distressed', or in places like Liverpool, South Lancashire and Tees-side, with such a high rate of unemployment . . . that they were demanding to be so scheduled. . . .

We marched into Leicester with the men's boots coming to pieces. There was no money for new ones. So, on their own initiative, the Co-operative Society's boot repairers sat up all night and worked without pay to repair the boots, the Society giving the necessary material. . . . One boot repairer, pulling to pieces an appalling piece of footwear, remarked: 'It seems sort of queer doing your own job, just because you want to do it, and for something you want to help, instead of doing it because you'd starve if you didn't.'

Ellen Wilkinson, The Town that was Murdered, 1939

THE ROAD TO LONDON

A few high spots stand out . . . wealthy Harrogate, where the Territorial officers looked after us . . . or the awful days like the twenty mile stretch from Bedford to Luton when it rained solidly all day and the wind drove the rain in our teeth. . . . The one thing that mattered was the weather. The men were up at 6.30, the cooks having got up earlier to prepare breakfast. They had all slept together on the bare boards of a school or drill hall. . . . To keep spruce when men sleep in their clothes is difficult, but they managed it. Daily shaves were the order. Parade was at 8.45, with everything packed for the road. . . . Most of the men had been in the army, so we marched by army rules . . . fifty minutes to the hour and ten minutes' rest. The field kitchen cooked us a midday meal, when the weather let them. . . .

We had looked forward all the way to our march through London. . . . Actually, rain soaked us through to the skin. The pressmen told us consolingly that we all looked so utterly shabby and weary in our wet clothes that we presented London with the picture of a walking distressed area. . . .

When Parliament reassembled there were two petitions to be presented . . . one, bound in the book we had carried across England, of nearly 12,000 signatures. . . . The Jarrow petition stated that the town had been passing through a long period of industrial depression without parallel in its

istory . . . its shipyards closed, its steelworks denied the right to re-open.
Whereas formerly 8,000 workers were employed, only 100 were now at
work, and those on temporary schemes. 'The town cannot be left derelict,
and therefore your petitioners humbly pray that His Majesty's Government and this honourable House will realize the urgent need that work
should be provided for the town without delay.'

It was a tense moment. As many marchers as could be got in were
packed in the galleries. The members, flooded with postcards and letters
from their constituents, to whom we had appealed en route, were interested and sympathetic. But, of course, there could not be a debate. A
few questions were asked . . . and the House passed on to consideration
of other things. . . .

The actual presentation at best could only be a gesture. What mattered more, in a practical sense, was the crowded meeting of members of
all parties in the biggest committee room in the House of Commons to
hear the Mayor . . . and the Town Clerk state the case about the shipyards
and the steelworks. There was a dramatic moment when the Mayor held
up his chain of office. 'This chain', he said, 'was given to the town by Sir
Charles Mark Palmer. Its links form a cable, its badge is an anchor . . .
symbols in gold of the cables and anchors of the thousand ships we built
at Jarrow. Now, owing to National Shipbuilders' Security Ltd, the
Jarrow shipyard is closed. Ships for Britain's food and her defence will
be made in that famous yard no more. God grant the time may not come
when you members of Parliament will have need to regret that you allowed
the scrapping of this great national asset in the interest of the private
profit of a bank's shareholders.'

                    Ellen Wilkinson, *The Town that was Murdered*, 1939

A LABOUR JUMBLE SALE

(Lettice Cooper's novel *National Provincial* is a story of political
struggles in an industrial town. The main conflict is not between
Labour and Conservative but between the slow-moving Trade
Unionist, John Allworthy, and the young and impatient Tom Sutton.
John is on friendly terms with his enlightened Conservative employer,
Stephen Harding.)

On the evening of January 20th, 1936, Grace Allworthy stood in the
parish room of the Onslet Road Wesleyan Chapel behind a trestle table
heaped with old clothes. She was selling at a jumble sale to raise funds
for the South Aire division of the Labour Party. It was still possible to
do quite well out of a jumble sale in the poorest parts of the city, although

the plentiful supply of cheap, ready made clothes, had reduced the deman
for second hand goods in any other quarter. And quite right too, though
Grace. No woman ought to be dressed in another woman's leavings
She watched the customers who pressed against the front of the stall
Most of them were elderly women with shapeless figures and worn, lined
faces, but with unabated vitality. Their eyes were shrewd to assess the
quality of the clothes; the movements of their work-worn hands were
brisk. Love for them swelled in Grace's heart and brought hot tears to
the back of her eyes. They asked so little of life for themselves and
contributed so much. They kept humour and spirit unbroken.

One of them began to turn over a pile of old hats at the end of the
table. The hats were marked sixpence each. She pushed the heap away
from her and said to Grace,

'You 'aven't a red one, 'ave you, love? Or a green? I do like a bit o'
colour! Seems to make you feel brighter like.'

She was a thin slip of a woman with greying hair, cut short, and a
sallow wedge of face in which two brown eyes sparkled undaunted.

'I'm afraid that's all we've got,' Grace said, and then paused. Growing
hot in the stuffy room she had taken off her own cherry red felt hat, and
thrown it down on the bench beside her. She was seized by one of the
sudden impulses for which John had laughed at her in her girlhood, and
which she had never outgrown.

'Stop a bit, love!' she said. 'There's one here, fallen down behind.
A nice bright red! Try it on!'

'Is that one of the sixpennies?'

Grace nodded. . . .

'I'll take it!' Recklessly stuffing her beret into the pocket of her old
coat, Mrs Cookson tipped Grace's red hat a little further over one eye-
brow, winked gaily at Mrs Wade, and walked over to the pile of worn
stair carpets, brass rods, pictures with cracked glass and oddments of
china in the middle of the room.

Grace picked out the least battered from the pile of hats and dropped
a sixpence into the bowl.

It was late when she went out to catch the tram. Her legs ached with
standing, and her back with stooping, but her spirits were high in the
glow of successful activity. They had made nine pounds. Her pleasure
in the result gave way to a mood of anger that these things should be
necessary. Tom Sutton had jeered the other evening at a revolution built
on jumble sales. Ah, but he was a daft lad, that was just the sort of thing
that a revolution in England would be built on, small efforts and small
sacrifices! It was better than having it built on dead and maimed bodies!

He had said that their Labour Party Division was very like a parish. And Stephen Harding had said that everything in England that was any good was run on the lines of a parish, it was the natural rhythm of the people. Well, the Labour Party funds had been made up out of pennies, and pennies that could ill be spared. Grace, who had seen it grow from a handful of men to one of the most important movements in the world, knew well enough what sacrifices, what self-denial and loyalty and devotion had gone to build it. And then for Tom to jeer. . . . Grace shook with anger, with a desire to put Tom across her knee and smack him.

Lettice Cooper, National Provincial, 1938

A NEW CHAPTER IN OUR HISTORY

The new House of Commons assembled for the first time yesterday and performed the customary ceremonies attendant on the election of a Speaker. . . . In a Chamber crowded to its utmost capacity there was an atmosphere of eager expectation, and an evident sense that this was a day to which in future years men might look back as the opening of a new chapter in the Nation's history. . . . In the political complexion of the House there has been no such radical transformation since the Liberals were returned to power in 1906. The Labour Party taking office with their present commanding majority are for the first time able to assume the burden of the King's Government without dependence on the support of any party or group but their own.

The Times leader, 2 August 1945

'THE RED FLAG' AT WESTMINSTER

George Lansbury may have passed on, but it was Poplar that was responsible yesterday for the singing of the 'Red Flag' in the Commons.

W. H. Guy, the M.P. who succeeds to George's seat, could not resist it.

When the Tories, seeing Winston enter the House, greeted him with 'For he's a Jolly Good Fellow' Guy said to George Griffiths, the miner who throughout the war supported Churchill with an unflinching loyalty, 'We can't let them get away with that! If you start the "Red Flag", I'll conduct it.'

So he waved his arms while Griffiths . . . started 'The people's flag is deepest red' and his Labour colleagues stood up and joined in.

It was T. G. Thomas, the young schoolmaster who won Cardiff Central, who spoke to me of the emotion he felt while he sang the Socialist Anthem which had heartened so many in the dark days, and which he had learned from the pioneers in his childhood.

'How they sang it in the Rhondda after the election!' he said. 'How the crowds cheered and how the old people wept with joy! I little dreamed I should live to be an M.P. on a day like this.'

The *Daily Herald*, 2 August 1945

THE STORY OF THE 'RED FLAG'

Years ago, I used to see, almost every day in Fleet Street, Jim Connell, who wrote the words in 1889, little dreaming they would become so famous—a defiance of privilege and an eternal inspiration to those who challenged it.

Connell, who used to say 'I was educated under a hedge for a few weeks' and who had been everything from a navvy and a journalist to a poacher, wrote the 'Red Flag' amid the thrill of the dock strike.

With Irish humour, he fitted the words to the old Jacobite air 'The White Cockade' . . . someone else chose the tune 'Maryland'.

Hannen Swaffer in the *Daily Herald*, 2 August 1945

(*Historical note.*—The *Red Flag* had been sung once before in the House of Commons, but not from the Government benches. It was sung in defiance during the early twenties by the small group of Opposition Labour M.P.s.)

WE HAVE FOUGHT A GOOD FIGHT

We have assembled for our Annual Conference in an historical year for our Party. It is the year of Jubilee. Fifty years ago—in September 1899 —the Trades Union Congress meeting at Plymouth . . . carried a resolution that laid the foundations of the Labour Party. That resolution instructed the Parliamentary Committee of Congress to convene a conference of 'All the Trade Union, Co-operative, Socialist and other working class organisations to devise ways and means for the securing of an increased number of Labour members in the next Parliament'.

That conference was held in February 1900 and the Labour Representation Committee was formed. That was the beginning of this great Party to which we are privileged to belong and which is now the greatest Social Democratic Party in the world. . . .

Today, as we enter on our Jubilee Year, we salute the memory of the pioneers, and not only the leaders, whose names we revere, but also of all those others, unknown and unhonoured in their day, whose loyalty built the Party. They had to fight hard and long to build a party, against all the forces of wealth and privilege. To join the Party in those days was to risk one's livelihood, to be victimised and despised, but hardest of all was their fight against the ignorance and apathy of the poor.

We, who are the members of the Party, have entered into a great inheritance. The best tribute we can pay to the memory of those who blazed the trail is to re-dedicate our lives to the service of the Movement. And more—we must preserve and strengthen that combination of movements upon which it is founded.

We come into this Party, some as Trade Unionists, some as Cooperators, and some as Socialists and in these days most of us as all three.

The framers of that 1899 resolution set themselves a modest aim—to increase the number of Labour members in the next Parliament. A year later, in the General Election of 1900, 15 candidates stood under the Banner of the Labour Representation Committee. They polled an aggregate of 62,700 votes. Two of them were returned to Parliament. Forty-five years after, in the General Election of 1945, Labour polled 12 million votes, and returned 393 members to Parliament. To have won political power and to have secured a majority over all other parties in less than half a century is one of the greatest democratic movements in history.

We meet today in the same hall in which we assembled in conference 4 years ago. . . . At that Conference we adopted our programme and we returned to our constituencies to fight a General Election. We fought and won. Might I ask you and the country—Has the Labour Government been faithful to its trust? I believe we can honestly claim that our record proves it. Today we look back upon 4 years of Labour rule. They have been 4 years of hard work and 4 years of solid achievement. We have not yet completed our term. We have already so far progressed with implementing our programme that it is safe to prophesy that when we seek a renewal of our mandate we shall be able to claim that we have done all that we promised to do. . . .

I would make another claim for our work during these 4 years. It is for the new and splendid chapter written into the history of our country by the massive programme of economic and social advancement we have carried through. We have fought the good fight, we have kept the faith, but the journey has only just begun.

James Griffiths, M.P., giving the chairman's address at the Labour Party Conference in Blackpool, 6 June 1949

2. With Songs to Battle

This song shall be our parting hymn
The Red Flag

THE SONG OF THE LOWER CLASSES

We plough and sow—we're so very, very low
That we delve in the dirty clay
Till we bless the plain—with the golden grain,
And the vale with fragrant hay.
Our place we know—we're so very low
'Tis down at the landlord's feet,
We're not too low—the bread to grow,
But too low the bread to eat.

Down, down we go—we're so very, very low,
To the hell of deep-sunk mines,
But we gather the proudest gems that glow
When the crown of the despot shines.
And whenever he lacks—upon our backs
Fresh loads he deigns to lay:
We're far too low to vote the tax,
But not too low to pay.

We're low, we're low—mere rabble, we know,
But at our plastic power,
The mould at the lordling's feet will grow
Into palace and church and tower—
Then prostrate fall—in the rich men's hall
And cringe at the rich man's door:
We're not too low to build the wall,
But too low to tread the floor.

We're low—we're low—we're very, very low,
Yet from our fingers glide
The silken flow—and the robes that glow

130

Round the limbs of the sons of pride.
And what we get—and what we give
We know, and we know our share:
We're not too low the cloth to weave,
But too low the cloth to wear.

                    Ernest Jones (a Chartist leader) (1819–69)

THE MARCH OF THE WORKERS

What is this, the sound and rumour? What is this that all men
      hear,
Like the wind in hollow valleys when the storm is drawing near,
Like the rolling on of ocean in the eventide of fear?
            'Tis the people marching on.

Whither go they, and whence come they? What are these of
      whom ye tell?
In what country are they dwelling 'twixt the gates of heaven and hell?
Are they mine or thine for money? Will they serve a master well?
            Still the rumour's marching on.

Forth they come from grief and torment; on they wend toward
      health and mirth,
All the wide world is their dwelling, every corner of the earth.
Buy them, sell them for thy service! Try the bargain what 'tis
      worth,
            For the days are marching on.

These are they who build thy houses, weave thy raiment, win thy
      wheat,
Smooth the rugged, fill the barren, turn the bitter into sweet,
All for thee this day—and ever. What reward for them is meet
            Till the host comes marching on?
. . .
Many a hundred years passed over have they laboured deaf and
      blind;
Never tidings reached their sorrow, never hope their toil might
      find.
Now at last they've heard and hear it, and the cry comes down
      the wind,
            And their feet are marching on.

O ye rich men, hear and tremble! for with words the sound is rife:
'Once for you and death we laboured; changed henceforward is
    the strife.
We are men and we shall battle for the world of men and life;
    And our host is marching on.'

. . .

'Is it war, then? Will ye perish as the dry wood in the fire?
Is it peace? Then be ye of us, let your hope be our desire.
Come and live! for life awaketh, and the world shall never tire;
    And hope is marching on.

'On we march then, we the workers, and the rumour that ye hear
Is the blended sound of battle and deliverance drawing near;
For the hope of every creature, is the banner that we bear,
    And the world is marching on.'

    Hark the rolling of the thunder!
    Lo the sun! and lo thereunder
    Riseth wrath, and hope, and wonder,
      And the host comes marching on.

      William Morris, *Chants for Socialists*, 1884

THE FRANCHISE

(Song sung during the agitation for the farm labourer's vote,
1877.)

There's a man who represents our shire
In the Parliament House, they say,
Returned by the votes of farmer and squire
And others who bear the sway;
And farmer and squire, when laws are made,
Are pretty well cared for thus:
But the County Member, I'm much afraid,
Has but little care for us.
So we ought to vote, deny it who can,
'Tis the right of an honest Englishman.

Whenever a tyrant county beak
Has got us beneath his thumb,
For justice then he ought sure to speak—

But the County Member is dumb.
Whenever the rights of labour need
A vote on a certain day,
The County Member is sure to plead
And vote the contrary way.
So we ought to vote, deny it who can,
'Tis the right of an honest Englishman.

We ask for the vote, and we have just cause
To make it our firm demand;
For ages the rich have made all the laws
And robbed the poor of their land.
The Parliament men false weights have made,
So that Justice often fails,
And to make it worse, 'The Great Unpaid'
Must always fiddle the scales.
So we ought to vote, deny it who can,
'Tis the right of an honest Englishman.

Quoted by Joseph Arch, *The Story of His Life*, 1898

A DEATH SONG

What cometh here from west to east awending?
And who are these, the marchers stern and slow?
We bear the message that the rich are sending
Aback to those who bade them wake and know.
Not one, not one, nor thousands must they slay,
But one and all if they would dusk the day.

We asked them for a life of toilsome earning,
They bade us bide their leisure for our bread;
We craved to speak to tell our woeful learning;
We come back speechless, bearing back our dead.
Not one, not one, nor thousands must they slay,
But one and all if they would dusk the day.

They will not learn; they have no ears to hearken.
They turn their faces from the eyes of fate;
Their gay-lit halls shut out the skies that darken.
But, lo! this dead man knocking at the gate.
Not one, not one, nor thousands must they slay,
But one and all if they would dusk the day.

Here lies the sign that we shall break our prison;
Amidst the storm he won a prisoner's rest;
But in the cloudy dawn the sun arisen
Brings us our day of work to win the best.
Not one, not one, nor thousands must they slay,
But one and all if they would dusk the day.

William Morris, *Chants for Socialists*, 1884

THE RED FLAG

The people's flag is deepest red.
It shrouded oft our martyred dead,
And ere their limbs grew stiff and cold
Their heart-blood dyed its every fold.

(*Chorus*) Then raise the scarlet standard high,
Within its shade we'll live or die.
Though cowards flinch and traitors sneer,
We'll keep the red flag flying here.

With heads uncovered swear we all
To bear it onward till we fall.
Come dungeons dark or gallows grim,
This song shall be our parting hymn.

J. Connell, 1889

JERUSALEM

And did those feet in ancient time
Walk upon England's mountains green?
And was the holy Lamb of God
On England's pleasant pastures seen?

And did the Countenance Divine
Shine forth upon our clouded hills?
And was Jerusalem builded here
Among these dark Satanic mills?

Bring me my bow of burning gold!
Bring me my arrows of desire!
Bring me my spear! O clouds unfold!
Bring me my chariot of fire!

I will not cease from mental fight,
Nor shall my sword sleep in my hand,
Till we have built Jerusalem
In England's green and pleasant land.

William Blake (1757–1827)

THESE THINGS SHALL BE

These things shall be; a loftier race
Than ere the world hath known shall rise,
With flame of freedom in their souls,
And light of science in their eyes.

They shall be gentle, brave and strong,
To spill no drop of blood, but dare
All that may plant man's lordship firm
On earth and fire and sea and air.

They shall be simple in their homes
And splendid in their public ways,
Filling the mansions of the state
With music and with hymns of praise.

Nation with nation, land with land,
Inarmed shall live as comrades free,
Through every heart and brain shall throb
The pulse of one fraternity.

New arts shall bloom of loftier mould,
And mightier music fill the skies,
And every life shall be a song,
When all the earth is paradise.

J. A. Symonds (1840–93)

3. The Christian Socialist

'The Labour Movement is essentially religious.'
Keir Hardie

HE HATH SHEWED STRENGTH . . .

HE HATH SHEWED strength with his arm; he hath scattered the proud in the imagination of their hearts. He hath put down the mighty from their seats and exalted the humble and meek. He hath filled the hungry with good things and the rich he hath sent empty away.

St Luke 1, vv. 51–3

WHAT THEN SHALL WE DO?

And the people asked him [John] saying, What shall we do then? He answereth and saith unto them, He that hath two coats, let him impart to him that hath none: and he that hath meat let him do likewise. Then came also publicans and said unto him, Master, what shall we do? And he said unto them, Exact no more than that which is appointed you.

St Luke 3, vv. 10–13

A WARNING TO THE CAPITALIST

And he [Christ] said unto them, Take heed, and beware of covetousness; for a man's life consisteth not in the abundance of things which he possesseth. And he spake a parable unto them, saying, The ground of a certain rich man brought forth plentifully: and he thought within himself, saying, What shall I do, because I have no room where to bestow my fruits? And he said, This will I do: I will pull down my barns, and build greater; and there will I bestow all my fruits and my goods. And I will say to my soul, Soul, thou hast much goods laid up for many years, take thine ease, eat, drink and be merry. But God said unto him, Thou fool, this night thy soul shall be required of thee: then whose shall those things be, which thou has provided? So is he that layeth up treasure for himself, and is not rich toward God.

St Luke 12, vv. 15–21

. . . AND THE RICH YOUNG MAN

And behold one came and said unto him, Good Master, what good thing shall I do, that I may have eternal life? . . . Jesus said unto him, If thou wilt be perfect, go and sell that thou hast, and give to the poor, and thou shalt have treasure in heaven; and come and follow me. But when the young man heard that saying, he went away sorrowful, for he had great possessions.

St Matthew 19, vv. 16, 21–3

FOR I WAS HUNGRY . . .

And the King shall answer and say unto them, Verily I say unto you, Inasmuch as ye have done it unto one of the least of these my brethren, ye have done it unto me. Then shall he also say to them on the left hand, Depart from me, ye cursed, into everlasting fire. . . . For I was an hungred, and ye gave me no meat: I was thirsty, and ye gave me no drink; I was a stranger and ye took me not in; naked and ye clothed me not; sick, and in prison, and ye visited me not. Then shall they also answer him, saying, Lord, when saw we thee an hungred, or athirst, or a stranger, or naked, or sick, or in prison, and did not minister unto thee? Then shall he answer them saying, Verily, I say unto you, Inasmuch as ye did it not to one of the least of these, ye did it not to me. And these shall go away into everlasting punishment: but the righteous into life eternal.

St Matthew 25, vv. 40–6

TO EACH ACCORDING TO HIS NEED

And all that believed were together and had all things common; and sold their possessions and goods, and parted them to all men, as every man had need.

The Acts 2, vv. 44–5

And the multitude of them that believed were of one heart and of one soul; neither said any of them that ought of the things which he possessed was his own; but they had all things common. . . . Neither was there any among them that lacked; for as many as were possessors of lands or houses sold them, and brought the prices of the things that were sold, and laid them down at the apostles' feet; and distribution was made unto every man according as he had need.

The Acts 4, vv. 32, 34–5

FROM EACH ACCORDING TO HIS ABILITY

For as we have many members in one body, and all members have not
the same office; so we, being many, are one body in Christ, and every one
members one of another. Having then gifts differing according to the
grace that is given to us. . . .

St Paul's Epistle to the Romans, 12, vv. 4–6

NO FOOD FOR THE RENTIER

For even when we were with you, this we commanded you, that if any
would not work, neither should he eat. For we hear that there are some
which walk among you disorderly, working not at all. . . . Now them that
are such we command and exhort by our Lord Jesus Christ, that with
quietness they work, and eat their own bread. . . . And if any man obey
not our word by this epistle, note that man, and have no company with
him, that he may be ashamed.

St Paul, Second Epistle to the Thessalonians, 3, vv. 10–12, 14

INJUSTICE AND THE CHRISTIAN

The devout Christian, confronted with spectacle of wrong and injustice,
may draw either of two contrary conclusions. In the eyes of his religion
the miner or weaver is just as important as the landlord or the cotton
lord. Clearly then, one will argue, it is the duty of a Christian State to
prevent any class, however obscure and trivial its place in the world may
seem to be, from sinking into degrading conditions of life. Every soul
is immortal, and the consequences of ill-treatment and neglect in the brief
day of its life on earth will be unending. If, therefore, society is so
organised as to impose such conditions on any class, the Christian will
demand the reform of its institutions. For such minds Christianity provides a standard by which to judge government, the industrial and economic order, the life of society, the way in which it distributes wealth
and opportunities. . . . But some minds drew a different moral from the
equality that Christianity teaches. Every human soul is a reality, but the
important thing about a human soul is its final destiny, and that destiny
does not depend on the circumstances of this life. The world has been
created on a plan of apparent injustice by a Providence that combined
infinite power with infinite compassion. The arrangements that seem so
capricious are really the work of that Power. But the same Power has
given to the men and women who seem to live in such bitter and degrading

surroundings, an escape from its cares by the exercise of their spiritual faculties. It is those faculties that make all men equal . . . and no misery or poverty can prevent a soul from winning happiness in the world to come. Thus whereas one man looking out on the chaos of the world calls for reform, the other calls for contemplation: one says, Who could tolerate such injustice? the other says, Who would not rejoice that there is another world? One says, Give these people the conditions of a decent life; the other says, Teach them to read the Bible.

J. L. and B. Hammond, *The Town Labourer 1760–1832*, 1917

TWO CHRISTIANS AND 'LITTLE HELL'

(Hannah More and her sister were typical of Evangelical Christians at the end of the eighteenth century. This extract shows how far removed they were from the spirit which animated the first Christian Socialists fifty years later.)

The condition of these villages was such that one of them was popularly known as Botany Bay or Little Hell. In one place Hannah More mentions that the wages are a shilling a day; in another that two hundred people are crammed into nineteen hovels. Of another parish she writes: 'I will only add that we have one large parish of miners so poor that there is not any creature in it that can give a cup of broth if it would save a life. Of course, they have nothing human to look to but us. The clergyman, a poor saint, told me, when we set up our schools there twenty-five years ago, that eighteen had perished that winter of a putrid fever and he could not raise a sixpence to save a life.' Nowhere perhaps was there a better illustration of the . . . exploitation of the mass of a race by the classes holding economic and political power. Now the sisters More were benevolent women who put themselves to great trouble and discomfort out of pity for these villages, and yet from beginning to end of the *Mendip Annals* there is not a single reflection on the persons or system responsible for these conditions. It never seems to have crossed the minds of these philanthropists that it was desirable that men and women should have decent wages, or decent homes, or that there was something wrong with the arrangements of a society that left the mass of people in this plight. . . . The employers and gentry are sometimes blamed, it is true, in these pages, but they are only blamed for their want of sympathy with the efforts of the More sisters to teach religion. They are nowhere blamed for ill-treating their dependants, or told that they have any duties to them except the duty of encouraging them to listen to Hannah More on the importance of obedience, and on the claims to their regard and gratitude of a Providence that had lavished such attention upon them. . . .

The period covered by this Journal was marked by two famines; they are naturally both discussed by Hannah More . . . and her comments on them are characteristic: 'In suffering by the scarcity you have but shared in the common lot, with the pleasure of knowing the advantage you have had over many villages in your having suffered no scarcity of religious instruction.' It mattered little that wheat was at 134 shillings a quarter, so long as the labourers who were living on a shilling a day had the story of Cain and Abel at their fingers' ends.

J. L. and B. Hammond, *The Town Labourer 1760–1832*, 1917

THE COMING OF CHRISTIAN SOCIALISM

(The events of 10 April 1848, described elsewhere, left the Chartist Movement dispersed and discredited. On this day, too, the Christian Socialist Movement came into being, which was in the long run to have a greater influence than Chartism.)

The after-swell of the great European tide was washing even the remote shores of England. The demand for the Charter had been first formulated in 1838. After ten years of agitation it seemed possible that the forces of agitation might at last break forth into open explosion. Men wondered if London would exhibit the same scenes of violence as Paris or Berlin. The famous 10th of April was to see the monster petition escorted by a hundred thousand determined men from Kennington to Westminster; the evening might see barricades and fighting in the streets. Maurice, utterly opposed to the appeal to force, had joined the side of order, and offered himself with the multitude of the middle classes which enrolled themselves as special constables. Kingsley had hurried to London from his country parish to be present at the day of decision, to see if anything could be done even at the last moment to prevent a collision between the Chartists and the troops. Maurice sent him to Mr Ludlow, and on this day first arose the combination of that little band of reformers who were to become famous in the history of social progress under the title of the 'Christian Socialists'. 'The poor fellows mean well however much misguided' were Kingsley's first words. 'It would be horrible if there were bloodshed. I am going to Kennington to see what man can do. Will you go with me?'

There was nothing to be done. The demonstration in a few hours had passed from tragedy to farce. The crowding of London with troops, the enrolling of 150,000 special constables to guarantee the preservation of property, the lack of leadership among the workmen and their own weakness and irresolution, had rendered all prospect of violence negligible. The numbers who assembled proved ridiculously inadequate to the work which they proposed to accomplish. Rain fell steadily. The leaders fled. The crowd dispersed. The great petition crawled ingloriously to West-minster in a four-wheeled cab. The day closed in mockery and rejoicing. Kingsley ... knew too well the misery and hunger ravaging the masses of the poor to find any exultation in such an ending. . . . Maurice and the little company who had gathered round him in the later spring of 1848 were watching with profound anxiety the signs of the time. They were convinced of the need for action, of the burden of action laid upon them. Their first immediate step was to placard London with addresses to the workmen of England telling them that they had more friends than they knew of 'who love you because you are their brothers, and who fear God, and therefore dare not neglect you, his children'. In plain terms these placards informed their readers that the Charter would not make them 'free from slavery to ten-pound bribes, to every spouter who flatters self conceit, to beer and gin'. The workmen of England, thus addressed on impersonal hoardings, were lying crushed and forlorn in the failure of their great endeavour, and the ridicule which was being outpoured on the bogus names in the great petition. Such a collapse may perhaps account for a lack of resentment at these strange, ill-chosen lectures, delivered to them through the quaint medium of advertisement in the streets of London, by men who had hitherto done nothing to guarantee their sincerity and their sympathy.

From such unpromising beginnings they passed to more continuous effort. On May 6, 1848, appeared the first number of *Politics for the People*. It consisted of a tiny newspaper of sixteen pages, published weekly at a penny. It appealed definitely to the working classes, and to all those in England who felt the reality of the grievances from which the working classes suffered, and who realised the necessity of reform. From the first, 'physical force Chartism' was repudiated. The hope of the new time was to come from religion: and the appeal—sometimes passionate, sometimes bitter—was primarily to the Church and its ministers to take up the obligation of social improvement. 'We have used the Bible', cried Kingsley in an early number, 'as if it were a mere special constable's handbook, an opium dose for keeping beasts of burden patient while they were being over-loaded, a mere book to keep the poor in order.' Against such blasphemy he appealed to the prophets and the teaching of the New Testament, for vindication of 'justice from God to those whom men oppress; glory to God from those whom men despise'. . . . Seventeen numbers only were issued of *Politics for the People*. The circulation reached some two thousand a week; but there seemed no chance of it attaining an economic success. Advertisements were impossible, and the newspaper was boycotted by most respectable newsagents. It died before the end of that wonderful summer. . . .

C. F. G. Masterman, *Life of F. D. Maurice*, 1907

A SECOND ATTEMPT

In the spring of 1849 further efforts were undertaken. The great revolutionary movement had collapsed in Europe and the old order had been re-established in fire and blood. . . . The Christian Socialists refused to abandon the vision of the 'good time coming'. Meetings were arranged with some of the Chartist leaders in London. . . . [At one] Maurice went to the root causes of the whole random disorganisation of modern life, in a philosophy whose far reaching application, had they but understood it, would have scared many of the patrons of the new reforms. He denounced almost savagely the gospel of free competition, and set forth the contrary ideal of association as the law of the Christian Kingdom. 'Competition is put forth as the law of the universe', he wrote a little later. 'That is a lie. The time is coming for us to declare that it is a lie. The payment of wages under this competitive system has ceased to be a righteous mode of expressing the true relation between employer and employed.' The challenge, clear and definite and with no soft words of compromise, is flung down to the orthodox economy which was the child of the industrial revolution in early Victorian England. 'We may restore the old state of things,' cried this social prophet, 'we may bring in a new one. God will decide that. His voice has gone forth clearly bidding us come forward to fight against the present state of things. It is no old condition we are contending with, but an accursed new one, the product of a hateful, devilish theory which must be fought with to the death.'

The challenge, here deliberate, was immediately accepted. It was sufficiently outrageous that a clergyman should term himself a Chartist and ally himself with those who demanded votes for the lower orders. But when such a clergyman passed from political to economic questions, assailed the very fabric of society, openly advocated Socialism, and denounced as 'devilish' the comfortable creed upon which were based the wealth and security of the leisured class, it was evident that he could expect little but a long and furious warfare against one who stirred up the people to unimaginable ends. Socialism came to Maurice . . . in the form of encouragement of association or co-operation among the working classes themselves. It was not the formation of little secluded Utopias he desired, leading the communal life. Nor did he ever appeal to the state to come in to organise the industrial class. But he thought that, by uniting the workmen themselves into Co-operative Producing Associations, he could eliminate the profits of dead capital and abrogate the ferocity of the competitive struggle. . . . But Co-operation in those days wore a very different garb from that which clothes it today. This mild and beneficent business-organisation of distribution and production, now so sleepy and conservative, patronised by Bishops, extolled by all that is respectable and secure, appeared sixty years ago as a programme of violent and revolutionary change. Workmen uniting with workmen, as their own masters, repudiating the leadership of the intellectual and the rich, were in such unity to shake the very fabric of society. Ultimately they might succeed in abolishing those profits of capital without which an upper and middle class could not decently endure. In the eyes of such a class it was revolutionary, anti-Christian, communistic, cutting at the root of the natural relationship of master and man, employer and employed. It signified a lawlessness and independence at the basis of society which could only consummate in some enormous collapse and upheaval. The orthodox in business and politics and religion turned in disgust from these reckless men; whose theology was misty and vague, whose political economy was contemptible, who were encouraging blasphemy by the proclamation, not in the name of a barren atheism, but as the demand of the Divine Ruler of the universe, that the competitive system must be overthrown.

C. F. G. Masterman, *Life of F. D. Maurice*, 1907

CHOOSING A NAME

After eighteen months of comparative silence, since the cessation of *Politics for the People*, it was agreed that the practical measure should be accompanied by another step forward. Chartism by this time had become a dead thing; Socialism a living menace; and the defiant flag of Christian Socialism was nailed to the mast. The name was apparently adopted with a desire to offend the maximum number of persons on both sides; 'to commit us at once', says Maurice cheerfully, 'to the conflict we must engage in sooner or later with the unsocial Christians and the un-Christian Socialists'.

C. F. G. Masterman, *Life of F. D. Maurice*, 1907

A FIERY CLERIC

Maurice was below middle height, but with a dignity of bearing which removed all sense of smallness. His habits gave the impression of an abundance of nervous energy. He would start his walk with a little run, move violently about the room while dictating his books, attack the fire with a poker or clutch pillows in an unconscious embrace; all the while pouring forth a continuous stream of words. . . . 'There were times', says his son, 'when he could make his words sting like a lash and burn like a hot iron. When his wrath was excited by something mean or cruel, he would begin in a most violent manner to rub together the palms of his hands. He appeared at such moments to be entirely absorbed in his own reflections, and utterly unconscious of the terrible effect which the wild look of his face and the wild rubbing of his hands produced upon an innocent bystander. A lady who often saw him thus says that she always expected sparks to fly from his hands and to see him bodily on fire.'

C. F. G. Masterman, *Life of F. D. Maurice*, 1907

A VICTORIAN VICAR

(Charles Kingsley, who was born in 1819 and died in 1875, was vicar of a country parish near Reading and later Professor of Modern History at Cambridge. His novel *Yeast*, although a confused story, clumsily expressed, had a considerable influence on the Christian Socialist movement. It succeeded in showing that traditional ideas of the country as a place of innocence and contentment were quite untrue and that drastic change was needed there as much as in the towns.)

'Our good vicar is like the rest hereabouts. God knows, he stints neither time nor money—the souls of the poor are well looked after, and their bodies too—as far as his purse will go; but that's not far.'

'Is he ill-off then?'

'The living's worth some forty pounds a year. The great tithes, they say, are worth better than twelve hundred; but Squire Lavington has them.'

'Oh, I see!' said Lancelot.

'I'm glad you do, sir, for I don't,' meekly answered Tregarva. 'But the vicar, sir, he is a kind man, and a good; but the poor don't understand him, nor he them.' . . .

'But cannot he expose and redress these evils, if they exist?'

Tregarva twisted about again.

'I do not say that I think it, sir; but this I know, that every poor man in the vale thinks it—that the parsons are afraid of the landlords. They must see these things, for they are not blind; and they try to plaster them up out of their own pockets.'

'But why in God's name, don't they strike at the root of the matter, and go straight to the landlords and tell them the truth?' asked Lancelot.

'So people say, sir. I see no reason for it, except the one which I gave you. Besides, sir, you must remember, that a man can't quarrel with his own kin; and so many of them are their squire's brothers, or sons, or nephews.'

'Or good friends with him, at least.'

'Ay, sir, and to do them justice, they had need, for the poor's sake, to keep good friends with the squire. How else are they to get a farthing for schools, or coal-subscriptions, or lying-in societies, or lending libraries, or penny clubs? If they spoke their minds to the great ones, sir, how could they keep the parish together?'

'You seem to see both sides of a question, certainly. But what a miserable state of things, that the labouring man should require all these societies, and charities, and helps from the rich—that an industrious freeman cannot live without alms!'

'So I have thought this long time,' quietly answered Tregarva.

Charles Kingsley, *Yeast*, 1848

A VICTORIAN BANKER

'If I were a Christian,' said Lancelot, 'like you, I would call this credit system of yours the devil's selfish counterfeit of God's order of mutual love and trust. . . . Ask yourself, honestly, how can you battle against it, while you allow in practice, and in theory too, except in church on Sundays, the very falsehood from which it all springs—that a man is bound to get wealth, not for his country, but for himself; that, in short, not patriotism, but selfishness is the bond of all society. Selfishness can collect, not unite, a herd of cowardly wild cattle, that they may feed together, breed together and keep off the wolf and bear together. But when one of your wild cattle falls sick, what becomes of the corporate feelings of the herd then? For one man of your class who is nobly helped by his fellows, are not the thousand left behind to perish? Your Bible talks of society, not as a herd, but as a living tree, an organic individual body, a holy brotherhood, and kingdom of God. And here is an idol which you have set up instead of it.'

But the banker was deaf to all arguments. No doubt he had plenty, for he was himself a just and generous, aye and a God-fearing man in his way, only he regarded Lancelot's young fancies as too visionary to deserve an answer.

Charles Kingsley, *Yeast*, 1848

CONDITIONS IN THE COUNTRY, 1848

'Did you ever do a good day's farm work in your life? If you had, man or boy, you wouldn't have been game for much reading when you got home; you'd do just what these poor fellows do—tumble into bed at eight o'clock, hardly waiting to take your clothes off, knowing that you must turn up again at five o'clock the next morning, to get a breakfast of bread, and perhaps a dab of the squire's dripping, and then back to work again; and so on, day after day, sir, week after week, year after year, without a hope or a chance of being anything but what you are, and only too thankful if you can get work to break your back, and catch the rheumatism over.'

'But do you mean to say that their labour is so severe and incessant?'

'It's only God's blessing if it is incessant, sir, for if it stops, they starve, or go to the house to be worse fed than the thieves in gaol. And as for its being severe, there's many a boy as their mothers will tell you, comes home night after night, too tired to eat their suppers, and tumble, fasting, to bed in the same foul shirt which they've been working in all the day, never changing their rag of calico from week's end to week's end, or washing the skin that's under it once in seven years.'

'No wonder,' said Lancelot, 'that such a life of drudgery makes them brutal and reckless.'

'No wonder, indeed, sir: they've no time to think; they're born to be machines, and machines they must be; and I think, sir,' he added bitterly, 'it's God's mercy that they daren't think. It's God's mercy that they don't feel. Men that write books and talk at elections call this a free country, and say that the poorest and meanest has a free opening to rise and become prime minister, if he can. But you see, sir, the misfortune is, that in practice he can't; for one who gets into a gentleman's family, or into a little shop, and so saves a few pounds, fifty know that they've no chance before them, but day-labourer born, day-labourer live, from hand to mouth, scraping and pinching to get not meat and beer even, but bread and potatoes; and then, at the end of it all, for a worthy reward, half a crown a week of parish pay—or the workhouses. That's a lively hopeful prospect for a Christian man!'

Charles Kingsley, *Yeast*, 1848

A VICTORIAN SQUIRE

It had come at last. The squire was sitting in his study, purple with rage, while his daughters were trying vainly to pacify him. All the men-servants, grooms and helpers, were drawn up in line along the wall, and greeted Tregarva, whom they all heartily liked, with sly and sorrowful looks of warning.

'Here, you sir, you ——, look at this! Is this the way you repay me? I, who have kept you out of the workhouse, treated you like my own child? And then to go and write filthy, rascally, Radical ballads on me and mine! . . . This is your handwriting, you villain! you know it' (and the squire tossed the fatal paper across the table).

A ROUGH RHYME ON A ROUGH MATTER

The merry brown hares came leaping
Over the crest of the hill,
Where the clover and corn lay sleeping
Under the moonlight still.

Leaping late and early,
Till under their bite and their tread
The swedes, and the wheat, and the barley,
Lay cankered, and trampled, and dead.

A poacher's widow sat sighing
On the side of the white chalk bank,
There under the gloomy fir-woods
One spot in the ley throve rank.

She watched a long tuft of clover,
Where rabbit or hare never ran;
For its black sour haulm covered over
The blood of a murdered man.

The thought of the dark plantation,
And the hares and her husband's blood,
And the voice of her indignation
Rose up to the throne of God.

I am long past wailing and whining—
I have wept too much in my life;
I've had twenty years of pining
As an English labourer's wife.

A labourer in Christian England,
Where they cant of a Saviour's name,
And yet waste men's lives like the vermin's
For a few more brace of game.

There's blood on your new foreign shrubs, squire;
There's blood on your pointer's feet;
There's blood on the game you sell, squire,
And there's blood on the game you eat!

'You villain!' interposed the squire, 'when did I ever sell a head of game?'

You have sold the labouring man, squire,
Body and soul to shame,
To pay for your seat in the House, squire,
And to pay for the feed of your game.

You made him a poacher yourself, squire,
When you'd give neither work nor meat;
And your barley-fed hares robbed the garden
At our starving children's feet;

When packed in one reeking chamber,
Man, maid, mother and little ones lay;
While the rain pattered in on the rotting bride-bed,
And the walls let in the day;

When we lay in the burning fever
On the mud of the cold clay floor,
Till you parted us all for three months, squire,
At the cursed workhouse door.

We quarrelled like brutes, and who wonders?
What self-respect could we keep,
Worse housed than your hacks and your pointers,
Worse fed than your hogs and your sheep.

Our daughters with base-born babies
Have wandered away in their shame;
If your misses had slept, squire, where they did,
Your misses might do the same.

Can your lady patch hearts that are breaking
With handfuls of coals and rice,
Or by dealing out flannel and sheeting
A little below cost price?

You may tire of the gaol and the workhouse,
And take up allotments and schools,
But you've run up a debt that will never
Be repaid us by penny-club rules.

In the season of shame and sadness,
In the dark and dreary day,
When scrofula, gout and madness,
Are eating your race away;

When to kennels and liveried varlets
You have cast your daughter's bread;
And worn out with liquor and harlots,
Your heir at your feet lies dead;

When your youngest, the mealy-mouthed rector,
Lets your soul rot asleep to the grave,
You will find in your God the protector
Of the freeman you fancied your slave.

She looked at the tuft of clover,
And wept till her heart grew light;
And at last, when her passion was over,
Went wandering into the night.

But the merry brown hares came leaping
Over the uplands still,
Where the clover and corn lay sleeping
On the side of the white chalk hill.

He turned to go. The squire, bursting with passion, sprung up with a terrible oath, turned deadly pale, staggered, and dropped senseless on the floor.

Charles Kingsley, *Yeast*, 1848

BEAR ONE ANOTHER'S BURDENS

The points in which Christian and Socialistic collectivism are at one are simple and fundamental. As, however, we must proceed carefully in this matter, we may state these points of resemblance under three heads.

(1) Both rise from the deeps of an emotion, the emotion of compassion for misfortune, as such. This is really a very important point. Collectivism is not an intellectual fad, even if erroneous, but a passionate protest and aspiration: it arises as a secret of the heart, a dream of the injured feeling, long before it shapes itself as a definite propaganda at all. The intellectual philosophies ally themselves with success and preach competition, but the human heart allies itself with misfortune and suggests communism.

(2) Both trace the evil state of society to 'covetousness', the competitive desire to accumulate riches. Thus, both in one case and the other, the mere possession of wealth is in itself an offence against moral order, the absence of it in itself a recommendation and training for the higher life.

(3) Both propose to remedy the evil of competition by a system of 'bearing each other's burdens' in the literal sense, that is to say, of levelling, silencing and reducing one's own chances, for the chance of your weaker brethren. The desirability, they say, of a great or clever man acquiring fame is small compared with the desirability of a weak and broken man acquiring bread. The strong man is a man, and should modify or adapt himself to the hopes of his mates. He that would be first among you, let him be the servant of all.

These are the three fountains of collectivist passion. I have not considered it necessary to enter into elaborate proof of the presence of these three in the Gospels. That the main trend of Jesus' character was compassion for human ills, that he denounced not merely covetousness but riches again and again, and with an almost impatient emphasis, and that he insisted on his followers throwing up personal aims and sharing funds and fortune entirely, these are plain matters of evidence presented again and again, and, in fact, of common admission.

G. K. Chesterton, from his *Notebooks*, c. 1895

A CHRISTIAN VIEW OF PROPERTY

There is nothing inherently wrong or unchristian in the ownership of private property; it is only when the nature of that ownership is such as to enable the arbitrary act of one individual to affect adversely the life and standards of another, that there is a danger and a problem which calls for our attention as Christians.

Now there are three ways of dealing with this problem. The first is to accept the danger and to attempt to moderate or eliminate it by the conversion of all people to true Christian ideals in human relationships, so that the danger is overcome by the goodness of the individual. . . .

The second is for the community or State to step in and so regulate conditions of tenants and employees as to remove as much of the danger as possible. In other words, for the State to protect the individuals against what is recognised as the inevitable danger of the situation. . . .

It is perhaps worth discovering the reason for our reliance upon the State's protection. The basic assumption is that the community as a whole is more likely to be Christian minded in these matters than the individual. The community, unlike the individual, is not tempted by profit or by the desire to gain personal power, and so can examine the relationships in an impartial manner, and with an eye to justice and equity rather than to individual advantage. The State is, in fact, accepted as the nearest that we can get to an impartial judge in any matter.

The third alternative is to remove the danger by abolishing all types of private property that give one individual power over another and to place that property in the hands of a democratically controlled State. . . .

It is the comparative failure of the first two alternatives stated that has made many people regard the third alternative as preferable and as more likely to make it possible to apply Christian principles in industry. I believe this myself, with one proviso, which is that the democracy controlling the State's actions, must be imbued with the Christian spirit.

From the Christian point of view there seem to be no fundamental arguments which can be raised against our third alternative. I know of no Christian principle or teaching which lays down the sanctity of private property, though there are many which deal with human relationships.

Certainly, the other alternatives have been tried over long periods. The first, absolutely free enterprise relying on the Christian beliefs of the individuals to moderate their actions, resulted in the scandals of child employment in the mills and mines and compelled the State . . . to introduce the second alternative of State control of industrial relationships. This has been helped by a strong defensive Trade Union Movement for the protection of the workers, but even so, none of us can be satisfied with the pre-war conditions, particularly as regards the inability of industry to employ great numbers of the people or to accept responsibility for the unemployed.

Sir Stafford Cripps, Towards a Christian Democracy, 1945

THE CHRISTIAN ELEMENT IN SOCIALISM

I have said, both in writing and from the platform many times, that the impetus which drove me first of all into the Labour movement, and the inspiration which has carried me on in it, has been derived more from the teachings of Jesus of Nazareth, than from all other sources combined. Labour men cannot afford, even if they were inclined, to neglect Christianity. A fact so potent in the history of the world, which has influenced not merely the life but the thought of a whole continent, which has its origin, by common consent, in the teachings and life of a Common Working Man, must necessarily appeal to all who are seeking to-day to make life more worthy of its high purposes than it has been in the past. . . .

. . . I say, therefore, that from the Socialist and Labour man Christ demands at least sympathetic consideration. It is true, He founded no party, He formulated no economic doctrine; but He laid down principles so broad and deep that when these come to be applied, as they one day will be applied when the world grows wiser, not only will poverty due to lack of bread have disappeared, but poverty due to the accumulation of riches shall also have disappeared from the world.

. . . If I were called upon to define Christianity in a single sentence, I would say that Christianity represents sacrifice having its origin in love. And the Christian who professes the Christian faith is thereby under obligation to make whatever sacrifice may be necessary in order to remove sin, suffering and injustice from the lives of those around him. It is not enough to pray to God; it is a mere mockery to sing hymns; unless our lives are consecrated to the services of God through humanity. . . .

. . . The Labour movement in its very essence is essentially religious. The men and the women who are in it are not working for themselves; they know perfectly well that all they can do is but to create the beginning of a condition of things which will one day bring peace and happiness and freedom and a fuller life for those who are to come after us. It

s hard to be misjudged by the smug, respectable, church-going, pleasure-
loving people, who regard Labour men and Labour movements as in-
pired by self-seeking and selfishness.

Keir Hardie, 1910

THE CHRISTIAN SOCIAL UNION, 1908

This was one of the pioneer societies of its kind in the Church. Its members were told by the scoffers that they took themselves rather too
seriously, especially when they produced a 'White List' of London
tailors who were known to pay fair wages; and the West End tailors
would raise supercilious eyebrows and cough discreetly when, before
ordering a summer suit, dapper young curates from S. George's, Hanover
Square, or Holy Trinity, Sloane Street, would ask them with a pathetic
lack of confidence whether their firm was 'on the C.S.U. White List'; or
when members of the Union flung away their cups and saucers and
allowed only leadless glaze on their tables and sideboards—but at least
they were honest in their hope that by doing so they were helping to
reduce the appalling number of deaths from lead poisoning in the pot-
teries. . . .

F. A. Iremonger, William Temple, His Life and Letters, 1948

COMPETITION IS UNCHRISTIAN

This is not an economic question. It is a question touching the nature
of human personality. It asks what are the deepest and most potent
motives in the human soul. The question is not economic—to the
Christian it is religious. . . .

If Christianity is to be applied to the economic system, an organization which rests primarily on the principle of competition must give way
to one which rests primarily on co-operation. . . .

The question of the competitive principle is driven down into the
Labour market, so that men compete against each other for the right to
work which is the right to live. Go and see it at work in the London
Docks. If one man is to secure the means of feeding himself and his
family, he must be depriving another. Is that an exhibition of Brotherhood? Such a system embodies no principle but selfishness and mutual
antagonism. . . .

William Temple, then a deacon, at the Pan-Anglican
Conference, 1908

DAMN YOUR CHARITY!

A primary concern of the Church is to develop in men a Christian character. . . . At present . . . the Church cannot without betraying its own trust,
omit criticism of the economic order or fail to urge such action as may be
prompted by that criticism. . . .

The existing system is challenged on moral grounds. . . . The banner
so familiar in earlier unemployed or socialist processions—'Damn your
charity; we want justice'—vividly exposes the situation as it was seen by
its critics. If the present order is taken for granted or assumed to be
sacrosanct, charity from the more or less fortunate would seem virtuous
and commendable; to those for whom the order itself is suspect or worse,
such charity is blood-money. Why should some be in the position to
dispense and others to need that kind of charity?

. . . The Christian cannot ignore a challenge in the name of justice.
The moral quality of the accusation brought against the economic and
social order involves the Church in 'interference' on pain of betraying
the trust committed to it. . . . Why should some of God's children have
full opportunity to develop their capacities in freely chosen occupations,
while others are confined to a stunted form of existence, enslaved to types
of labour which represent no personal choice but the sole opportunity
offered?

The suffering caused by existing evils makes a claim upon our sympathy which the Christian heart and conscience cannot ignore. Before
the outbreak of war there were three main causes of widespread suffering
—bad housing, malnutrition, and unemployment. The varied forms of
suffering which bad housing causes are easy to imagine in part, but few
who have had no personal knowledge of it are able to imagine the whole
—the crushing of a woman's pride in her home through the ceaseless
and vain struggle against dirt and squalor; the nervous fret; the lack of
home comforts for the tired worker; the absence of any space for children to play. The bad conditions in slum quarters are not chiefly due to
the people living there. . . . The toleration of bad housing is a wanton
and callous cruelty.

Malnutrition is a direct result of poverty and ignorance. It produces
enfeebled bodies, embittered minds and irritable spirits; thus it tells against
good citizenship and good fellowship. Children are the most obvious
sufferers, but those who have suffered in this way as children seldom come
later to full strength or to physical and spiritual stability. . . .

Unemployment is the most hideous of our social evils. . . . The worst
evil of such unemployment . . . is its creating in the unemployed a sense

that they have fallen out of the common life . . . they are not wanted! That is the thing that has power to corrupt the soul of any man not already far advanced in saintliness. Because the man has no opportunity for service he is turned in upon himself and becomes, according to his temperament, a contented loafer or an embittered self-seeker. It has not been sufficiently appreciated that this moral isolation is the heaviest burden and most corrosive poison associated with unemployment: not bodily hunger but social futility. . . . The only real cure for unemployment is employment. . . . Christian sympathy demands this.

> William Temple, Archbishop of York, *Christianity and Social Order*, 1942

PORTRAIT OF A CHRISTIAN

(Lord Overtoun—millionaire chairman of a chemical firm whose workers had been on strike. He was a well-known Liberal, a philanthropist and President of the Y.M.C.A.)

Lord Overtoun gives £10,000 a year in charity. Ten thousand a year is about £27 8/. a day, £1.2.10 an hour. Lord Overtoun gives out of the fullness of his Christian charity 22/10 an hour in furtherance of God's work; to his workmen, as an act of justice, he gives fourpence! . . .

For it will scarcely be believed, but it is none the less true, that there are *no meals allowed* these men [the workers in his chemical factories]. From six in the morning until six at night, without a stoppage. . . . Food has to be snatched in mouthfuls as best the men can whilst carrying on their never-ceasing task. With their hands soiled with the poisonous chemicals they handle, inhaling a poison-laden atmosphere, they 'dine' in the fashion here stated. Twelve hours every day and *seven days every week*. For there is no rest for these men. If a man dares to stay away from work on Sunday to attend Church or Chapel he is punished by being compelled to lose Monday's wages also. Lord Overtoun is a great man with the Sunday Rest and Lord's Day Observance Societies. When the Glasgow Corporation proposed to run Sunday cars to enable the citizens to get out from their streets and slums to spend a few hours in the country a deputation from the societies named waited upon the Town Council to enter an indignant protest against this desecration of the Lord's Day. Lord Overtoun headed that deputation!

> Keir Hardie, 1899

THE MAKING OF A SOCIALIST

(Among Low Churchmen in the middle of the nineteenth century the Christian Socialist views of Charles Kingsley had gained
much support. Among High Churchmen later in the century the
predominant influence was that of Charles Gore. As first principal
of Pusey House, the Anglo-Catholic institution founded in 1884, and
subsequently as Bishop of Oxford, he was largely responsible for the
spread of Radical opinions within the university, though Socialism
was never in Britain, as it was on the Continent, an academic movement.)

At Oxford the first political event that came to operate on his mind with
overwhelming force was the heroic effort of Joseph Arch, the Warwickshire peasant, to organise and improve the lot of agricultural labourers,
in 1872. Gore never forgot Joseph Arch. Circumstances and the obtuse-
ness of Victorian squires and country clergy combined to make Arch
critical of the Church. Gore reckoned this a tragedy. 'The squirearchy',
he wrote in 1925, 'was not by any means a bad lot, nor the clergy, but
they lacked imagination.' Their apathy towards the conditions of the
labourers disgusted him. 'We always seem to see the truth about the
things when it is too late.' The Church ought to have thrown all its
weight into the scale on behalf of Arch's campaign. It is interesting to
record that Gore was not alone among High Churchmen in supporting
Arch's efforts. In its review of the year 1874 the *Church Times* compared Arch's work sympathetically with the Peasants' Revolt under
Richard II and regretted that no clerical champion had come forward from
the outset, like John Ball, to direct this more peaceful protest against
rural injustice. After Arch, the undergraduate Radical became conscious
of F. D. Maurice. . . . Later still, on turning to the Fathers, he began to
discover some of the extremely critical sentiments upon wealth that are
expressed in the Christian tradition, and reflected more and more on the
implications of our Lord's teaching on the subject.

G. L. Prestige, *Life of Charles Gore*, 1935

. . . AND HIS PROGRESS

The Labour demonstrations of 1887 in London—which brought the
name of John Burns prominently before the public notice, cost its owner
six weeks' imprisonment for alleged resistance to the police, and led to
the closing of Trafalgar Square to free speech—elicited a fierce epistle
from Holland [an Oxford don and Anglican priest, Gore's most intimate

friend]. 'Don't believe one word the Papers tell you of these unhappy Trafalgar Square meetings. I never read such brazen lies. The crisis has all come about through outraged spirit—I never saw a crowd look more innocent of revolution in my life: and there was no disturbance to London—or to the traffic—until the Police smashed their heads. The Government seem bent on manufacturing a Revolution—I have seldom felt so sad, or so mad, at a political wickedness.' Gore's sympathies lay on the same side as Holland's. When the affair was being discussed during lunch at Pusey House, an undergraduate guest was horrified to hear Gore remark, 'It's a pity they did not loot the West End'.

G. L. Prestige, *Life of Charles Gore*, 1935

STRIKERS WELCOME!

(In November 1889 Gore caused great alarm among Conservative circles in Oxford by entertaining at Pusey House the General Secretary of the Dockers' Union and the part organizer of the great Dock Strike of that year, Ben Tillett.)

Gore's motive was to insist . . . on 'the apostleship of justice and the responsibility of wealth'. As he said to the Pan-Anglican Congress in 1908, 'we must identify ourselves with the ideal of socialistic thoughts'. He possessed a 'permanently troubled conscience' about social short-comings. He 'raged for righteousness', and it was largely his earnest faith in the importance of carrying out Christian teaching in human life which endeared him to Nonconformists in years to come. But when he proclaimed adherence to socialistic thought, it was a moral, not merely a political co-operation which he had in mind. At Tillett's meeting Gore carefully stated that the object was to acquire first-hand information about the recent strikes; he also testified to the gladness with which he had witnessed 'the self-sacrifice' of the stevedores, who had undertaken a sympathetic strike in support of the other men. He saw in the Labour movement, headed by such men as Keir Hardie and George Lansbury, a righteous claim for what he called 'justice not charity' . . .

Too much had been heard of the rights of property. The Christian had a threefold duty to society. As a worker he must contribute his service to the community; shirkers and triflers in any class of society were not only neglecting their duty to man but failing also to recognise the claim of God. As owner or employer, the Christian should be taught to recognise as a fundamental principle of religion that the first charge on any industry must be the proper maintenance of the labourer—an idea expressed in popular language by the phrase 'a living wage'. As consumer, no Christian had the right to demand commodities at a price incompatible with the adequate remuneration of the workers or with proper conditions of industry.

G. L. Prestige, *Life of Charles Gore*, 1935

MEN BEFORE MEDALS

Leaders in political campaigns for the protection of workers in dangerous or sweated industries did not have to ask twice for his support; his action now outran the strict principles of the Christian Social Unionism, which took no sides but concentrated on investigation. He won them recruits, distributed the information which they had collected, preached in their interest at the Abbey, and helped to raise them funds. At the height of the agitation against the poisoning of workers in the china and earthenware trades, resulting from the employment of lead glaze in the process of manufacture, a representative of the Women's Trade Union League called at Little Cloisters in despair at the need for £100 to carry on the crusade. Gore preached a sermon for them, allocating the collection, which he took in person, to the cause, and the £100 was raised. Again the funds were exhausted, and again the lady called in Little Cloisters. All collections had already been allocated. Gore bent his head over his desk in deep reflection. Then suddenly he pulled out a drawer, and took from it medals of gold and silver which he had won at school; these should be sold for the fund.

G. L. Prestige, *Life of Charles Gore*, 1935

A BISHOP SHOPS AT THE CO-OP

In general, he confined himself to preaching right principles and stimulating those more directly concerned in the promotion of actual political measures. But on occasion he came down personally in the arena. When cases of injustice to individuals were reported to his notice, he made careful investigation, and took such steps as he could to have the wrong set right. He once became a shareholder in a large London store, solely in order to attend the shareholders' meeting and to protest against the oppressive treatment of employees. He was keenly interested in the Co-operative movement and purchased everything he could from shops of that type. . . .

G. L. Prestige, *Life of Charles Gore*, 1935

THE LABOUR GOOD SAMARITAN

(Geoffrey Bing was replying to Conservative complaints that foreign visitors to this country were able to receive free treatment under the National Health Service.)

arlier on, when we were discussing other matters, there was some dis-
ussion on ethical values, and in the course of some researches, which I
appened to be making in the Library on another matter, I came across
n old book in the reference department, which contained a passage
/hich . . . dealt with a stranger and a foreigner, who was on a journey to
place called Jericho. In the course of the journey he fell among thieves
nd was wounded and left for dying. Then it happened that two members
f the ruling class passed, and they, realising that in the interests of
ational economy they should restrict their personal expenditure, passed
im by on the other side. It happened that a little later there came some
ntutored fellow from an outlandish part, from what I suppose would
oughly correspond in the Palestine of those days to Wales in this
ountry . . . [who] without making any proper enquiries at all as to the
rigin of the stranger, stooped and at once gave him medical attention.
Not only that, but he made a small monetary payment towards his sup-
ort, and, worse than that, he said—I have taken the exact words,

'Take care of him; and whatsoever thou spendest more, When I
come again, I will repay thee',

hus leaving the way open for a supplementary estimate. This parable
as been quoted time and time again to show the contrast between the
rudent conduct of the ruling class and the reckless extravagance of the
rdinary man, who was prepared to squander not only his own money,
ut that of his fellows on helping a mere stranger.

Geoffrey Bing, House of Commons, 19 October 1949

PEOPLE BEFORE PROFITS

How far . . . is it true that the primary concern of those who control production is so to direct it that all engaged in it find in their activity a truly
human life, and that the needs of the public are met? How often are these
questions discussed at Boards of Directors? Is it not evident that the
primary concern is for profits out of which dividends may be paid to
shareholders? . . . The consumer ought not to come in only or chiefly as
a means to the interest of the producer; his interest ought to be para-
mount. . . .

To many it appears evident that we have allowed the making of profit, which is necessary as a means to the continuance of the industry, to get into the first place which properly belongs to the supply of human need —the true end of industry. . . . Instead of finance existing to facilitate production and production existing to supply needs, the supply of need is made the means to profitable production, and production itself is controlled as much as it is facilitated by finance. . . .

If that is true it is the duty of Christians to . . . demand a remedy

Archbishop Temple, *Christianity and Social Order*, 1942

THE CHURCH'S TASK

The Church itself must show faith in its own message, regardless of all cost; for either the Christianity in which we believe is no more than the whited sepulchre of the Pharisees, or else it is the most real thing in our lives. No Church dares preach social salvation unless it works for social justice.

As for the rest, the hardest part of our task will be to convince the world that no private or selfish interest is to be allowed to stand in the way of the full application of the principles in which we believe. These principles must be given preference over material gain and advantage.

Sir Stafford Cripps, *Towards a Christian Democracy*, 1945

THE CHRISTIAN AND THE CAPITALIST

Our whole contention is that the existing system is unjust; it is heavily weighted in favour of capital. And it is to be remembered that under the present system the wage-earners bear the losses to a great, often a quite unjustly great extent; for the bankruptcy of a firm means unemployment for its employees. . . . Whatever the system, those who have a surplus to invest and invest it, must bear the main risk of loss.

It should not be possible to 'make a living' (let alone a fortune) out of the manipulation of money. . . . There seems in fact to be as strong a case for converting the Bank of England and the Joint Stock Banks into publicly administered institutions as there is for the State's monopoly of minting money.

Archbishop Temple, *Christianity and Social Order*, 1942

THE CHRISTIAN AND THE LANDLORD

The land legislation of the Old Testament results from the principle that the land in a special sense belongs to God. This principle appears in our

Common Law in the doctrine that only the King has full Dominion over land; only its Use is granted to landlords. . . .

There is good reason to insist more strongly on this principle. In the case of urban sites it will lead toward public ownership, for there is little service, if any, that the owner of urban sites can render which cannot as well or better be rendered by the public authority. There is no reason why we should pay certain citizens large sums of money for merely owning the land on which our cities are built . . . the case for public ownership is at this point very strong.

Land not beneficially used should involve liability to fine, or, in extreme cases, to forfeiture. . . . In no case should land be regarded as a purely personal possession. How often we hear of an estate being 'mortgaged up to the hilt' because some heir to the property was a wastrel! . . . Overburdened estates should be compulsorily liquidated.

Archbishop Temple, *Christianity and Social Order*, 1942

HOW THE CHURCH WENT ASTRAY

Christianity in its early days was the champion of the downtrodden and the oppressed; it was the faith of the common people, not merely asserting their equality in a life hereafter, but emphasising the equal brotherhood of all men on earth. It was preached as an integral part of the life of the people on earth, and its power was derived in no small degree from its conception of the presence of God in the midst of the people, helping and encouraging them to strive, so that their wrongs might be righted and their sufferings alleviated.

By the nineteenth century, and indeed long before, apart from the recurrent religious revolutions, the Church had settled down into an acceptance of society as it was and had ceased to be revolutionary or even progressive in its outlook. It thus lost touch with the hearts of the people, becoming something external and imposed and out of sympathy with the masses, so losing its moral leadership. The parson in this country was looked upon as the squire's junior colleague and not as one of the people. The carpenter and the fisherfolk had stepped up into a superior position and so lost their close contact with the common folk.

The result of all this was to place the churches in a false position. Christianity tended to become a religious cult having little bearing upon the material side of ordinary life or with politics and economics.

By the more influential, the churches were tolerated so long as they did not interfere in political or economic matters, which were held to be outside their sphere, thus emphasising their isolation from the human

F

problems of this world. They might promise what rewards they liked in the world to come, but they must not work or carry out propaganda for practical improvements in the lot of the masses in this world.

These at least were the impressions that I derived from my experience, which included at that time membership of my Parochial Church Council, of the Archidiaconal Conference, the Diocesan Conference and the Church Assembly.

Sir Stafford Cripps, *Towards a Christian Democracy*, 1945

WHAT ARE WE *DOING*?

As a matter of practical politics—what is our so-called Christianity doing? Men are still rather encouraged to get drunk than otherwise; the poor are not housed, nor the naked clothed nor the hungry fed. And yet nearly everyone in England professes to believe that one at least of the sentences of final condemnation is 'I was a stranger and ye took me not in', etc. Take another instance: it is a certain fact that in rich parishes the people who go to church most are the most selfish. And yet our Lord said 'Not everyone that saith unto *me*, Lord, Lord, shall enter into the kingdom of heaven: but he that *doeth* the will of my *Father*'—i.e. his duty to his neighbour. I might give instances for ever: but to put it shortly, the Church forgets that Christianity is not an attitude of mind, but a type of life; a man's spirit is known not by his opinion (creeds, etc.) but by his actions and general conduct.

William Temple, then a layman, at Oxford, *c.* 1904

BEFORE GOD, WE *ARE* EQUAL

There belongs accordingly to every member of the human family an equal and eternal spiritual value. That is the ruling idea. Differences of function and capacity among men involve subordination of one to another. Jesus shows no signs of hostility to 'inequality' in this sense. But in spiritual value all are equal. There are no privileged persons who have a right to think of themselves as more important in God's sight than their fellows, or to exploit others for their own profit. . . . He treats wealth or the accumulation of property and avarice, the acquisitive passion, as an evil, an almost insuperable obstacle to entrance into the kingdom. . . . Indifference to the needs of the miserable, brings upon itself the divine sentence of judgement—'Depart, ye cursed'. Always He is plainly on the side of the humble and the poor.

Bishop Gore, *Christ and Society*, 1928

NO HOPE FOR THE HYPOCRITE

In every settled society a certain standard of respectability or of 'good form' comes into being. . . . But all such social standards of good behaviour tend always to stress outward conformity rather than inward motive, and also to appraise highly all that maintains the settled order and to brand with infamy what tends to upset it—such as outrages on life and property and lawless lust. . . . But any such distinction between disreputable and respectable sins plainly Jesus Christ absolutely refuses to allow. In His eyes avarice, pride, refusal to forgive, hypocrisy, are at least as bad as fornication or adultery or violence. . . . It is on the respectable sins that He lays the greater stress.

Bishop Gore, *Christ and Society*, 1928

MEMBERS ONE OF ANOTHER

What fellowship means in material matters [in the Early Church] is made very plain. Every man is to work for his living. 'If a man will not work, neither let him eat.' But those who cannot work are to be provided for out of the common fund. Old and helpless persons who have relations of their own should, indeed, find their support from them and not be forced to come upon the Church; but for the resourceless the Church must provide. And those who are rich and who earn more than enough to support their own families are to be willing contributors to the common fund. The love of money—the desire to accumulate wealth—is a root of every kind of evil. The relation of one to another is to be that of members in one body, in which, if one member suffers, all the members suffer with it.

Bishop Gore, *Christ and Society*, 1928

CAPITALISM IS UNNATURAL

It is not only that the contrasts between luxurious and idle wealth and ignominious poverty at the extremes of society are as startling as ever, but also, and much more, that that on which the wholesome and peaceful life of a community depends—the sense of security in employment and a confident expectation of a just return for work done—is conspicuously lacking for the great mass of our workers. In former times the sense of security depended, so far as it existed, on the confidence the workers felt in the good will of the individual masters. Now, though the phrase 'I am determined to be master in my own business' is still heard it has less and less true meaning. There is in most businesses no individual who is master. There are a number of workers with hand and with brain and there are managers: but the *owners* are for the most part unknown shareholders and large-scale financiers, very often themselves without any knowledge of the industry or interest in it, save as a means of profitable employment of capital. This is such an unnatural and unjust condition of things that it cannot be expected to last.

Bishop Gore, *Christ and Society*, 1928

CHRISTIAN OR CAPITALIST?

I am conscious that in the whole of this argument I am 'up against' . . . a protest based on the assumption that, whereas all these and the like suggested reforms are 'socialistic' and tend to undermine the possibility of acquiring and maintaining large fortunes, absolutely at the control of individual owners, to put them into force would destroy the motive which is probably the greatest motive in industry—the desire to become a very rich man, wielding the power which riches can always claim, and having the right to hand on down the succession of generations both the acquired wealth and its advantages.

There are many things to be said in criticism of such an ideal. It is certainly in the deepest sense opposed to the teaching of Christ. Also it seems contrary to experience to suppose, that, if a man feels that it is on the whole worth his while to do his best, the energy he exhibits will depend on a precise calculation of how much financial profit he will obtain. . . . What is really of most importance for the remedying of inveterate social evils is the deepening and development of the sense of justice—that is, the demand that social arrangements should be so remoulded and redirected as that every one born into citizenship should have a fair chance of making the best of himself: and that our present industrial and educational and legal arrangements contradict manifestly and on a wide scale this demand of justice—that they have been fashioned by the false philosophy which made the acquisition of material wealth the end of industry instead of the good of the industrial society, and thereby have ministered to the satisfaction of a small propertied class to the detriment and dissatisfaction of the great majority. The privileged classes for the most part—in terror at the prospect of a socialist or communist revolution—appear to have hardened themselves into a blind adherence to their privileges and the refusal of demands involving any fundamental reform: and the 'disinherited' classes to have lapsed into a permanent condition of discontent—sometimes savage, sometimes sullen, but more often cynical.

Bishop Gore, Christ and Society, 1928

PACIFISM AND THE LABOUR PARTY

(The Labour Party has always contained a convinced minority of pacifists. Of these the most notable was George Lansbury, who eventually resigned from his position as leader, when the Party decided to advocate resistance to the Italian invasion of Abyssinia even at the risk of war.)

The following is a summary of my speech at the Conference at which my position was discussed:

'... There is one thing that brings me to this microphone today [October 1935] and that is an overwhelming conviction, since I was a boy, that force is no remedy.... I believe that force never has and never will bring permanent peace and permanent goodwill to the world. I believe also that we in our Movement have really said that in dealing with our own striving for Socialism. We have said to the workers: "We are sorry for your plight, but you must wait until we have converted the rest of the people to our point of view." I have gone into mining areas, I have gone into my own district when people have been starving or semi-starving; I have stood in the midst of dockers who have been on the verge of starvation (before there was any "dole" or Poor Law Assistance, excepting the workhouse), and I have said to them: "No, you must not rise, you must have no violence, you must trust to the winning of this through public opinion." I have never at any time said to the workers of this country: "You must take up either arms, or sticks, or stones, in order to force your way to the end that you seek to attain." And when I am challenged on these issues, I say to myself this: I have no right to preach pacifism to starving people in this country and preach something else in relation to people elsewhere.... I have never under any circumstances said that I believed you could obtain Socialism by force....

'I have spoken for Socialism on many an occasion, and the stock argument against me by Christians and Jews and people of all religious faiths, and of no religious faiths, has been: "Oh, Socialism, it is a fine ideal, my boy, but you have got to change human nature first." Well, I have never succumbed to that about Socialism, and I am not going to succumb to it about war....

'Christianity is the realist principle of life, because it says: "We are willing that you shall carry out the doctrine of those who are strongest, helping with the strength of their brain and their power the weak." I know that you will say to me: "Say that to Mussolini, or say that to Hitler." If I had had power during this period I would have gone and faced these men at Geneva and I would have let the world know what it was I was proposing to do.

'This is no mere ideal; it is no greater international ideal than the national ideal of common service for each other within our own nation. We have got somewhere and at some time to begin, and I want our people to begin. And that is the message that somehow I must put to the world wherever people will hear me. . . .

'If mine were the only voice in this Conference, I would say in the name of the faith I hold, the belief I have that God intended us to live peaceably and quietly with one another. If some people do not allow us to do so, I am ready to stand as the early Christians stood, and say: "This is our faith, this is where we stand, and, if necessary, this is where we will die." '

George Lansbury, *My Quest for Peace*, 1938

4. The Great Blinding Light

That night I became a Socialist.
Edith Summerskill

THE FUTURE PRIME MINISTER . . .

(In autumn, 1907, Clement Attlee became the resident leader
of the Haileybury House, a boys' club in the East End of
London. At this time he was still a Conservative.)

CONTACT WITH BOYS and with older people in the district brought Attlee
to a state of mind in which he was at once appalled by the contrast between
life in Stepney and life in Putney, Haileybury, Oxford—everywhere that
he had previously known it—and convinced that no justification for this
could be found in the false belief that the working classes were morally
and intellectually inferior. Poverty, he now realised, was obviously due
to some evil trick of fate and not, in the overwhelming majority of cases,
to individual sin. . . . The beginnings of new beliefs, or prejudices as his
political enemies might call them, were already crowding in upon him.
He was filled with a sense of wrongs to be righted, quite how, he knew
not at this stage, and of warm fellowship for those he had previously dis-
trusted or even despised. Within a few months the existing social system
had lost a complacent supporter and seen an enemy, enthusiastic if not
bitter, arise in his place. Attlee had abandoned the 'comfortable Tory
faith' with which he had first gone to Limehouse. . . .

The stark poverty and utter insecurity of life in the East End were the
first and most obvious but not the only factors which jolted Attlee's mind
away from the rut in which it had been moving. Many of the men in
Limehouse were dockers or building labourers—both casual trades in
which they never knew when they were going to do a day's work and
when they were going to stand idle. Even those in regular employment,
such as railwaymen, were lucky if they made £1 a week; with rents at 7/6
or 10/- for two rooms this left little margin and meant, in practice, that
the man's income had always to be supplemented by his wife and older
children. The woman stitched away for some 'sweat-shop' owner and
earned perhaps 7/6 a week. The boys worked ten or twelve hours a day
in some blind-alley job and took home 5/- at the end of the week.

167

Even with these contributions few families were far above the level of bare subsistence. They were never able to accumulate any reserves. In times of unemployment or, for some casual workers, even in bad weather, they fell into debt and borrowed at exorbitant rates of interest; repayment absorbed whatever surplus good times brought. The shadow of eviction by the landlord was never far away, and families were not infrequently turned out into the streets and left without home or money. The next meal was often an uncertain event . . .

Lack of amenities made life in Stepney even more unpleasant. The overcrowding in the borough was frightful. A population of 300,000 was herded into less than 1,700 acres, more than twelve times as many people to the acre as would be budgeted for in a town-planning scheme today. Two or three families were often crowded into the small back to back houses that are characteristic of the area. There was a great shortage of open spaces. Almost every available square yard had been developed to yield the last penny of profit. . . .

All this shocked Attlee, but had it not been accompanied by other simultaneous discoveries, it might merely have sent him back to more westerly and more prosperous regions of London, depressed and despairing. If the squalor was deeper than he had imagined, so was the courage of those who endured it higher. 'The next thing I discovered was the fine characters of many of the boys, the heroism of the struggle with poverty, the unselfishness and neighbourly kindness which existed in a poor district. I found also that boys of this class were no different from boys of any other class except that they were up against life at an earlier age.' . . .

He was never again to believe that charity, however well organised, could provide even an incomplete answer. . . . Co-partnership and co-operation were his next tentative solutions. . . . Co-partnership it seemed would free the worker from the evils of exploitation without any violent economic upheaval and without disturbing too much the comfortable middle-class background from which Attlee had sprung, or the comfortable middle-class life that he was used to living. . . . This easy faith lasted just long enough for him and his brother to get a few suits very badly made at a tailor's establishment run on co-partnership lines. He began to see too clearly the strength of the forces he was fighting, to believe that they could be defeated by easy or half-hearted attacks. He realised that the social work he himself was performing in Limehouse could never be more than ambulance work, and that it would be dishonest otherwise to regard it. He grew contemptuous of his own vacillations and of the queasiness that was still making him avoid the radical solution of full public ownership. . . . Attlee saw also that half-hearted pecking at the problem and romantic utopianism were equally unlikely to achieve results; nor could the new Jerusalem be imposed from above. It was only by stirring up the great mass of the people and getting them to exert their power through their elected representatives that social justice could be secured. And he came to see that Webb's State Socialism and detailed planning formed a necessary framework for the new society that was to be built.

Today it is difficult to imagine the magnitude assumed by the step he was about to take. Middle-class Socialists were a thousand times more rare in 1906 than in 1946 or even 1936. The vast majority of well to do people in England not only held Socialist beliefs to be mistaken; it was almost beyond their comprehension that sensible men could entertain such dangerous nonsense. . . .

In the autumn of the same year [1907] within a few weeks of the date of his move from Putney to Haileybury House, he and his brother Tom walked into the offices of the Fabian Society, in Essex Street off the Strand, and said they wished to become members. . . . Attlee took a more decisive step into Socialist politics, and certainly into working class politics, when in January, 1908, he became a member of the Stepney branch of the Independent Labour Party.

. . . On the following Wednesday evening he found himself sitting round a stove in a small and grimy East London Church hall, in the company of eight or ten working men. He was attending his first branch meeting of the I.L.P.

. . . 'In two years', he wrote, 'the rather cynical Conservative had been turned into an unashamed enthusiast for the cause of Socialism.'

Roy Jenkins, *Mr Attlee*, 1948

THE FUTURE PRIMATE

. . . Temple had always been on the side of the under-dog. None of his relatives or friends can remember a time when this was not so. In his seventh year [1888] he was staying with his parents for their holiday in the Lakes, and the hotel had provided roast chicken for lunch—a dish of which he was specially fond. Somehow, in the course of conversation, it was mentioned that the servants were not allowed chicken, whereupon Temple put down his knife and fork and burst into tears. It was not easy for his parents to understand this sudden breakdown, and their answer to his 'Why not?' has not survived. But the questions 'Why?' and 'Why not?' began to batter at the doors of his heart and brain—surely the eternal justice of things was being flouted if, while he was enjoying roast chicken in the dining-room, the servants below stairs were being fobbed off with a beef stew! It was no more than an incident—and grimmer experiences were to follow. Nearly twenty years later a Sweated Industries Exhibition was held at Oxford. Here Temple saw the results of a *laissez-faire* industrial system; match-boxes made at the rate of 2*d*. a gross, the worker having to find paste, hemp (for tying up), and firing to dry wet boxes, spending 2 hours a day in fetching and returning her work, and receiving 8*s*. a week for 10 hours' toil a day; trousers which were basted, machined, finished, and pressed at a net wage of 6*s*. a week for 12 hours' hard daily work; artificial flowers for the making of which the worker provided her own paste, and earned an average of 10*s*. a week for a 14-hour day; stall after stall decked with the produce of free enterprise, including one devoted to the wages and hours that prevailed in the industry of 'Bible-folding'. Temple, in co-operation with the Christian Social Union, was responsible for collecting the committee which organized the Exhibition, and in the handbook he wrote:

'It is the system which is foul and rotten. Producer, capitalist, consumer—all are entangled in the meshes of its net. While we prate about the spread of refinement; . . . while we glory in an Empire whose Flag is said to stand for Justice—we are convicted by the facts at our own doors, of stupid coarseness, of ignorant insensibility, and of wanton oppression. We form Army Corps, we build "Dreadnoughts"; we discuss endlessly what metaphysics are to be taught to children in our schools. But if we listen, there is still the desolate cry of the Son of Man: "I am hungry and ye give me no meat." . . .'

At last Temple discovered what he never ceased to believe was the true answer to his question. Why—why did there exist, side by side, extremes of misery and luxury, of sweated labour and wild extravagance, of squalor and the ordered comforts of a decent home? Could the answer be, merely because all but a few of his fellow countrymen were too ignorant, too idle, and too selfish to put an end to it—to a state of things which could have no place in any decent human order, still less in the divine order of eternal justice called the Kingdom of God—and to set up another in its place? There was nothing in the present system—or the lack of one—fixed unalterably by the laws of nature or economics, or sacrosanct by any law of God. Good will, good sense, and good work were all that was needed to change it. And what of the few who knew, and cared, and tried? At least he could throw in his lot with them, and share their task of destroying and rebuilding. In 1907, while still a layman, he describes to his mother a Sunday he spent in Leicester:

'. . . I then sped away to the other end of the town, to the Labour Church, where I took the chair. . . . Then tea . . . then again to the Labour Church. I had meant to repeat my Extension Lecture on "Socialism and Education", but they had been getting a deal of abuse from some clergy at that end of the town, and were very keen for me to talk on "Socialism and Christianity". So I did; and began by exhorting them to set a Christian example to the church folk who abused them by not "reviling again". They are not all Christians (in metaphysics) at that Labour Church, but I have seldom felt so near the real presence of pure religion. To-night I talk to the Church Socialist League.'

. . . early in 1918 he announced to the Lower House of Canterbury Convocation that he had joined the Labour Party. He had for some years questioned whether the clergy should attach themselves to any political group but that doubt was now resolved, and he was glad to make clear a week or two later (in an article in the *Daily News*) a distinction which he believed to be valid. After stating that there were two marks by which a 'truly spiritual movement' could be known, freedom and fellowship, he went on:

'Now the Labour Movement is essentially an effort to organize society on the basis of freedom and fellowship. As such it has a right to claim the sympathy of the Church. The Labour Party is a different thing: that is a political organization, and the Church as a whole must not be attached to any political party—not even to the Tory Party. But churchmen ought to consider very carefully the formulated programme of the Labour Party, and whether they should individually subscribe to it. Here is a party which has at least put forward an outline scheme of reconstruction in national and international life. It is a scheme based on moral ideals. We must not support it simply because we sympathize with the motives behind it: but if we believe that these motives are, on the whole, applied with wisdom, we have no right to stand aside. We must go in and help.'

F. A. Iremonger, *William Temple, His Life and Letters*, 1948

AND THE FUTURE EDITOR

In the meantime, I myself, having begun my writing career hoping to be a poet, had graduated through most branches of newspaper work to the position of financial and economic correspondent of the *Evening Standard*. I found myself after a little while fascinated by the activities of the City and by the, as it seemed to me, frequently anti-social consequences of those activities upon the lives of ordinary people. Study of these activities confirmed me intellectually in the Socialism I had previously embraced on human grounds.

Francis Williams, *Press, Parliament and People*, 1946

A BISHOP JOINS THE PARTY

. . . Should you think me wrong, if I were to resign this bishopric with a view to retiring, probably to London or near it, to read and write and preach? . . . I have almost made up my mind to resign. It is partly that Broad and High and Low and Conservative are all against me. So I stick. Also I'd like to join the Labour Party.

Charles Gore, Bishop of Oxford, to William Temple, January 1919

. . . AND AN AUTHORESS

We returned to an England [December 1924] politically very different from that which we had left, for Mr Baldwin had replaced Mr MacDonald as Prime Minister, and the Conservative Party, numbering over four hundred in contrast to the hundred and fifty-two of discredited Socialism, were comfortably settled in office for another five years.

In spite of this debacle, I definitely became, for the first time, a member of the Labour Party when I had been in England for two or three weeks. My first vague realisation that poverty was the result of humanity's incompetence, and not an inviolable law of nature, had come with the sixteen-year-old reading of Carlyle's *Past and Present*, and though, during the War, my consciousness of political programmes and antagonisms was dim, I had seen the poor, the meek and the modest, the young, the brave and the idealistic, all those in fact who always are too easily enchanted by high-sounding phrases—giving their lives and their futures in order that the powerful might have more power, the rich grow richer, the old remain in comparative security.

For years now, since the War, I had been to Geneva and worked hopefully in the cause of the League; I had heard statesmen at the Assembly giving lip-service to peace and then going back to their own countries to support preparations for war; I had seen the delegates who really cared for peace ideals . . . always in a minority; I had watched protocols and pacts brought forward, piously applauded and in practice turned down. I had heard disarmament lauded to the skies while everywhere countries were increasing their armaments, and had realised that few were better and a great many worse than ourselves, who annually spent nearly five hundred million pounds upon the causes and consequences of war, and then declared that we couldn't afford a national maternity service. I had now travelled through Germany and Austria, and Czechoslovakia and Hungary; I had been in the occupied areas, and had talked to the Quakers in Essen and Vienna, and although a League of Nations existed, and French statesmen, like British and Japanese and Italian, sang hymns of praise to Geneva, I had found everywhere oppression, the conqueror grinding down the conquered by hunger and humiliation, . . . hatred and fear dominant in a Europe vowed to charity and co-operation, and everywhere countries casting envious or resentful eyes upon their neighbours' territories. I had witnessed all this until there seemed to be no words in which to describe the situation, but the sad, disillusioned words of Ecclesiastes: 'So I returned, and considered all the oppressions that are done under the sun: and behold the tears of such as were oppressed, and they had no comforter; and on the side of their oppressors there was power; but they had no comforter.'

And at last I had come to believe that, although men did change slowly, and left the evidence of their progressive modifications in statutes and treaties, no change would come soon enough to save the next generation from the grief and ruin that had engulfed my own so long as the world that I knew endured—the world of haves and have-nots; of owners and owned; of rich and poor; of Great Powers and little nations, always at the mercy of the wealthy and strong; of influential persons whose interests were served by war, and who had sufficient authority to compel politicians to precipitate on behalf of a few the wholesale destruction of millions. So it was that I became a Socialist, in the belief that membership of the Labour Party would help me to work for a new order based upon the discipline of man's strongest instinct—his instinct for possession.

Vera Brittain, *Testament of Youth*, 1933

A PICTURE OF THE PRESENT

It was the suffering of a woman which finally drew me into the political world. One wet, cold night many years ago, at the age of 22, a newly qualified doctor, I went to attend my first confinement. Very nervous, I arrived with my new black bag. My knock was answered by the young husband, pallid and shabby, with the familiar signs of long unemployment upon him. He took me upstairs to a room, stripped of all but the bare necessities of life; there lay the patient, on a mattress, covered by a threadbare blanket—a girl of my own age in labour with her second child. By the bed stood a cot, and standing grasping the wooden bars was a child, with bulging forehead and crooked legs, the classic picture of rickets, a disease of under-nourishment.

The young mother clutched my hand with her own moist, bony fingers, on which she wore a greenish brass wedding ring, twisted round with cotton to prevent its falling off. In that room that night I became a Socialist—I joined in the fight. Not against a class, but against a system, a system which accepted unemployment as the natural order of things, a system which permitted one-third of the population between the two wars to suffer from some degree of under-nourishment, a system which refused to accept responsibility for the welfare of the most helpless among us.

The aim my party set itself many years ago was to remove poverty, hunger and insecurity from the lives of the people. That is what we are seeking to do now that we have been put into power by the people. . . .

Dr Edith Summerskill, M.P., in a broadcast. From *The Listener*, 8 April 1948

. . . AND A VISION OF THE FUTURE

What I mean by Socialism is a condition of society in which there should be neither rich nor poor, neither master nor master's man, neither idle nor overworked, neither brain-sick brain workers, nor heart-sick hand workers, in a word, in which all men would be living in equality of condition, and would manage their affairs unwastefully and with the full consciousness that harm to one would mean harm to all—the realisation at last of the meaning of the word Commonwealth. . . .

Now this view of Socialism which I hold today, and hope to die holding, is what I began with; I had no transitional period, unless you may call such a brief period of political radicalism during which I saw my ideal clear enough, but had no hope of any realisation of it. That came to an end some months before I joined the (then) Democratic Federation, and the meaning of my joining that body was that I had conceived a hope of the realisation of my ideal. If you ask me how much of a hope, or what I thought we Socialists then living and working would accomplish towards it, or when there would be effected any change in the face of society, I must say, I do not know. I can only say that I did not measure my hope, nor the joy that it brought me at the time. For the rest, when I took that step I was blankly ignorant of economics; I had never so much as opened Adam Smith, or heard of Ricardo, or of Karl Marx. I had read some of Mill . . . in which he attacks Socialism in its Fourierist guise. In those papers he put the arguments, as far as they go, clearly and honestly, and the result, as far as I was concerned, was to convince me that Socialism was a necessary change, and that it was possible to bring it about in our own days. Those papers put the finishing touch to my conversion to

Socialism. Well, having joined a Socialist body (for the Federation soon became definitely Socialist) I put some conscience in trying to learn the economic side of Socialism, and even tackled Marx, though I must confess that, whereas I thoroughly enjoyed the historical part of *Capital*, I suffered agonies of confusion of the brain over reading the pure economics of that great work. Anyhow, I read what I could, and will hope that some information stuck to me from my reading; but more, I must think, from continuous conversation with such friends as Bax and Hyndman and the brisk course of propaganda meetings which were going on at the time and in which I took my share.

... In this telling how I fell into practical Socialism I have begun, as I perceive, in the middle, for in my position of a well to do man, not suffering from the disabilities which oppress a working man at every step, I feel that I might never have been drawn into the practical side of the question if an ideal had not forced me to seek towards it. For politics as politics, i.e. not regarded as a necessary if cumbersome and disgustful means to an end, would never have attracted me, nor when I had become conscious of the wrongs of society as it now is, and the oppression of poor people, could I have ever believed in the possibility of a partial setting right of those wrongs. In other words, I could never have been such a fool as to believe in the happy and 'respectable' poor. But the consciousness of revolution stirring amidst our hateful modern society prevented me, luckier than many others of artistic perceptions, from crystallising into a mere railer against 'progress' on the one hand, and on the other from wasting time and energy in any of the nervous schemes by which the quasi-artistic of the middle classes hope to make art grow when it has no longer any root, and thus I became a practical Socialist....

Perhaps some of our friends will say, what have we to do with these matters of history and art? We want by means of Social-Democracy to win a decent livelihood, we want in some sort to live, and that at once. Surely any one who professes to think that the question of art and cultivation must go before that of the knife and fork (and there are some who do propose that) does not understand what art means, or how that its roots must have a soil of a thriving and unanxious life. Yet it must be remembered that civilisation has reduced the workman to such a skinny and pitiful existence, that he scarcely knows how to frame a desire for any life much better than that which he now endures perforce. It is the province of art to set the true ideal of a full and reasonable life before him, a life to which the perception and creation of beauty, the enjoyment of real pleasure that is, shall be felt to be as necessary to man as his daily bread.

William Morris, *How I became a Socialist*, 1894

THE LAND REFORMER

Out of the open West came a young man of less than thirty to this great city of New York. He was small of stature and slight of build. His alma mater had been the forecastle and the printing office. He was poor, unheralded, unknown. He came from a small city rising at the western golden portals of the country to set up here, for a struggling little newspaper there, a telegraphic news bureau, despite the opposition of the combined powerful press and telegraph monopolies. The struggle was too unequal. The young man was overborne by the monopolies and his little paper crushed.

This man was Henry George and the time was 1869.

But, though defeated, Henry George was not vanquished. Out of this struggle had come a thing that was to grow and grow until it should fill the minds and hearts of multitudes and be as 'an army with banners'.

For in the intervals of rest from his newspaper struggle in this city the young correspondent had musingly walked the streets. As he walked he was filled with wonder at the manifestations of vast wealth. Here, as nowhere that he had dreamed of, were private fortunes that rivalled the riches of the fabled Monte Cristo. But here, also side by side with the palaces of the princely rich, was to be seen a poverty and degradation, a want and shame, such as made the young man from the open West sick at heart.

Why in a land so bountifully blest, with enough and more than enough for all, should there be such inequality of conditions? Such heaped wealth interlocked with such deep and debasing want? Why, amid such superabundance, should strong men vainly look for work? Why should women faint with hunger, and little children spend the morning of life in the treadmill of toil?

Was this intended in the order of things? No, he could not believe it. And suddenly there came to him—there in daylight, in the city street— a burning thought, a call, a vision. Every nerve quivered. And he made a vow that he would never rest until he had found the cause of, and if he could, the remedy for, this deepening poverty amid advancing wealth.

> Henry George, jnr., on his father: preface to 25th Anniversary
> Edition of *Progress and Poverty*

. . . AND THE LABOUR PROPHET

Socialists are born as well as made. . . . I have had, from my earliest recollection, a keen sympathy for all kinds of 'bottom dogs' and a rather pugnacious resentment against all kinds of bullies. I learnt the meaning of poverty in a lean and sharp school and the blessings and indignities of labour were made manifest to me at an early age. . . . Indeed I was a thorough democrat and an out and out radical before I was out of my teens, and when I joined the 'Sunday Chronicle' I was something more than a Radical, for having perceived that competition was a failure . . . I had . . . devised an economic scheme of my own. . . .

Some time in 1888 or 1889 I was writing upon some Social question in the 'Chronicle' when a Manchester workman wrote to say that the only remedy was Socialism. I replied by condemning Socialism. Then a Liverpool workman wrote to say that I evidently did not know what Socialism was. . . . Therefore I wrote to my Liverpool friend and asked for some books on Socialism, at the same time saying that I would study the question, and that if Socialism seemed to me just and wise I would not be ashamed nor afraid to say so. The man sent me a pamphlet by Hyndman or Morris. I read it. I saw directly that this collectivist idea was the very thing I had been looking for. . . . Therefore I was a Socialist and said so.

Robert Blatchford, from A. N. Lyons's biography, 1912

THE GREATEST OF THEM ALL

Twenty-three years ago I made my first public appearance as an agitator. As the years went on, the question that has troubled me from my boyhood, presented itself with increasing pertinacity. 'Why is there so much poverty in the midst of abundance?' As a boy in the pit, I puzzled over and discussed the matter with many who, like myself, thought it strange. Everybody said things were as they were because they could not be otherwise. There had always been poverty and there always would be poverty. Even men who were poor said and believed that and accepted the existing order as something unchangeable and part of the laws of Nature.

With wider experience and broader outlook I began to see that poverty did not arise from the niggardliness of Nature, nor was it any part of the scheme of Divine Providence, but solely and exclusively the outcome of the wrong relations between man and his fellows.

I was not then [1888] a Socialist. Just thinking in my own stupid way, I came to the conclusion that if there were a system of society in which co-operation, not competition, and common ownership rather than individualistic aggression obtained, the change would be for the better. I can remember how the idea grew that the prime necessity was that the workers of the country should obtain control of the legislative machinery, for it seemed to me, as it still does, a self-evident proposition that the class which made the laws would also own the wealth.

Keir Hardie, 1902

5. Know Your Enemy!

The poverty of the poor is not an accident.
Ellen Wilkinson

THE PROFIT MOTIVE IN WALES, 1847

THE COMMISSIONERS ON EDUCATION [1847] gave this account of the housing: 'Even the physical condition of the people seems almost as if contrived for the double purpose of their degradation and the employers' profit. Some of the works are surrounded by houses built by the companies without the slightest attention to comfort, health or decency, or any other consideration than that of realising the largest amount of rent from the smallest amount of outlay. I went into several of this class of houses in the north part of my district and examined them from top to bottom. Men, women and children of all sexes and ages are stowed away in the bedrooms, without curtains or partitions, it being no uncommon thing for nine or ten people not belonging to the same family to sleep together in this manner in one room. In one instance I found three men sleeping in a sort of dungeon, which was nine feet by six feet in dimensions, without any light or air except through a hole in the wall, not a foot square, which opened into another room occupied by some women. . . . An immense rent in comparison to the accommodation is paid to the company or master for these miserable places. . . . There is neither drainage nor even light in the streets, although coal is close at hand. Nevertheless these places are little worse than others.'

In other places the Report described mud cabins, 'in many instances a deserted cowshed converted into a human habitation'; or beds used in turn by different sets of workers; or houses in Merthyr, the centre of the iron trade, where 'an open, stinking and nearly stagnant gutter, into which the house refuse is, as usual, generally flung, moves slowly before the doors'.

In these districts the citizen was so lost in the profit seeker that men who were founding great families sought to make fraudulent gain out of their shops, and even out of their schools. They preferred their workmen to spend their money on drink, because they were afraid it might otherwise be used to strengthen their combinations.

J. L. and B. Hammond, *The Rise of Modern Industry*, 1925

THE PROFIT MOTIVE AND TOWN-PLANNING

(Despite frequent Commissions and Reports no legislation concerning Town Planning was passed by successive Conservative and
Liberal Governments during the nineteenth century. Free enterprise
in housing continued to be protected from 'bureaucratic meddling'
with the result that huge slum areas still disgrace most of our larger
cities.)

The town of the industrial age, without beauty or method, marked the
spirit of this age just as truly as St Paul's cathedral marked the spirit of
the Renaissance, or the cathedral of Durham the spirit of the Crusades.
It expressed a concentration in which religion, beauty, leisure, the life of
the spirit, or the life of the senses, were all held to be rivals to the stern
life of selfish duty. The purpose of man's life was not to fight or to pray,
to contemplate or to create, to enjoy or to become, but to make profits,
profits for himself, if a master, profits for another, if a servant. This was
man's duty, and it was the duty of society to put no obstacle in his
way....

   This concentration led to the complete neglect of the most urgent tasks
of the age. In the first twenty years of the nineteenth century, the population of Manchester increased from 94,000 to 160,000; of Bolton from
29,000 to 50,000; Leeds more than doubled its population between 1801
and 1831; Bradford, which had 23,000 inhabitants in 1831, grew grass in
its streets at the end of the eighteenth century. Oldham, which had
38,000 inhabitants in 1821, had three or four hundred in 1760. In the
twenty years from 1801 to 1821 the population of Lancashire grew from
672,000 to 1,052,000; in the next twenty years it grew to 1,701,000. The
population of Merthyr increased from 7,700 to 35,000 between 1801 and
1841, and that of the two counties of Glamorgan and Monmouth from
126,000 to 305,000. Industry was accumulating dense masses of people
into particular districts, where the workman was shut up in melancholy
streets, without gardens or orchards. England was passing from a
country to a town life, as she passed from a peasant to an industrial
civilization. What this meant is clear if we compare the state of the towns
as revealed in the health statistics, with that of the country districts. In
1757 Dr Percival put the death rate for Manchester at 1 in 25, for Liverpool at 1 in 27. In Monton, a few miles from Manchester, the ratio was
at that time 1 in 68, at Horwich, between Bolton and Chorley, 1 in 66, at
Darwen, three miles from Blackburn, 1 in 56. The Industrial Revolution
was to spread the conditions of town life over places like Monton,
Horwich and Darwen.

The problem of arranging and controlling the expansion of the towns was thus the most urgent of the problems created by the Industrial Revolution. Its importance was illustrated by a picture of some cottages near Preston published by the Health of Towns Commission in 1844. These cottages stood in two rows, separated by little backyards, with an open sewer running the whole length. The picture was given as an example of dangerous and disgusting drainage. But this is not its chief significance. One would suppose that these huddled cottages, without gardens of any kind, were built in a crowded town, where not an inch of space was available for amenities. They were in fact in the open country. Clearly then there was more here than a problem of drainage, for if it were left to private enterprise to develop this district, under the guidance of an uncontrolled sense for profit, these rows would spring up all round, and Preston would have another slum on its hands. This is what happened in the new industrial districts. When the Health of Towns Commission investigated towns like Manchester, they were told that the worst evils were not the evils of the past, for new Manchester was reproducing the slums and alleys of the old, and spreading them, of course, over a far wider surface. Of no other problem was it so true that neglect by one generation tied the hands and the mind of the next.

J. L. and B. Hammond, *The Rise of Modern Industry*, 1925

THE SPIRIT OF THE AGE

(The following passage refers particularly to the period about 1850 but is true of the whole nineteenth century.)

Thus England asked for profits and received profits. Everything turned to profit. The towns had their profitable dirt, their profitable smoke, their profitable slums, their profitable disorder, their profitable ignorance, their profitable despair. The curse of Midas was on this society: on its corporate life, on its common mind, on the decisive and impatient step it had taken from the peasant to the industrial age. For the new town was not a home where man could find beauty, happiness, leisure, learning, religion, the influences that civilize outlook and habit, but a bare and desolate place, without colour, air or laughter, where man, woman and child worked, ate and slept. This was to be the lot of the mass of mankind; this the sullen rhythm of their lives. The new factories and the new furnaces were like the Pyramids, telling of man's enslavement, rather than of his power, casting their long shadow over the society that took such pride in them.

J. L. and B. Hammond, *The Rise of Modern Industry*, 1925

THE GLORIES OF FREE ENTERPRISE

The problem of life is 'Given a country and a people, show how the people can make the most of the country and themselves'. Before we go on, let us try to judge how far we in Britain have succeeded in answering the problem.

The following are facts which no man attempts to deny:

1. Large numbers of honest and industrious people are badly fed, badly clothed, and badly housed.

2. Many thousands of people die every year from preventable diseases.

3. The average duration of life amongst the population is unnaturally short.

4. Very many people, after lives of toil, are obliged to seek refuge in the workhouse, where they die despised and neglected, branded with the shameful brand of pauperism.

5. It is an almost invariable rule that those who work hardest and longest in this country are the worst paid and the least respected.

6. The wealthiest men in our nation are men who never did a useful day's work.

7. Wealth and power are more prized and more honoured than wisdom, or industry, or virtue.

8. Hundreds of thousands of men and women, willing to work, are unable to find employment.

9. While on the one hand wages are lowered on account of over-production of coal, of cotton, and of corn, on the other hand many of our working people are short of bread, of fuel and of clothing.

10. Nearly all the land and property in this country are owned by a few idlers, and most of the laws are made in the interests of those few rich people.

11. The national agriculture is going rapidly to ruin to the great injury and peril of the State.

12. Through competition millions of men are employed in useless and undignified work, and all the industrial machinery of the nation is thrown out of gear, so that one greedy rascal may overreach another.

And we are told that all these things must remain as they are, in order that you may be able to 'get a living'.

What sort of living do you get? . . .

As to work. You are employed in a factory for from 53 to 70 hours a week. Some of your comrades work harder, and longer, and in worse places. Still, as a rule, it may be said of all your class that the hours of labour are too long, that the labour is monotonous, mechanical and

severe, and that the surroundings are often unhealthy, nearly always disagreeable, and in many cases dangerous. . . .

As a rule, your work is hard and disagreeable.

Now, what are your wages?

I don't mean how many shillings a week do you get; but what *life* do
you get as the reward of your toil?

You may get 15 shillings a week, or a pound, or 25 or 35 shillings, or
two pounds; but the question is, how do you *live*? What will your
money *buy*?

As I have shown already, you do not get enough leisure, nor enough
fresh air, nor enough education, nor enough health, and your town is
very ugly and very dirty and very dull. . . .

Come we now to the home. Your houses are not what they should be.

I do not allude to the inferior cottage—*that* is beneath notice. Here in
Manchester we have some forty thousand houses unfit for habitation.
But let us consider the abode of the more fortunate artisan. It has many
faults. It is badly built, badly arranged, and badly fitted. The sanitation
is bad. The rooms are much too small. There are no proper appliances
for cleanliness. The windows are not big enough. There is a painful
dearth of light and air. The cooking appliances are simply barbarous.

Again, the houses are very ugly and *mean*. The streets are too narrow.
There are no gardens. There are no trees. Few working-class families
have enough bedrooms, and the bathroom is a luxury not known in
cottages.

In fine, your houses are ugly, unhealthy, inconvenient, dark, ill-built,
ill-fitted and dear.

This is due in a great measure to the cost of land. I will tell you soon
why land is so expensive. . . .

Poor Mrs John Smith, her life is one long slavery. Cooking, cleaning,
managing, mending, washing clothes, waiting on husband and children,
her work is never done. And amid it all she suffers the pains and anxieties
of child-bearing, and the suckling of children. There are no servants, and
few workers, so hard wrought and so ill-paid as the wife of a British
artisan. What are her *hours of labour*, my Trade Union friend? What
pleasure has she, what rest, what prospect? . . .

And now we come to the last item in your life, your recreation. Here,
Mr Smith, you are very badly served. You have hardly anything to amuse
you. Music, art, athletics, science, the drama, and nature are almost denied
to you. A few cheerless museums filled with Indian war clubs, fag ends
of tapestry and dried beetles; a few third-rate pictures, a theatre or two

where you have choice between vulgar burlesque and morbid melodrama, a sprinkling of wretched music halls, one or two sleepy night-schools, a football field, and sometimes—for the better paid workers—a cricket ground, make up the sum of your life's pleasures. Well—yes, there are plenty of public houses and you can gamble. The betting lists and racing news have a corner in all the respectable papers. . . .

The chief causes of the evils I have pointed out to you, John, are competition, monopoly and bad management. . . . Go into any street and you will see two or three carts delivering milk. A cart, a pony, and a man to carry milk to a few houses; and one postman serves a whole district; as one milkman and one horse could, were it not for competition.

Again, in each house there is a woman . . . washing clothes for one family. And the woman is over-worked . . . and the house is made horrible by steam and the odours of burnt fat. So with all the things we do and use. We have two grocers' shops next door to each other, each with a staff of servants, each with its own costly fixtures. Yet one big store would do as well, and would save half the cost and labour. Fancy a private post office in every street. How much would it cost to send a letter from Oldham to London?

So now let me tell you roughly what I suggest as an improvement on things as they now are. . . . I would make all the land, mills, mines, factories, works, shops, ships and railways the property of the people.

Robert Blatchford, Merrie England, 1895

THE TOWN THAT WAS MURDERED

The poverty of the poor is not an accident, a temporary difficulty, a personal fault. It is the permanent state in which the vast majority of the citizens in any capitalist country have to live. . . . Men are regarded as mere instruments of production and their labour is a commodity to be bought and sold. In capitalist society vast changes can be made which sweep away the livelihood of a whole town overnight, in the interests of some powerful group, who need take no account of the social consequences of their decisions. . . . Generalizations are not proof. The idea of this book is to take one town, which has been through the whole process —the rise of capitalist industry, its heyday, and the rationalization period after the first world war—and to give a picture of capitalism at work. For the purpose the ancient town of Jarrow serves as a curiously complete example. . . .

Jarrow has seen the rise and fall of a great coal industry, the growth of

one of the great shipyards of Europe ... and its extinction. For in its hey-
day Palmer's Shipyard at Jarrow led the way in shipbuilding technique.
At the end of the [Great] War it had a payroll of 10,000 men. Twenty
years later a blue official paper addressed 'Palmer's Shipyard, Ellison
Street, Jarrow' was returned with the pencilled scrawl 'Not known.
Gone away!'—the last letter of the Palmer file at Somerset House.

The bitterness of the passing of this great enterprise is that its fall was
due to no national emergency, but to serve the immediate interests of a
certain group. . . .

One thing is constant through the whole story of Jarrow—through
boom and slump, through so-called prosperity and the consequent
distress—and that is the poverty of the working people of Jarrow. They
built vast fortunes for others. They remained at subsistence level ... and
many are now below even that.

Ellen Wilkinson, *The Town that was Murdered*, 1939

A HOSPITAL FOR JARROW

One other hospital had been built in the town, the Palmer Memorial
Hospital. The story of that dates back to 1865, when a meeting was held
in Jarrow to discuss the provision of a memorial to the first wife of Charles
Mark Palmer. Collections had already been started to purchase a stained-
glass window for the church. . . . the tough and blunt manager of the
Shipyard suggested that a memorial hospital would be the best tribute.
He quoted instances of men injured in the Shipyard who had to suffer
agonizing pain en route from the works to the hospital. Of twenty accident
cases which were sent to Newcastle Infirmary, eight died on the way.
Another speaker said that their lives were jolted out of the injured men. A
workman present gave the case of a fellow worker who had his arm
severely damaged at 7 a.m. but did not reach the Infirmary till 11 a.m.
The pain drove him mad and he died two days later. . . .

No one seems to have suggested that as Palmer had been paid that year
nearly three-quarters of a million in cash and shares in the business now
capitalized at two millions, the care of their badly injured workmen might
have been regarded as a necessary expense by the firm. . . . Jarrow, of
course, was not the only town where insanitary conditions prevailed
during the period of nineteenth-century capitalism . . . where the health
of the workers was not even considered where profit was to be made.
. . . It is no wonder that men like Palmer were Liberals believing in 'free
trade', 'free labour', 'freedom of the subject' when these doctrines

relieved them of any consideration for the welfare, even the elementary needs of housing, sanitation and medical care, of their 'free workers'.

Ellen Wilkinson, *The Town that was Murdered*, 1939

BENEVOLENCE IS NO EXCUSE

From George Robert Stephenson ... down to the Cadburys and Nuffields of our own day, the benevolent capitalist has been an interesting feature of the British industrial landscape. His benevolence has not been allowed to interfere with profit. In fact, the resulting increased profit has been an argument for the benevolence. But the belief that disinterested capitalists do exist; the fact that if any employer shows the least tendency that way his men are prepared to give him credit far in excess of any virtue he actually possesses, has played a not inconsiderable part in the development of the more conservative aspects of British trade-unionism.

Ellen Wilkinson, *The Town that was Murdered*, 1939

THE WASTEFULNESS OF CAPITALISM

Business men denounce the very idea of planned socialism as inefficient and wasteful. But under capitalism shipbuilding seems to be as wasteful as it could be. Productive capacity in one great yard has to be maintained to handle an output of 60,000 tons per year, and yet there are times when only 1620 tons are launched. To ensure ability to deal with the highest possible demand, men and productive resources are left lying idle during the greater part of the trade cycle. For the men the industry accepts no responsibility. It seeks however to compensate the owners of the capital by charging such prices during the good years as will make it possible to pay a fair average return to its investors.

Before the war the 'bad times' in Jarrow meant hardships to the workmen and their families which are difficult for us to realize. As a shipbuilding programme was completed, and if no further work was ready, men were discharged from the yard. Their number increasing as the slump developed, and unable to find work elsewhere, they had to prepare to exist until the 'good times' and of course without any unemployment benefit. The whole town lost its purchasing power when the gates of Palmer's closed. The march of the trade cycle seemed as inevitable as the plague. There is a grim fatalism about the way in which the workmen prepared for the bad time. . . . Two, three or more families would move together into one house. . . . the overcrowding was appalling. Large families were herded together in one room. . . . This overcrowding and the inadequate nourishment led to effects which are continually bewailed by the medical officer of health. In 1884 the local officer prefaced his report with: 'The lamentable depression of trade in the borough, with the consequent distress among the working classes, has had an appreciable effect upon the mortality statistics of the year.'

Ellen Wilkinson, *The Town that was Murdered*, 1939

A TOUR OF THE EAST END SLUMS

If you go and look upon these women you will feel suddenly stricken old. Look at their mean and meagre dress, look at their warped figures, their furrowed brows, their dim eyes. . . . The thought that rose up most distinctly in my mind was 'What would these poor creatures do without the *gin*?'

When I hear honourable members prating in the House about 'Imperial questions' I think of the famished seamstress, the unemployed docker, the girl (with the jaws eaten away by phosphorus) whom the honourable gentleman represents. When I see beautiful sculptures and paintings of Greek womanhood I remember how, coming out of an art gallery . . . I saw a white haired old Englishwoman carrying a great bag of cinders on her bent old back. I ask myself questions about that Bridge of Sighs where London women drown themselves in their despair. . . .

My companion took me to a bridge across a kind of dock, and told me it was known thereabouts as 'The Bridge of Sighs'. There is a constable there on fixed point duty. Why? *To prevent the women from committing suicide.*

The suicides were so numerous, he said, that special precautions had to be taken. And since the constable had been there, so eager are the women to quit the best of all possible worlds that they have been known to come there at night with a couple of women friends and to leap into the deep, still water while those friends engaged the constable in conversation.

Robert Blatchford, *Not Guilty: A Plea for the Bottom Dog*, 1906

A TOUR OF STAFFORDSHIRE

At Cradley I saw a white-haired old woman carrying half a hundred-weight of chain to the forgers round her shoulders; at Cradley I saw women making chain with babies sucking at their breasts; at Cradley I spoke to a married couple who had worked 120 hours in one week and had earned 18 shillings by their united labour; at Cradley I saw heavy chain strikers who were worn out old men at 35; at Cradley I found women on strike for a price which would enable them to earn twopence an hour by dint of labour which is to work, what a battle is to a Bank Holiday review. At Cradley the men and women are literally being worked to death for a living that no gentleman would offer his dogs.

Thence to the domestic workshops. Old women, young girls, and mothers working as if for dear life. Little children, unkempt and woe-begone, crouching amongst the cinders. No time for nursing or house-wifery in the chain trade. These women earned from 6 shillings to 9 shillings a week. Some of them are, I see, in an advanced state of preg-nancy.

And what pleasures have these people; what culture and beauty in their lives? This: Were they ever so anxious to 'improve their minds' what leisure have they, what opportunity? Their lives are all swelter and sleep. Their town a squalid, hideous place, ill-lighted and unpaved —the paths and roads heel-deep in mire. Their houses are not homes— they have neither comfort, nor beauty, but are mere shelters and sleeping pens.

In all the place there is no newsroom nor free library, nor even a concert hall or gymnasium. There is no cricket ground, no assembly room, no public bath, no public park, no public garden. Throughout all that sordid, dolorous region I saw not so much as one tree, or flower bed, or fountain. Nothing bright or fair on which to rest the eye.

But there are public houses. . . .

Robert Blatchford, *Not Guilty: A Plea for the Bottom Dog*, 1906

A POSTSCRIPT ON WEALTH

The worship of wealth as an end in itself left no room for the vital sense of joy in creation. It [the nineteenth century] was an age of creation, but it was not the spirit of creation that men admired. It is one of the ironies of history that this age admired itself for every reason but the right one. What men praised was the great civil order which had survived all the storms of the Revolution, and had made property more secure than any other system in the world. The immense energy that might have created a society of free men was admired just because it had created a society in which so few men were free. Similarly a false value was put on all the discoveries and institutions of the time. To the modern mind the truest thing that was said about the Industrial Revolution was said by Doherty in *The Voice of the People*: that if life was to be enriched by the new industry, machinery must be made subordinate to the men who used it.

The political economy of the age valued the new industry as offering rapid and tempting prizes to the spirit of gain which was regarded as the great motive power of human progress. The ideal workman was the man who set his heart on making money, and had no higher purpose in his toil and in his abstinence from pleasure. The religion of the age assigned one virtue to the working classes, the virtue of bearing with Christian patience 'the inconveniences of a lower station': inconveniences that were steadily increasing. Economist and Evangelical alike judged every movement by the single standard of its reactions on the existing order. It was left to a few independent spirits to question this amazing complacency, to ask the Evangelicals whether ninety out of a hundred of their fellow-citizens had been born for no other purpose than to practise the virtue of resignation; to ask the economist whether the workman was to have no other god in life than the law of supply and demand, to be worshipped with impartial enthusiasm whether it found him employment or whether it put him in the workhouse; to ask the politician whether a government whose dominant object is to preserve its own existence fulfils any large or noble purpose in the world.

J. L. and B. Hammond, closing chapter of *The Town Labourer, 1760–1832*, 1917

6. What is Socialism?—Introduction

Socialism is a system of government eminently wise, just and practical.
Robert Blatchford

WHAT IS SOCIALISM?

IF A CELESTIAL intelligence were now to look down from heaven on the earth with the power of observing every fact about all human beings at once, he might ask, as the newspaper editors are asking as I write, what that Socialism is which influences so many lives? He might answer himself with a definition which could be clumsily translated as 'a movement towards greater social equality, depending for its force upon three main factors, the growing political power of the working classes, the growing social sympathy of many members of all classes, and the belief, based on the growing authority of scientific method, that social arrangements can be transformed by means of conscious and deliberate contrivance'. He would see men trying to forward this movement by proposals as to taxation, wages, and regulative or collective administration; some of which proposals would prove to be successfully adapted to the facts of human existence and some would in the end be abandoned, either because no nation could be persuaded to try them or because when tried they failed. But he would also see that this definition . . . is not 'Socialism' as it exists for the greater number of its supporters. The need of something which one may love and for which one may work has created for thousands of working men a personified 'Socialism', a winged goddess with stern eyes and drawn sword to be the hope of the world and the protector of those that suffer. The need of some engine of thought which one may use with absolute faith and certainty has also created another Socialism, not a personification, but a final and authoritative creed. Such a creed appeared in England in 1884, and William Morris took it down in his beautiful handwriting from Mr. Hyndman's lectures. It was the revelation which made a little dimly educated working man say to me three years later, with tears of genuine humility in his eyes, 'How strange it is that this glorious truth has been hidden from all the clever and learned men of the world and shown to me'.

Graham Wallas, *Human Nature in Politics*, 1908

TOO GOOD TO BE TRUE?

Socialism seemed too good to be true: it was passed by as merely the old optimism foolishly running its head against the stone wall of modern science. But Socialism now challenges individualism, scepticism, pessimism, on their own ground of science. The science of the production and distribution of wealth is political economy. Socialism appeals to that science, and turning on Individualism its own guns, routs it in incurable disaster. Henceforth the bitter cynic who still finds the world an eternal and unimprovable doghole, with the placid person of means who repeats the familiar misquotation 'the poor ye shall have always with you', lose their usurped place among the cultured, and pass over to the ranks of the ignorant, the shallow, and the superstitious. As for the rest of us, since we were taught to revere proprietary respectability in our unfortunate childhood, and since we found our childish hearts so hard and unregenerate that they secretly hated and rebelled against respectability in spite of that teaching, it is impossible to express the relief with which we discover that our hearts were all along right, and that the current respectability of today is nothing but a huge inversion of righteous and scientific social order weltering in dishonesty, uselessness, selfishness, wanton misery, and idiotic waste of magnificent opportunities for noble and happy living. It was terrible to feel this, and yet to fear that it could not be helped—that the poor must starve and make you ashamed of your dinner—that they must shiver and make you ashamed of your warm overcoat. It is to economic science—once the Dismal, now the Hopeful —that we are indebted for the discovery that though the evil is enormously worse than we knew, yet it is not eternal—not even very long lived, if we only bestir ourselves to make an end of it.

Bernard Shaw, *Essays in Fabian Socialism*, 1889

CAPITALISM IS UTOPIAN

It is not sufficiently realised, that the Capitalist system is quite as Utopian, quite as artificial, quite as much a paper system founded on essays and treatises by clever idealist writers, as Socialism. Its elaborately worked out theory was that the solution of the great problem of how to keep our huge population alive in response to their necessary first prayer 'Give us this day our daily bread' is to make the material sources of production private property, enforce all voluntary contracts made under this condition, keep the peace between citizen and citizen, and leave the rest to the operation of individual self-interest. This, it was claimed, would guarantee to every worker a subsistence wage whilst providing a rich leisured class with the means of upholding culture, and saturating them with money enough to enable them to save and invest capital without personal privation. . . . The Theory worked wonderfully in the sphere of production and trade. It built up our factory system, our power machinery, our means of transport and communication, which have made the world a new world. . . . Unfortunately these unprecedented achievements in production and finance have been accompanied by a failure in distribution so grotesquely inequitable and socially disastrous that its continuance is out of the question. Desperate attempts are being made everywhere by redistributive taxation, State regulation of wages, and factory legislation, to remedy or at least palliate it, within the limits of the Capitalist system. But redistributive taxation within Capitalist limits means dole for idleness instead of wages for productive work; and regulation of wages and factories does not help the unemployed. . . .

. . . No other remedy than the transformation of Capitalistic society into Socialistic society has so far been able to stand examination.

Bernard Shaw, *Essays in Fabian Socialism*, 1889

THE NATURE OF PROPERTY

I recently had a debate with a distinguished Roman Catholic priest . . . [who] told me he thought I had only scored one point during the whole affair. . . .

. . . that one point of mine arose over a question of property. I said that I was a Socialist . . . just because I was in favour of individual, private, property. I said that my main complaint against capitalism was that it had deprived by far the greater part of the British people of any individual, private, property worth talking about. I quoted him those figures about four-fifths of us dying with property worth less than £100. . . .

The point is that there are two quite different sorts of private property. The one sort is private property in the means of production: private property in a factory, or a mine, or in the land. And the other sort is private property in 'consumers' goods', in food and clothes and furniture, in houses, in motor-cars, in every sort of thing which we actually use and consume.

. . . endless confusion arises from a failure to distinguish between these two kinds of private property. It ought to be impossible to mix them up. For there is one rule for distinguishing between them. Private property of the first sort—private property in the means of production—carries an income with it; private property of the second sort—private property in consumers' goods—does not carry an income with it.

For instance, if you own £500 worth of shares in the Austin motor factory in Birmingham, you will get an income from these shares. But if you own an Austin motor-car, price £500, no one will dream of paying you anything because you own that motor-car. . . . There you have the distinction.

Now, you get paid an income if you own shares in the Austin factory because the Austin factory is part of the means of production of the country. You do not get paid an income if you own an Austin motor-car, because a motor-car is not part of the means of production. It is a consumer's good.

The economic system which is commonly called socialism—and this is the system which we can put in the place of capitalism—involves abolishing the first sort of private property, in order to increase vastly the second sort of private property.

John Strachey, *Why you should be a Socialist*, 1938

NON-CLASS NOT WORKING CLASS

The working class is not a class; it is the nation. This being so, it is a degradation of the Socialist movement to drag it down to the level of a mere struggle for supremacy between two contending factions. We don't want 'class conscious' Socialists; we want conscious Socialists, men and women who are conscious of their Socialism, and why they are Socialists. This 'class war' and 'class-conscious' phrasing is, then, I submit, harmful to the cause of Socialism; harmful because it misrepresents the movement; harmful because it makes it impossible for other than working people to join the Socialist ranks without being accused by their fellows of treachery and of wearing the uniform of the enemy; harmful because it distracts attention from the real issue, and fosters a belief that mere class hatred will transform Society. The less a person knows about Socialism the more likely he is to cover up his ignorance by shouting 'class war' in lieu of sober argument. . . .

Socialism declares war upon a system, not upon a class.

Keir Hardie, 1904

JOHN SMITH GETS HIS ANSWER

John Smith, do you know what Socialism is? You have heard it denounced many a time, and it is said that you do not believe in it; but do you know what it is?

G

Good or bad, wise or foolish, it is all I have to offer as a remedy for the many evils of which I have been complaining.

Good or bad, wise or foolish, Socialism is the only remedy in sight. None of its opponents, none of your friends, the members of Parliament, old trade union leaders, Tory and Liberal editors, parsons, priests, lawyers and men of substance have any remedy to offer at all.

Some of them are sorry or profess to be sorry, that there is so much misery in the land; some of them offer a little mild charity, some a little feeble legislation, but there is no great radical cure to be heard of except Socialism. . . .

But before I tell you what Socialism is, I must tell you what Socialism is not. For half our time as champions of Socialism is wasted in denials of false descriptions of Socialism; and to a large extent the anger, the ridicule, and the argument of the opponents of Socialism are hurled against a Socialism which has no existence except in their own heated minds.

Socialism does not consist in violently seizing upon the property of the rich and sharing it out amongst the poor.

Socialists do not propose by a single Act of Parliament, or by a sudden revolution, to put all men on an equality, and compel them to remain so. Socialism is not a wild dream of a happy land where the apples will drop off the trees into our open mouths, the fish come out of the rivers and fry themselves for dinner, and the looms turn out ready-made suits of velvet with golden buttons without the trouble of coaling the engine. Neither is it a dream of a nation of stained-glass angels, who never say damn, who always love their neighbours better than themselves, and who never need to work unless they wish to.

No, Socialism is none of those things. It is a scientific scheme of national Government, entirely wise, just, and *practical*. . . . Practical Socialism is so simple that a child may understand it. It is a kind of national scheme of co-operation, managed by the State. Its programme consists, essentially, of one demand, that the land and other instruments of production shall be the common property of the people, and shall be used and governed by the people for the people.

Make the land and all the instruments of production State property; put all farms, mines, mills, ships, railways, and shops under State control, as you have already put the postal and telegraphic services under State control, and Practical Socialism is accomplished. . . . That which has been done with the post-offices may be done with mines, trams, railways, and factories.

The difference between Socialism and the state of things now in existence will now be plain to you.

At present the land—that is, England—does not belong to the people —to the English—but to a few rich men. The mines, mills, ships, shops, canals, railways, houses, docks, harbours, and machinery do not belong to the people, but to a few rich men.

Therefore the land, the factories, the railways, ships and machinery are not used for the general good of the people, but are used to make wealth for the few rich men who own them.

Socialists say that this arrangement is unjust and unwise, that it entails waste as well as misery, and that it would be better for all, even for the rich, that the land and other instruments of production should become the property of the State, just as the post-office and the telegraphs have become the property of the State.

Socialists demand that the State shall manage the railways and the mines and the mills just as it now manages the post-offices and the telegraphs.

Socialists declare that if it is wicked and foolish and impossible for the State to manage the factories, mines and railways, then it is wicked and foolish and impossible for the State to manage the telegraphs.

Socialists declare that as the State carries the people's letters and tele-grams more cheaply and more efficiently than they were carried by private enterprise, so it could grow corn and weave cloth and work the railway systems more cheaply and more efficiently than they are now worked by private enterprise.

Socialists declare that as our Government now makes food and clothing and arms and accoutrements for the army and navy and police so it could make them for the people.

Socialists declare that as many corporations make gas, provide and manage the water-supply, look after the paving and lighting and cleansing of the streets, and often do a good deal of building and farming, so there is no reason why they should not get coal, and spin yarn, and make boots, and bread and beer for the people.

Socialists point out that if all the industries of the nation were put under State control, all the profit, which now goes into the hands of a few idle men, would go into the coffers of the State,—which means that the people would enjoy the benefits of all the wealth they create.

This, then, is the basis of Socialism, that England should be owned by the English, and managed for the benefit of the English, instead of being owned by a few rich idlers, and mismanaged by them for the benefit of themselves.

But Socialism means more than the mere transference of the wealth of the nation to the nation.

Socialism would not endure competition. Where it found two factories engaged in under-cutting each other at the price of long hours and
low wages to the workers, it would step in and fuse the two concerns into
one, save an immense sum in cost of working, and finally produce more
goods and better goods at a lower figure than were produced before.

But Practical Socialism would do more than that. It would educate the
people. It would provide cheap and pure food. It would extend and ele-
vate the means of study and amusement. It would foster literature and
science and art. It would encourage and reward genius and industry. It
would abolish sweating and jerry work. It would demolish the slums
and erect good and handsome dwellings. It would compel all men to do
some kind of useful work. It would re-create and nourish the craftsman's
pride in his craft. It would protect women and children. It would raise
the standard of health and morality; and it would take the sting out of
pauperism by paying pensions to honest workers no longer able to work.

Why nationalise the land and instruments of production? To save
waste; to save panics; to avert trade depressions, famines, strikes and
congestion of industrial centres; and to prevent greedy and unscrupulous
sharpers from enriching themselves at the cost of the national health and
prosperity. In short, to replace anarchy and war by law and order. . . .

I will now give you one example of the difference between Socialism
and the existing system. . . . Under existing conditions what is the state of
the salt trade?

The mines are owned and carried on by a number of firms, each of
which competes against all the rest.

Result: Most of the small firms ruined; most of the large firms on the
verge of ruin. Salt-boilers, the workmen, working twelve hours a day
for 3 shillings, and the public wasting more salt than they use.

Put this trade under State control. They will cease to make salt to
waste; they will establish a six hours day and they will raise the wages of
the men to, say, two pounds a week.

To pay these extra wages they will abolish all the unnecessary middlemen and go-betweens. The whole industry will be placed under one
management. A vast number of clerks, agents, travellers, canvassers and
advertisers will be dispensed with, the salaries of the managers will be
almost entirely saved, and the cost of distribution will be cut down by
fully seventy-five per cent.

The same system would be pursued with other industries. Take the
soap trade.

There is one firm which spends over £100,000 a year in advertisement, and the head of that firm makes £100,000 a year in profits. Social-

ism would save all that advertisement, and would pay a manager a reasonable salary and produce the soap at less than its present cost, whilst paying the workers good wages for shorter hours than they now work.

You will observe that under Practical Socialism there would be wages paid; and . . . the wages of managers would be higher than the wages of workmen; and the wages of artists, doctors and other clever and highly trained men would be higher than those of weavers or navvies.

Robert Blatchford, *Merrie England*, 1895

HOW IT CAN BE DONE

How can Socialism be accomplished? . . . The first thing to do is to educate the people in Socialism. Let us once get the people to understand and desire Socialism, and I am sure we may very safely leave them to secure it.

The most useful work which Socialists can do at present is the work of education and organisation.

Socialism will not come by means of a sudden coup. It will grow up naturally out of our surroundings and will develop naturally and by degrees. But its growth and its development may be materially hastened.

It always amuses me to hear the intensely practical person demand, How are you going to do it? When will you make a start? Where do you propose to leave off?

My dear Mr Smith, it is too late to ask when we are going to begin. We *have* begun. We, or rather they, began long ago. Nearly all law is more or less Socialistic, for nearly all law implies the right of the State to control individuals for the benefit of the nation. But of late years the law has been steadily becoming more and more Socialistic. I will give you a few examples.

The abolition of toll bars and bridge tolls was Socialistic action, for it made the roads and bridges common property.

Most of the Building Acts, by virtue of which streets must be of a specified width, back to back houses are forbidden, and so on, are Socialistic, for they take away from the property owner the power to do as he likes with his own.

The Truck Acts are Socialistic, for they deny the employer the power to swindle his workmen. The Factory Acts are Socialistic, for they deny the employer the power to work women and children to death.

The Compulsory and Free Education Acts are Socialistic. The Acts which compel the inspection of mines and factories, the inspection of boilers, the placing of a load line on ships and the granting of relief to paupers, are all Socialistic Acts, for they all interfere with the 'freedom of contract' and the 'rights of the individual'. Finally, the acquirement of the postal and telegraphic arrangements by the State, and the establishment of corporate gas and water works are Socialistic measures, for they recognise the Socialistic principle of common ownership, production and distribution.

You will see then, that Socialism has begun, so that the question of where to begin is quite superfluous. . . .

Robert Blatchford, Merrie England, 1895

WHY ARE WE POOR?

. . . discontent has led to a research into the causes productive of the poverty, and this has disclosed the fact that poverty is due exclusively to the private monopoly of land and capital and to the production of commodities for profit and not for use. Production for Profit is the formula of commercialism; production for Use that of Socialism. Having got this far, the other question to be settled was: Is Socialism desirable in other respects, or are there disadvantages connected with it which would outweigh the abolition of poverty which would undoubtedly follow its adoption? To this question only experience can give the final answer, but if such dangers lurk behind Socialism, not only are they not apparent, but to some of us, Socialism is not only a good system of political economy, but a philosophy of life altogether beautiful. If experience should prove that a system based on love, fraternity, and service is bad, then woe betide this hapless old world.

Keir Hardie, 1896

LIBERALISM IS NOT ENOUGH

. . . Of every two working men who attain the age of sixty-five years one dies a pauper, whilst two million pass through the books of the relieving officers every year. One-third of the working-class population are housed under conditions which would bring disgrace upon a savage tribe. Want of employment and irregularity of work are chronic, and it has been demonstrated on the unbiased testimony of men of standing and position, such as Charles Booth and Seebohm Rowntree, that the earnings of thirty per cent of the working-class population when in full work, and during a period of good trade, are not sufficient to furnish a standard of comfort equal to what obtains in the workhouse or the jail. If this be the best that the combined efforts of Liberalism and Toryism can effect for the nation, it would seem to be about time for some change to be tried.

Keir Hardie, 1903

... The minimum wage and the like are good so far as they go; but they don't go far. The colliers have had their big strikes; they have been well organised; they have won a living wage; they have tried sliding scales, arbitration and conciliation boards; and despite them all they are to-day as badly off as ever. And I would have them note this fact: So long as they tolerate private ownership of land and capital, and leave competition to fix the selling price of coal and the wage of the miners, they can never permanently improve their position. It would be just as easy for the nation to own and regulate the production of its coal and food as it is to own and regulate the postal system.

This is what is meant by Socialism.

Keir Hardie, 1896

HOW LONG, O LORD?

When will the time come when honest and clear-seeing men will grow sick of all this chaos of waste, this robbing of Peter to pay Paul, which is the essence of Commercial war? When shall we band together to replace the system whose motto is 'The devil take the hindmost' with a system whose motto shall be really and without qualification 'One for all and all for one'?

Who knows but that the time may be at hand, but that we now living may see the beginning of that end which shall extinguish luxury and poverty? When the upper, middle, and lower classes shall have melted into one class, living contentedly a simple and happy life.

How can we of the middle-classes, we the capitalists, and our hangers-on, help them? By renouncing our class, and on all occasions when antagonism rises up between the classes casting in our lot with the victims; with those who are condemned at the best to lack of education, refinement, leisure, pleasure and renown; and at the worst to a life lower than that of the most brutal of savages—in order that the system of competitive commerce may endure. .... It is true that at present Capitalist Society only looks on Socialism in England with dry grins. .... I can offer you a position which involves sacrifice ... and I earnestly beg you, those of you who are convinced of the justice of our cause, not to hang back from active participation in a struggle which—who ever helps or who ever abstains from helping—must beyond all doubt end at last in Victory.

William Morris, *Art and Socialism*, 1884

LET US GO FORWARD TOGETHER

Well, since our aim is so great and so much to be longed for, the substituting throughout all society of peace for war, pleasure and self-respect for grief and disgrace, we may well seek about strenuously for some means for starting our enterprise; and since it is just these means in which the difficulty lies, I appeal to all socialists, while they express their thoughts and feelings about them honestly and fearlessly, not to make a quarrel of it with those whose aim is one with theirs, because there is a difference of opinion between them about the usefulness of the details of the means. It is difficult or even impossible not to make mistakes about these, driven as we are by the swift lapse of time and the necessity for doing something amidst it all. So let us forgive the mistakes that others make, even if we make none ourselves, and be at peace amongst ourselves, that we may the better make War upon the monopolist.

William Morris, *Communism*, 1903

THE ONLY ANSWER

Have we not all read a dozen 'grave warnings' from our learned bankers, our earnest railway chairmen, and our oh! so humanitarian company directors? How often have these gentlemen assured us: 'No one is more appalled by unemployment than we are; but unfortunately it is all a very, very difficult and complex problem. Human wisdom has as yet discovered no solution for it. All we can do is to wait patiently in the hope that some day some wonderfully clever man will invent a way, if not to overcome, then at any rate to mitigate, the problems of unemployment and industrial depression.' All the oceans of talk of that sort have been, and are, nothing more nor less than excuses for doing nothing. The truth is that the thing could be done tomorrow if anyone in authority really had the mind to do it. But it could only be done on the condition that those in authority put some ideal before the making of profits.

... If we were to put the ... ideal of the love and welfare of our fellow-men before profits, we should solve our economic problem. (And that is Socialism.)

John Strachey, *A Faith to Fight For*, 1941

THE MEANING OF SOCIALISM

By Socialism I mean a form of society in which men and women are not divided into opposing economic classes, but live together under conditions of approximate social and economic equality, using in common the means that lie to their hands of promoting social welfare. Socialism, as I understand it, means four closely connected things—a human fellowship which denies and expels distinction of class, a social system in which no one is so much richer or poorer than his neighbours as to be unable to mix with them on equal terms, the common ownership and use of all the vital instruments of production, and an obligation upon all citizens to serve one another according to their capacities in promoting the common well-being. Nothing is Socialism that does not embrace all these four things; and, given the means of realising these four, nothing further is needed to make a Socialist society.

G. D. H. Cole, *The Simple Case for Socialism*, 1935

THE DANGERS OF 'GRADUALISM'

Nor have Socialists a belief that Socialism, even to the extent to which its institutions can be foreseen, can spring suddenly into being full and complete. Whether the advance towards it be rapid or slow, it is bound on all accounts to be by stages. Even where, as in Russia, Socialist control has been ushered in by revolution and preceded by an almost entire dissolution of the old order, Socialist institutions and ways of living cannot be built in a day. They have to be developed by stages, as enough people become ready to accept them and have strength and skill to build them up. Still more, if Socialism comes in, not through war and revolution as it did in Russia, but by peaceful conquest of power, as we hope it may in Great Britain, must its coming be by steps and stages so contrived as to keep the old order still working until the new institutions can be got ready to take its place. That conservation of the old order during the process of transition to the new is the hardest part of the task for those who seek to bring in Socialism by evolutionary means; for it cannot be easy to keep the two systems working smoothly side by side. Indeed it cannot be done at all without strong government animating the whole system with a single conscious driving force in the direction of Socialism.

In the ranks of the Socialist movement there has been much controversy over the question of 'gradualism' in Socialist policy; and a good deal of this controversy has been beside the mark. If 'gradualism' means only that Socialism cannot be brought in at a blow, then every sensible

Socialist is a gradualist. If, however, it means that a society can slide by imperceptible gradations from a capitalist to a Socialist system, then 'gradualism' is at fault; for such a view misses out the vital importance of conscious human purpose, of the striving of millions of ordinary people towards the realisation of a new way of life, as the indispensable driving force towards a Socialist society. The coming of Socialism means for the whole people a change of mind and heart and not merely a change of machinery. It means a conscious will towards equality and good fellow-ship that will stir the imaginations of the young and make men and women ready and eager to work and sacrifice for their ideal. Without this impul-sion behind it, Socialism cannot be brought into existence; and if, with-out this, we get 'socialistic' changes in the machinery of society, we shall not therewith be getting Socialism. For Socialism is in its essence not mainly a new gospel of mechanical efficiency, but a way of life.

The danger of 'gradualism' is that its exponents, conceiving the change as one of machinery and administration, that can be made by barely noticeable stages, without shock to the minds and habits of the people, will fail to arouse the enthusiasm and the strength that are needed for every great adventure. The force of habit and of tradition is very great: most of us live mainly under it for most of our lives. Now the habits and traditions of to-day are built on the requirements and adaptations of the past. So far from showing that human nature never changes, they are the crystallisation of past changes that were revolutionary in their day. Of these existing habits and traditions very many must be taken up almost without outward change into the way of living of the new social order; for no social order can be made at all except on the foundations laid by the past. But habits once rooted in men outlive their use: traditions that were once fountains of lively development turn into frozen monuments to the past. Men cannot live without habits and traditions; but they must be always making new ones if they are to live well.

Enthusiasm based on glowing belief that is a blend of intellect and emo-tion is the active force that brings new habits and traditions to birth. Intellect by itself makes no movements; for intellect alone can never tell us what we *ought* to do. *Ought* is a matter of emotion and sentiment— not of sheer intellect alone. But men's emotions are stirred to great deeds not by little things but only by great hopes and high beliefs. Unless men passionately want and value freedom, fellowship, class equality, comrade-ship in using and enjoying the great resources that lie ready to their hands, they will not succeed in achieving Socialism in any real sense. Collectivism of a sort they may achieve. For the technical forces of modern industrialism are driving them incessantly towards collective forms of administration. But collectivism is as compatible with the Slave State as with Socialism; and if we seek Socialism without assiduously preaching to mankind a new way of living together we are in grievous danger of making only the Slave State where bureaucrats will rule and the quality of life decay.

Our Socialism is, then, ardent, passionate, an affair of the heart as well as of the mind. We are in love with Socialism—with the vast new opportunities it offers for living together on terms of which no one of us will need to feel ashamed, of assuring to one and all, so far as in our knowledge lies, the means to health and strength and balanced growth of body and of mind, of doing away with all those twists and miseries of living that come of undernourishment, starvation of mental strength and hope, uneasiness at the sense of the crookedness of human dealing, thwarted personality and sheer disillusionment and loss of faith in life. That these ills can be conquered must be our faith, which is at bottom the simple belief that, given opportunity, most men will respond to an appeal to decent feeling and be ready to give as good as they get and often more.

That is what our 'gradualists' are apt to miss, where our 'extremists' get at least a glimpse of it.

G. D. H. Cole, *The Simple Case for Socialism*, 1935

ALL MEN TO COUNT AS ONE

I ask no one to call himself a Socialist unless he wants society to recognise other men's claims as no less valid than his own. Socialism is an imaginative belief that all men, however unequal they may be in powers of mind and body or in capacity for service, are in a really significant sense *equal*, not merely before the law but one with another. They are equal as brothers and sisters are equal, the strong with the weak, the foolish with the wise—and the bad with the good, so far as men are good or bad in any final sense. Luck no social system can ever eliminate: there will be lucky ones and unlucky ones under Socialism as there are to-day. Differences of quality and attainment, too, will exist, however society is organised. There will be waste of genius, square pegs in round holes, backslidings and misfortunes due to passion and evil impulses under any social system. But we can at least greatly improve the chances of well-being and bring them nearer to equality between man and man. We can give everyone a much fairer start, a far more even chance of making the best of body and mind, and therewith a far better hope of escaping the doom of body or mind twisted awry by forces of nurture and environment. There is immense scope for increasing the sum of human happiness, even though, whatever we do, much unhappiness is bound to remain. The reason—the only valid reason—for being a Socialist is the desire, the impassioned will, to seek the greatest happiness of the greatest number. . . .

Our job is to promote happiness by promoting, not for a few but for all, those means to happiness which are most capable of being maximised by collective action. The only arguments against Socialism that are worth considering are those in which it is alleged that Socialists are mistaken in believing that the collective control of social forces can increase the sum of human well-being. All other arguments turn out on analysis to be mere defences of vested 'rights' and claims to superiority over other men. One cannot argue with a man who really holds that the rights of property are sacred irrespective of their social expediency, any more than it was possible to argue with the upholders of the Divine Right of Kings. Men can and do believe disinterestedly in the Divine Right of Property, just as some men used to believe disinterestedly in the Divine Right of Kings. But, ninety-nine times out of a hundred, behind the assertion of absolute right lies vested interest; and vested interest has not seldom an uneasy conscience that may weaken or even paralyse its resistance when we expose it for what it is. If the upholders of absolute right stick to their guns, they cannot be driven out by argument. But as soon as they invoke expediency to buttress absolutism, we Socialists can have them on the hip.

G. D. H. Cole, *The Simple Case for Socialism*, 1935

7. What is Socialism?—The Land for the People

The earth is the Lord's, and therefore not the landlord's.
Steward D. Headlam

LAND SHOULD BE AS FREE AS AIR

THE EQUAL RIGHT of all men to the use of land is as clear as their equal right to breathe the air—it is a right proclaimed by the fact of their existence. For we cannot suppose that some men have a right to be in this world and others no right. If we are all here by the equal permission of the Creator, we are all here with an equal right to the enjoyment of his bounty, with an equal right to the use of all that nature so impartially offers. This is a right which is natural and inalienable; it is a right which vests in every human being as he enters the world, and which during his continuance in the world can be limited only by the equal rights of others. There is on earth no power which can rightfully make a grant of exclusive ownership in land. If all existing men were to unite to grant away their equal rights, they could not grant away the rights of those who follow them. For what are we but tenants for a day? Have we made the earth that we should determine the rights of those who after us shall tenant it in their turn. . . . Let the parchments be ever so many, or possession ever so long, natural justice can recognise no right in one man to the possession and enjoyment of land that is not equally the right of all his fellows. Though his titles have been acquiesced in by generation after generation, to the landed estates of the Duke of Westminster the poorest child that is born in London today has as much right as has his eldest son. The puniest infant that comes wailing into the world in the squalidest room of the most miserable tenement houses, becomes at that moment seized of an equal right with the millionaires. And it is robbed if the right is denied.
Henry George, *Progress and Poverty*, 1879

HOW IT CAN BE DONE

There is but one way to remove an evil and that is to remove its cause. Poverty deepens as wealth increases, and wages are forced down while productive power grows, because land, which is the source of all wealth and the field of all labour, is monopolised. To extirpate poverty, to make wages what justice commands they should be, the full earnings of the labourer, we must therefore substitute for the individual ownership of land a common ownership. Nothing else will go to the cause of the evil —in nothing else is there the slightest hope. This, then, is the remedy for the unjust and unequal distribution of wealth apparent in modern civilisation, and for all the evils which flow from it: I propose to show that this simple measure is not only easy of application; but that it is a sufficient remedy for all the evils which, as modern progress goes on, arise from the greater and greater inequality in the distribution of wealth—that it will substitute equality for inequality, plenty for want, justice for injustice, social strength for social weakness, and will open the way to grander and nobler advances of civilisation. . . . I thus propose to show that the laws of the universe do not deny the natural aspirations of the human heart; that the progress of society might be, and if it is to continue, must be, toward equality, not toward inequality; and that the economic harmonies prove the truth—'We are made for co-operation, like feet, like hands, like eyelids, like the rows of the upper and lower teeth'.

Henry George, *Progress and Poverty*, 1879

WHY COMPENSATE A THIEF?

The anti-slavery movement in the United States commenced with talk of compensating owners, but when four millions of slaves were emancipated, the owners got no compensation, nor did they clamour for any. By the time the people of any such country as England are sufficiently aroused to the injustice and disadvantages of individual ownership of land to induce them to attempt its nationalisation, they will be sufficiently aroused to nationalise it in a much more direct and easy way than by purchase. They will not trouble themselves about compensating the proprietors of land. . . . The truth is, and from this truth there can be no escape, that there is and can be no just title to an exclusive possession of the soil, and that private property in land is a bold, bare enormous wrong, like that of slavery. The majority of men in civilised communities do not recognise this, simply because the majority of men do not think. With them whatever is is right, until the wrongfulness has been frequently pointed out, and in general they are ready to crucify whoever first attempts this.

Henry George, *Progress and Poverty*, 1879

THE ALCHEMY OF RENT

The widow is gathering nettles for her children's dinner; a perfumed seigneur, delicately lounging in the Œil de Bœuf, hath an alchemy whereby he will extract from her the third nettle and call it rent.

Thomas Carlyle, quoted by Henry George

BY WHAT WARRANT?

Consider for a moment the utter absurdity of the titles by which we permit to be gravely passed from John Doe to Richard Roe the right exclusively to possess the earth, giving absolute dominion as against others. . . . In England they go back to the Norman conquerors. Everywhere, not to a right which obliges, but to a force which compels. And when a title rests but on force, no complaint can be made when force annuls it. Whenever the people, having the power, choose to annul those titles, no objection can be made in the name of justice.

Has the first comer at a banquet the right to turn back all the chairs and claim that none of the other guests shall partake of the food provided, except as they make terms with him? Does the first man who presents a ticket at the door of a theatre and passes in, acquire by his priority the right to shut the doors and have the performance go on for him alone? Does the first passenger who enters a railroad car obtain the right to scatter his baggage over all the seats and compel the passengers who come in after him to stand up? . . . The comparative handful of proprietors who own the surface of the British Islands would be doing only what English law gives them full power to do, and what many of them have done on a smaller scale already, were they to exclude the millions of British people from their native islands. And such an exclusion, by which a few hundred thousand should at will banish thirty million people from their native country, while it would be more striking would not be a whit more repugnant to natural right than the spectacle now presented, of the vast body of the British people being compelled to pay such enormous sums to a few of their number for the privilege of being permitted to live upon and use the land which they so fondly call their own.

Henry George, Progress and Poverty, 1879

EPITAPH ON A LANDLORD—THE DUKE OF HAMILTON

The dead Duke 'owned' the greater part of Lanarkshire, and, with the exception of the small estate of Kilmichael, the whole of the island of

Arran. The latter he kept as a game preserve, and, with the exception of
a few places near the shore, would not allow houses to be built upon it.
Arran is one of the most beautiful and might be one of the most pleasant
health resorts in the country; but this man, who is now dead, was able to
say, and did say, that the place should not be used by his fellow-country-
men either in health or weakness. . . .

. . . he let his minerals to company after company, until his income
from this one estate and this one source alone amounted to £114,000 a
year. The miner received as low as sevenpence for digging and sending
to the surface one ton of coal. The Duke, who gave his permission to
dig the coal, received exactly double—fourteen pence.

What were the claims which this man had upon society that he should
be able to tax society to the extent here indicated? He came from a long
line of ancestors whose historic record proves that they were vacillating,
shifty, and treacherous when it served their purpose. . . . It is not easy to
discover in any of these things any claim to our gratitude. . . .

And yet a people professing to be 'democratic' and self-governing
submit to a rule under which this dead man was able, not only to extract
hundreds of thousands a year from the wealth produced by their labour,
but to say that they should not be able to labour at all without his permission. . . . His successor is a young man who has held some appointment in the Royal Navy. He will now enter upon all the powers formerly
possessed by the dead 'nobleman'. Liberal may succeed Tory, and Tory
succeed Liberal in the seat of power—all of them representing the common people—and yet the power of territorial magnates such as the one
in question will remain unchecked. Truly we are a great people, democratically governed.

Keir Hardie, 1895

WHERE DOES THE MONEY COME FROM?

We have now to consider a very important question, viz., have the rich
any *right* to their riches?

I have already laid it down as my guiding principle that a man has a
right to all the wealth that he creates by the exercise of his own unaided
faculties; and to no more. . . .

How do men grow rich? . . .

The Duke of Plaza Toro owns an estate. The rent roll is £30,000 a
year. Where does the money come from?

The estate is let out to farmers, at so much per acre. These farmers
pay the duke his £30,000 a year. Where do the farmers get it from?

The farmers sell their crops, and out of the purchase money pay the rent. How are the crops raised?

The crops are raised by the agricultural labourers, under the direction of the farmers.

That is to say, that the rent is earned by labour—by the labour of the farmer and his men. The duke does nothing. The duke did not make the land, nor does he raise the crops. He has therefore no *right* to take the rent at all.

The man who gets rich on ground rent gets rich on the labour of others.

Robert Blatchford, *Merrie England*, 1895

WHY DO WE COMPLAIN?

Now, John, what are the evils of which we complain? Lowness of wages, length of working hours, uncertainty of employment, insecurity of the future, low standards of public health and morality, prevalence of pauperism and crime, and the existence of false ideals of life.

I will give you a few examples of the things I mean. It is estimated that in this country, with its population of 36 millions, there are generally about 700,000 men out of work. There are about 800,000 paupers. Of every thousand persons who die in Merrie England over 900 die without leaving any property at all. About 8 millions exist always on the borders of destitution. About 20 millions are poor. More than half the national income belongs to about 10 thousand people. About 30 thousand people own 55 fifty-sixths of the land and capital of the kingdom, but of 36 millions of people only 1½ millions get above £3 a week. The average income per head of the working classes is about £17 a year, or less than 1 shilling a day. . . .

Political orators and newspaper editors are very fond of talking to you about 'your country'. Now, Mr Smith, it is a hard practical fact, that you have not got any country. The British Islands do not belong to the British people; they belong to a few thousands—certainly not half a million—of rich men. . . .

It would be just as reasonable for a few families to claim possession of the sea and the air, and charge their fellow creatures rent for breathing or bathing, as it is for those few families to grab the land and call it theirs. As a matter of fact we *are* charged for breathing, for without a sufficient space of land to breathe on we cannot get good air to breathe.

If a man claimed the sea, or the air, or the light as his, you would laugh at his presumption. Now, I ask you to point out to me any reason for private ownership of land which will not act as well as a reason for private ownership of sea and air.

So we may agree that no man can have any *right* to the land. And if a man can have no right to the land, how can he have a right to sell the land? And if I buy a piece of land from one who has no right to sell it, how can I call that land mine? . . .

The landlord does *not* 'create the value' of the estate. The value of an estate consists in the industry of those who work upon it. To say that Lord Blankdash has farm lands or town property worth £50,000 a year means that he has the legal power to take that money from the factory hands and farm workers for the use of that which is as much theirs as his.

I suppose you are aware that no 'value' can be got out of an estate without labour. If you doubt this, take a nine acre field, fence it in, and wait until it grows crops. You know it will *never* grow crops, unless some one ploughs it and sows it.

No; even if you have land and capital you cannot raise a single ear of corn without labour. Take your nine acre field. Put in a steam plough, a sack of seed, a harrow, and a bank book, and wait for crops. You will not get a stalk of corn. A poor labourer with a broken shovel and a piece of thorn bush will raise more wheat in his little patch of back garden than all the capital of England could get out of all the acres of Europe without labour. . . .

Do you ever think about these things? Do you know the difference between the land law and the patent laws and copyright?

A nobleman owns an estate. He draws £30,000 in rent from it annually. He and his family before him have drawn that rent for five or six centuries, and the land is still his.

But if John Smith of Oldham invents a new loom and patents it, his patent right expires in fourteen years. For fourteen years he may reap the fruits of his cleverness. At the end of that time anyone may work his patent without charge. It has become public property; this is the law.

Or John Smith of Oldham writes a book. The book is copyright for forty years, or for the life of the author and seven years after.[1] Whilst it is copyright no one can print the book without John's leave, and so John may make money by his cleverness. But at the end of that time the copyright lapses and the book becomes public property. Anyone may print it then.

Now you see the difference between land law and patent law. The landlord's patent *never* runs out. The land *never* becomes public property.

[1] Now fifty years.

The rent is perpetual. And yet the landlord did not make the land; whereas John Smith *did* invent the loom.

Mr Smith, if you *are* a practical, hard-headed man, I think I may leave you to study the land question for yourself.

Robert Blatchford, *Merrie England*, 1895

8. What is Socialism?—The Economic Answer

Socialism is a particular way of organising the economic life of the world.
John Strachey

AWAY WITH THE MIDDLEMEN

THE WORKER has nothing to sell but his labour, and he must sell that to the middleman. Now, suppose a middleman wants a potato patch dug up; and suppose there are two men out of work. Will the middleman pay one of the men a just price, and charge the labour to the consumer of the potatoes? No. He will ask the men what they will do it for, and give the work to the man who will do it at the lower price. Nor is that the end of the mischief. Say one man gets the work at 3 shillings a day. The other man is still unemployed. He therefore goes to the middleman and offers to do the work for 2 shillings a day. Then the other man is thrown out of work and must go in for one and six a day, or starve.

And so we see that competition amongst the workers reduces the workers' wages, and either increases the middleman's profits or lowers the price of potatoes.

It would pay the workers better to combine. Then they might force the middleman to pay one of them 5 shillings a day, which they could share. By this means they would each have two shillings and sixpence a day, whereas competition between them would result in one of them working for one shilling and sixpence a day and the other getting nothing. This is the idea of the trade unionist. . . .

Take the case of a tram-guard working, say, sixteen hours a day for one pound a week. That man is being robbed of all the pleasure of his life. His wife and children are being deprived of necessary food and comfort. Now there ought to be two guards working eight hours at £2 a week. If the tram company makes big dividends the increased cost should come out of those dividends. If the dividend will not pay it, the fares should be raised. If the public cannot afford to pay bigger fares they ought to walk. At present supposing the dividends to be low, the public are riding at the expense of the tram-guard's wife and children.

Robert Blatchford, *Merrie England*, 1895

SOCIALISM GIVES US A CHANCE

Socialism is a particular way of organising the economic life of the world. All the differences between it and capitalism are founded on the fact that, under capitalism, a small group of private persons owns the means of production, while, under Socialism, they are owned by everybody. It is this change in ownership which makes it possible to get rid of those scourges, such as undernourishment, slumps, unemployment . . . which afflict the world today. None of these things can be got rid of without this change in the ownership of the means of production and capital, of the country.

Now Socialism is not Utopia. The establishment of a socialist society does not suddenly make people into saints or heroes. They remain imperfect men and women. Therefore all sorts of troubles, of difficulties and of struggles, remain in existence. But the point is this. *Socialism gives us a chance*. What we make of this chance is our affair. Socialism can only make a job available for everybody and guarantee everybody who is willing to work a decent living wage with the opportunity to rise to the top of his chosen vocation.

John Strachey, Why you should be a Socialist, 1938

WHAT IS PROFIT?

The next thing we have to discover is, What is profit? Profit is the excess price received for an article over the price paid for it.

If a man sells a thing for more money than he buys it for the balance is profit.

You will see, then, that men may make profit either upon their own work or upon the work of others.

As a rule profit is not made by the producer of an article, but by some other person commonly called the 'middleman' because he goes between the producer and the consumer; that is to say, he, the middleman, buys the article from the maker, and sells it to the user, at a profit.

In some cases, and to some extent, this profit is fair. For example, a costermonger buys fish in the market, carries it into the city and sells it at a profit. That profit is his wage, and pays him for his work as a distributor or carrier of goods from the producer to the user.

But when the middleman becomes a capitalist; when he buys fish on the Kentish beach by the ton and sells it at a profit to the shopkeeper and the coster, making for himself a couple of thousand a year, while the fisherman and the coster can hardly keep body and soul together, that is not a fair profit at all.

Why? Just look at it in this light. Here are four persons concerned in the fishery trade.

1. The fisherman, or getter.
2. The middleman, or dealer.
3. The coster, or carrier.
4. The consumer, or user.

Now, can you see any *reason* why of these four people the middleman, who does nothing but sign cheques, should fare so much better than the others?

We have three persons engaged in getting the fish from the sea to our doors. Is it fair that he who does the least work should have the most money? Is the work done by, or rather done *for*, the middleman, so much more valuable to the public than the work of the fisherman and the coster?

Robert Blatchford, Merrie England, 1895

USEFUL WORK VERSUS USELESS TOIL

Therefore, since we have, as it were, a pair of scales in which to weigh the work now done in the world, let us use them. Let us estimate the worthiness of the work we do, after so many thousand years of toil, so many promises of hope deferred, such boundless exultation over the progress of civilisation and the gain of liberty.

Now, the first thing as to the work done in civilisation and the easiest to notice is that it is portioned out very unequally amongst the different classes of society. First, there are people—not a few—who do not work, and make no pretence of doing any. Next, there are people, and very many of them, who work fairly hard, though with abundant easements and holidays, . . . and lastly, there are people who work so hard that they may be said to do nothing else than work, and are accordingly called 'the working classes', as distinguished from the middle classes and the rich, or aristocracy, whom I have mentioned above.

. . . As to the class of rich people doing no work, we all know that they consume a great deal while they produce nothing. Therefore, clearly, they have to be kept at the expense of those who do work, just as paupers have, and are a mere burden on the community. . . .

. . . As to the middle class, including the trading, manufacturing and professional people of our society, they do, as a rule, seem to work quite hard enough. . . . [but] . . . the commercial and manufacturing part of them, the most powerful part, spend their lives and energies in fighting amongst themselves for their respective shares of the wealth which . . . the genuine workers provide for them. . . . Besides this obvious burden on the producers and the scarcely less obvious one of domestic servants, there is first the army of clerks, shop-assistants, and so forth, who are engaged in the service of the private war for wealth, which, as above said, is the real occupation of the well to do middle class. This is a larger body of workers than might be supposed, for it includes amongst others all those engaged in what I should call competitive salesmanship, or, to use a less dignified word, the puffery of wares, which has now got to such a pitch that there are many things which cost far more to sell than they do to make.

William Morris, *Useful Work versus Useless Toil*, 1885

WASTE

The power of producing wealth in any form is the power of producing subsistence. . . . A set of diamonds has a value equal to so many barrels of flour—that is to say it takes on the average as much labour to produce the diamonds as it would to produce so much flour. If I load my wife with diamonds it is as much an exertion of subsistence producing power as though I had devoted so much food to purposes of ostentation. If I keep a footman, I take a possible ploughman from the plough. The breeding and maintenance of a race-horse require care and labour which would suffice for the breeding and maintenance of many work horses.

Henry George, *Progress and Poverty*, 1879

HOW DO WE LIVE NOW?

How do we live, then, under our present system? Let us look at it a little.

And, first, please to understand that our present system of Society is based on a state of perpetual war. Do any of you think that this is as it should be? I know that you have often been told that the competition, which is at present the rule of all production, is a good thing, and stimulates the progress of the race; but the people who tell you this should call competition by its shorter name of *war* if they would wish to be honest, and you would then be free to consider whether or no war stimulates progress, otherwise than as a mad bull chasing you over your own garden may do. War, or competition, whichever you please to call it, means at the best pursuing your own advantage at the cost of some one else's loss. . . .

Let us pass to 'competition' between 'the organisers of labour', great firms, joint-stock companies; capitalists in short, and see how competition 'stimulates production' among them: indeed it does do that; but what kind of production? Well, production of something to sell at a profit, or say production of profits; and note how war commercial stimulates that; a certain market is demanding goods; there are, say, a hundred manufacturers who make that kind of goods, and every one of them would if he could keep that market to himself, and struggles desperately to get as much of it as he can, with the obvious result that presently the thing is overdone, and the market is glutted, and all that fury of manufacture has to sink into cold ashes. Doesn't that seem something like war to you? Now for the producer; I mean the real producer, the worker; how does this scramble for the plunder of the market affect him? The manufacturer, in the eagerness of his war, has had to collect into one neighbourhood a vast army of workers, he has drilled them till they are as fit as may be for his special branch of production, that is, for making a profit out of it, and with the result of their being fit for nothing else: well, when the glut comes in that market he is supplying, what happens to this army, every private in which has been depending on the steady demand in that market, and acting, as he could not choose but act, as if it were to go on for ever? You know well what happens to these men: the factory door is shut on them. What becomes of them? Nay, we know that well enough just now. But what we don't know, or don't choose to know, is that this reserve army of labour is an absolute necessity for commercial war; if *our* manufacturers had not got these poor devils whom they could draft on to their machines when the demand swelled, other manufacturers in France, or Germany, or America, would step in and take the market from them. . . .

As nations under the present system are driven to compete with one another for the markets of the world, and as firms or the captains of industry have to scramble for their share of the profits of the markets, so also have the workers to compete with each other—for livelihood; and it is this constant competition or war amongst them which enables the profit-grinders to make their profits, and by means of the wealth so acquired to take all the executive power of the country into their hands. But here is the difference between the position of the workers and the profit-makers: to the latter, the profit-grinders, war is necessary; you cannot have profit-making without competition, individual, corporate, and national; but you may work for a livelihood without competing; you may combine instead of competing.

I have said war was the life breath of the profit-makers; in like manner, combination is the life of the workers. The working classes cannot even exist as a class without combinations of some sort. The necessity which forced the profit grinders to collect their men first into workshops working by the division of labour, and next into great factories worked by machinery, and so gradually drew them into the great towns and centres of civilisation, gave birth to a distinct working class. . . . They are combining to produce wares of which the profit of a master forms an essential part, instead of goods for their own use; as long as they do this, and compete with each other for leave to do it, they will be, and will feel themselves to be, simply a part of those competing firms I have been speaking of; they will be in fact just a part of the machinery for the production of profit; and so long as this lasts it will be the aim of the masters or profit-makers to decrease the market value of this human part of the machinery; that is to say, since they already hold in their hands the labour of dead men in the form of capital and machinery, it is their interest, or we will say their necessity, to pay as little as they can help for the labour of living men which they have to buy from day to day; and since the workmen they employ have nothing but their labour-power, they are compelled to underbid one another for employment and so enable the capitalist to play his game.

. . . Now observe, I said that to the existence of the workers it was combination, not competition, that was necessary, while to that of the profit-makers, combination was impossible and war necessary. The present position of the workers is that of the machinery of commerce, or in plainer words its slaves; when they change that position and become free, the class of profit-makers must cease to exist; and what will then be the position of the workers? Even as it is they are the one necessary part of society, the life-giving part; the other classes are but hangers-on who live on them. But what should they be, what will they be, when they, once for all, come to know their real power, and cease competing with one another for livelihood? I will tell you: they will be society, they will be the community. And being society—that is, there being no class outside them to contend with—they can then regulate their labour in accordance with their own real needs.

There is much talk about supply and demand, but the supply and demand usually meant is an artificial one; it is under the sway of the gambling market; the demand is forced, as I hinted above, before it is supplied; nor, as each producer is working against all the rest, can the producers hold their hands, till the market is glutted and the workers, thrown out on the streets, hear that there has been over-production, amidst which over-plus of unsaleable goods they go ill-supplied with even necessaries, because the wealth which they themselves have created is 'ill-distributed' as we call it—that is, unjustly taken away from them. . . . Well, now, what Socialism offers you in the place of these artificial famines, with their so-called over-production, is, once more, regulation of the markets; supply and demand commensurate; no gambling and consequently (once more) no waste; not overwork and weariness for the worker one month and the next no work and terror of starvation, but steady work and plenty of leisure every month.

William Morris, *How We Live and how We Might Live*, 1888

THE MEANING OF INHERITANCE

Inheritance means that one man may be given for nothing the legal right to command for a lifetime (and even after) the services of a group of his fellow men. An inherited income, in effect, gives a man the right to invoke the whole legal and armed forces of the State in order to compel a certain number of his fellow citizens to work in perpetuity to satisfy his needs and desires. It means neither more nor less than this. For when a man of property dies a certain proportion of the national income is, so to speak, going begging. Somebody has to get it, and it must be decided who. The possibilities are either to devote it to the service of the needs of the community as a whole, or to a particularly necessitous or deserving section of it, or to a certain favoured individual or individuals. The choice of a third method in preference to the other two is what we call inheritance.

The fact of inheritance reinforces and clinches the case against un-earned income. Inheritance gives a man an unearned income that is not even a reward for his own savings. He is not paid for saving out of income at all, but merely for not consuming his capital. And he never accumu-lated that capital, but received it as a free gift. That he should therefore receive a large income merely in return for not consuming his capital, when another man who received none has to work hard for a small income, is a plain injustice and absurdity. Suppose a man on a desert island had five sons, and left all the land to one of them. That one might live in idleness on a 'rentier' income for the rest of his life; and the rentier income would consist of the commodities produced by his four labouring brothers. The landowner would recline in his armchair and receive from his four brothers as 'rent' a piece of paper certifying that he had refrained from consuming the land; and he would hand this piece of paper back to his brothers in return for a substantial share of the annual produce of their labour. Such, when stripped of verbiage, is the institution of inherited property.

An institution like this, it may be argued, could not continue; the four labouring brothers would plainly rise up and compel their idle colleague to work or starve. Doubtless on a desert island they would. . . . If there were only one property owner and four workers, it would be easy enough for the four workers to impose their rights by force. But where there are 50,000 property owners and 50,000,000 workers, it is equally easy for the 50,000, who in any case have all the advantages of wealth, education, and power already in their hands, to defend by force what cannot be defended by reason.

Douglas Jay, The Socialist Case, 1937

KNOWING THE RIGHT PEOPLE

The concentration of wealth in a few hands means the concession to a few of enormous advantages of education and influence. All men do not start equal in looking for a job. It is, of course, true that a working man of extraordinary force and ability can rise in modern England or America to almost any position; and dukes have been found unable to secure admission to universities. But the fact remains that a man of anything but superlative ability cannot, if he starts as a miner, rise to be the chairman of an industrial combine; while the expensively educated public-school boy, though also of only normal ability, is quite capable of *holding* the company directorship which he has obtained by influence. The man of average ability in any walk of life, bus conductor or bank chairman, can *hold* his position when it is once gained. Brief familiarity with the average bus conductor will show that he would be quite capable of holding a banking directorship if his father had given it him; and the perusal of some of our company chairman's speeches will also show that if they had started as bus conductors they would certainly be there still. It would be absurd to suggest that there are no men of superior ability among company directors or doctors or lawyers. But it remains true nevertheless that it requires a man of exceptional ability to rise from the place where he started, and one of exceptional stupidity to fall below it.

Douglas Jay, The Socialist Case, 1937

THE NEED AND THE REMEDY

(*Fabian Essays in Socialism*, edited by Bernard Shaw and first published in 1889, had an effect as striking among the educated classes as
Merrie England among working people. The charge that Socialists
were merely impractical idealists or malicious traitors could clearly not
be sustained against these learned and brilliant authors, whose arguments have in fact never been answered.)

The unrestrained power of capitalism very speedily reduced a large part
of England to a deplorable condition. . . . There was not a savage in the
islands of the Pacific who was not better fed, happier, healthier and more
contented than the majority of the workers in the industrial parts of
England. . . . Medical inspectors reported the rapid spread of malforma-
tion of the bones, curvature of the spines, heart diseases, rupture, stunted
growth, asthma, and premature old age among children and young persons; the said children and young persons being worked by manufacturers without any kind of restraint. Manufacturing profits in Lancashire
were being at the same time reckoned at hundreds and even thousands
per cent. . . . Women and young children of six years old drew coal along
the passages of the mines, crawling on all fours with a girdle passing round
their waists, harnessed by a chain between their legs to the cart. A sub-
commissioner in Scotland reported that he 'found a little girl, six years
of age, carrying half a cwt; and making regularly fourteen long journeys a
day. The height ascended and the distance along the road exceeded in
each journey the height of St Paul's Cathedral.' . . . Such was a large part
of industrial England under the unrestrained rule of the capitalist. . . .

It was evident that capitalist monopoly must be restrained, reluctant as
English statesmen brought up under the commercial system were to interfere. . . . The first piece of labour legislation was the Morals and Health
Act of 1802, which interfered with the accommodation provided to children by the employers. The Cotton Mills Act was passed in 1819 partly
owing to the exertions of Robert Owen. It limited the age at which
children might work in factories; and it limited the time of their labour to
seventy-two hours per week. . . .

This brief and imperfect survey of the legislation which has destroyed
the regime of *laisser faire* is sufficient for my purpose to prove: (1) That
with private property in the necessary instruments of production, individual liberty . . . must be more and more restricted, i.e. that in our existing economic condition individualism is impossible and absurd. (2) That
even hostile or indifferent politicians have been compelled to recognise
this. (3) That unrestrained capitalism tends as surely to cruelty and op-

pression as did feudalism or chattel slavery. (4) That the remedy has been, as a matter of fact, of a Socialistic character, involving collective checking of individual greed and the paring of slices off the profits of capital in the interests of the working community. These four propositions can scarcely be contested. . . .

The fact that the modern capitalist may be not only useless but positively obstructive was well illustrated at a meeting of the shareholders of the London and South Western Railway on 7th February last. Three shareholders urged a reduction in third-class fares. The chairman pointed out the obvious fact that such a reduction would probably lower the dividend, and asked the meeting if that was what they wished. He was, of course, answered by a chorus of 'No, no!' and all talk of reduction of fares is at an end. Here is a plain sample . . . of the evident interests of the public being sacrificed to those of the capitalist.

That joint-stock capitalism is extending rapidly everyone knows. In the United States, according to Mr Bryce, the wealth of joint-stock corporations is estimated at one-fourth of the total value of all property. In England every kind of business, from breweries, banks and cotton mills, is falling into the hands of the joint-stock capitalist and must continue to do so. Twenty years ago who would have supposed that a brewery like that of Guinness or such a banking firm as Glyn, Mills and Co. would become a joint-stock company? Yet we know it is so today. Capitalism is becoming impersonal and cosmopolitan. And the combinations controlling production become larger and fewer. Barings are getting hold of the South African diamond fields; a few companies control the whole anthracite coal produce of Pennsylvania. Each one of us is quite 'free' to 'compete' with these gigantic combinations, as the Principality of Monaco is 'free' to go to war with France should the latter threaten her interests. The mere forms of freedom remain; but monopoly renders them nugatory. The modern State, having parted with the raw material of the globe, cannot secure freedom of competition to its citizens; and yet it was on the basis of free competition that capitalism rose. Thus we see that capitalism has cancelled its original principle—is itself negating its own existence. . . .

The individualist devotees of *laisser faire* used to teach us that when restrictions were removed, free competition would settle everything. Prices would go down, and fill the 'consumer' with joy unspeakable; the fittest would survive; and as for the rest—it was not very clear what would become of them, and it really didn't matter. . . . Where is 'free competition' now? Almost the only persons still competing freely are the small shopkeepers, trembling on the verge of insolvency, and the working men, competing with one another for permission to live by work. Combination is absorbing commerce. . . . A steel rail combination was some years ago formed among previously competing firms in America. This combination discovered that too many rails were being made and that prices were being cut. Accordingly, one of the mills in the combination—the Vulcan mill of St Louis—was closed and stood smokeless for years; its owners meanwhile receiving a subsidy of 400,000 dollars a year from the other mills in the combination for *not* making rails. This is how the owners of the Vulcan mill earned their 'wages of superintendence'. It is needless to add that no payment was made to the men for *not* working: they were thrown on the streets to meditate on the right to 'liberty and the pursuit of happiness', secured to them by the Declaration of Independence.

Or, again, take the case of the anthracite coal lands of Pennsylvania, occupying an area of some 270,000 acres, and held by the Reading Coal and Iron Company, the Leigh Valley Railroad, the Delaware and Hudson Railroad . . . and smaller firms and corporations tributary to these. The rich owners, popularly known as the 'coal barons', agree to fix absolutely the wholesale price of coal, always securing an immense rise just before the winter sets in. There is no such thing known or possible as free trade or open competition in the anthracite coal produce of America. . . .

The individualist who supposes that Free Trade plus private property will solve all economic problems is naturally surprised at these 'rings' which upset all his crude economic notions; and he very logically asks for legislation to prevent the natural and inevitable result of the premises with which he starts. It is amusing to note that those who advocate what they call self-reliance and self-help are the first to call on the State to interfere with the natural results of that self-help, of that private enterprise, when it has overstepped a purely arbitrary limit. Why, on ordinary commercial principles, should not a copper syndicate grasp all the copper in the world? It is merely the fittest surviving. The whole case against Socialism is assumed by its most intelligent opponents to lie in that Darwinian theory. And yet when the copper syndicate or the 'coal barons' survive, they rouse against themselves the fiercest and, from the commercial point of view, the most unreasonable antagonism. As sin when it is finished is said to bring forth death, so capitalism when it is finished brings forth monopoly. And one might as well quarrel with that plain fact as blame thorns because they do not produce grapes, or thistles because they are barren of figs. . . .

As regards the great combinations of capital, State action may take one of three courses. It may prohibit and dissolve them; it may tax and control them; or it may absorb and administer them. In either case the Socialist theory is *ipso facto* admitted; for each is a confession that it is well to exercise a collective control over industrial capital. . . . If the powers of acquisition . . . are to be restricted, what becomes of the 'incentive to industry', the 'reward of abstinence' and all the rest of the worn-out phrases which have so often done duty in the place of argument? . . .

And now, finally, what is the immediate policy for rational students of economics and genuine social reformers to adopt? . . . To all quack proposals they must offer a steady resistance. These proposals will take the form of attempts to bring back some economic condition out of which society has emerged. One quack will desire to revive the old British yeomanry; another will talk nonsense about 'Fair Trade'; a third will offer to the rustic 'three acres and a cow'; while a fourth will see salvation in getting rid of primogeniture . . . and 'planting' prosperous labourers on the soil—as though the labourers grow like trees. . . . Instead, therefore, of attempting to undo the work which the capitalists are unconsciously doing for the people, the real reformer will rather prepare the people, educated and organised as a true industrial democracy, to take up the threads when they fall from the weak hands of a useless possessing class.

William Clarke, *Fabian Essays in Socialism*, 1889

9. What is Socialism?—The Moral Answer

All decent men are nine-tenths Socialists to begin with, whether they know it, or not.'

Bernard Shaw

CAPITALISM BREEDS SELFISHNESS

. . . COMMERCIALISM tends to destroy the true and strengthen the false that is in us. For this reason it stands condemned. Socialism would reverse this order of things by taking away the incentives to selfishness and teaching each to find the highest good in ministering to the welfare of his neighbour. This is only possible when land and capital have ceased to be private property used to enrich its possessors—the few— and beggar and degrade all others—the many. For this reason the economic side of the question must be kept well to the front as a means to an end—with independent political action as one of the chief methods . . . of realising the means.

Here we have the philosophy underlying and inspiring the work of the I.L.P. It is a new Holy Crusade.

Keir Hardie, 1898

. . . CLASS WAR

Socialism, it cannot be too often repeated, has nothing whatever to do with class antagonism. The present system necessarily involves such class war, a fact which finds embodiment in Trade Unionism. But the object of Socialism is to abolish all such artificial class distinctions as our present method of wealth, production and ownership bring in its train. In the Socialist movement are landlords and capitalists, and the number, fortunately, is growing. These men accept Socialism for what it is, a great and ennobling principle. Under its operation they would lose their land and capital, but they would gain a sense of fellowship with the race which would make life a joy, and give it a fulness and depth at present unknown. Their gain, therefore, would be infinite, their loss infinitesimal. Private ownership of land and capital cannot be defended, since it leads to strife and discord where there should be fraternal unity, introduces poverty in the midst of plenty, and enslaves alike the worker and the wealth-possessor. Poverty enslaves the one and property the other, and Socialism will bring freedom to both.

Keir Hardie, 1901

WE MIDDLE-CLASS SOCIALISTS . . .

Let me give you a direct example of the slavery to competitive Commerce, in which we hapless folk of the middle-classes live. . . . I have long thought that one of the most revolting circumstances that cling to our present class-system, is the relation between us, of the well-to-do, and our domestic servants; we and our servants live together under one roof, but are little better than strangers to each other, in spite of the good nature and good feeling that often exists on both sides; nay strangers is a mild word; though we are of the same blood, bound by the same laws, we live together like people of different tribes. . . . Surely we of this educational century cannot be ignorant of what an education it would be for the less refined members of a household to meet on common easy terms the more refined once a day, at least; to note the elegant manners of well-bred ladies, to give and take in talk with learned and travelled men, with men of action and imagination; believe me that would beat elementary education.

. . . Note, as a token of this stupidity of our sham civilisation, what foolish rabbit warrens our well-to-do houses are obliged to be. . . . No wonder our houses are cramped and ignoble when the lives lived in them are cramped and ignoble also. . . .

Can we put luxury from us and live simple and decent lives? Yes, when we are free from the slavery of Capitalist-Commerce, but not before.

. . . At first sight, indeed, it would seem impossible to make men born under the present system of Commerce understand that labour may be a blessing to them; not in the sense in which the phrase is sometimes preached to them by those whose labour is light and easily evaded; not as a necessary task laid by nature on the poor for the benefit of the rich; not as an opiate to dull their sense of right and wrong, to make them sit down quietly under their burdens to the end of time, blessing the squire and his relations. . . . But the true doctrine that labour should be a real tangible blessing in itself to the working man, a pleasure even as sleep and strong drink are to him now; this one might think it hard indeed for him to understand, so different as it is to anything which he has found labour to be.

William Morris, Art and Socialism, 1884

H

WHAT WILLIAM MORRIS CLAIMED

What is it that I need, therefore, which my surrounding circumstances can give me—my dealings with my fellow men—setting aside inevitable accidents which co-operation and forethought cannot control, if there be such?

Well, first of all I claim good health . . . and I believe this claim for a healthy body for all of us carries with it all other due claims . . . for the poor suffer always from one disease—hunger; and at least I know this, that if a man is overworked in any degree he cannot enjoy the sort of health I am speaking of; nor can he if he is continually chained to one dull round of mechanical work, with no hope at the other end of it; nor if he lives in continual sordid anxiety for his livelihood, nor if he is ill-housed, nor if he is deprived of all enjoyment of the natural beauty of the world, nor if he has no amusement to quicken the flow of his spirits from time to time; all these things, which touch more or less directly on his bodily condition, are born of the claim I make to live in good health. . . .

Now the next thing I claim is liberal education: opportunity, that is, to have my share of whatever knowledge there is in the world according to my capacity or bent of mind, historical or scientific; and also to have my share of skill of hand which is about in the world, either in the indus-trial handicrafts or in the fine arts. . . . But also I know that this claim for education involves one for public advantages in the shape of public libraries, schools and the like . . . but these I claim very confidently, being sure that no reasonable community could bear to be without such helps to a decent life.

In order that my leisure might not degenerate into idleness and aimless-ness, I must set up a claim for due work to do. Nothing to my mind is more important than this demand. . . .

My last claim is that the material surroundings of my life should be pleasant, generous, and beautiful; that I know is a large claim, but this I will say about it, that if it cannot be satisfied, if every civilised community cannot provide such surroundings for all its members, I do not want the world to go on; it is a mere misery that man has ever existed . . . I feel sure that the time will come when people will find it difficult to believe that a rich community such as ours, having such command over external Nature, could have submitted to live such a mean, shabby, dirty life as we do.

And once for all, there is nothing in our circumstances save the hunting of profit that drives us into it. It is profit which draws men into enormous unmanageable aggregations called towns, for instance; profit which crowds them up when they are there into quarters without gardens or open spaces; profit which won't take the most ordinary precautions against wrapping a whole district in a cloud of sulphurous smoke; which turns beautiful rivers into filthy sewers; which condemns all but the rich to live in houses idiotically cramped and confined at the best, and at the worst in houses for whose wretchedness there is no name.

I say it is almost incredible that we should bear such crass stupidity as this; nor should we if we could help it. We shall not bear it when the workers get out of their heads that they are but an appendage to profit grinding, that the more profits that are made the more employment at high wages there will be for them, and that therefore all the incredible filth, disorder, and degradation of modern civilisation are signs of their prosperity. So far from that, they are signs of their slavery. When they are no longer slaves they will claim as a matter of course that every man and every family should be generously lodged; that every child should be able to play in a garden close to the place his parents live in; that the houses should by their obvious decency and order be ornaments to Nature, not disfigurements of it; for the decency and order above-mentioned when carried to the due pitch would most assuredly lead to beauty in building. All this, of course, would mean the people, that is, all society, duly organised, having in its own hands the means of production, to be *owned* by no individual, but used by all as occasion called for its use, and can only be done on those terms; on any other terms people will be driven to accumulate private wealth for themselves, and thus, as we have seen, to waste the goods of the community and perpetuate the division into classes, which means continual war and waste. . . .

William Morris, *How We Live and how We Might Live*, 1888

HAVING IT BOTH WAYS

We have just enough Socialism to protect the strong and give them power to oppress the weak. If a workman steals five shillings from the pocket of his employer, he gets sixty days in jail; if an employer steals a thousand pounds a year from the wages of his workers, he is made an elder in the kirk, . . . and invited to deliver lectures against Socialism. If a pirate attacks a merchant ship and carries off the merchandise, the power of the British Navy is at once employed to catch the depredator, and hang him up at the yard arm; if the merchant gets his goods to land, and cheats his customers by selling them at fifty per cent above their true value, we point to him as an example of a successful business man. If a wealthy man puts a thousand pounds into the purchase of a piece of land, the whole civil and military power of the State is at his disposal in helping him to compel his tenants to pay rent so as to give him a return for his money; if an agricultural labourer has put fifty years of his life into the cultivation of that same piece of land, making it yield of its increase sufficient to provide for the requirements of ten men like himself, he may have lived on meal and water all the time, and in the end be turned out to die like a dog in a ditch, and there is no law to interfere on his behalf. We State Socialists protest against all this. We say it is not the strong who need protection. We ask for such legislation as will protect the worker in the full enjoyment of the whole of the wealth produced by him. . . . We don't believe it possible to reconcile the antagonistic interests of the capitalist and the worker.

Keir Hardie, 1889

KNOWLEDGE IS OUR RIGHT

I have not come here as a suppliant. . . . I refuse to sit down at the rich man's door and beg for crusts. . . . I demand for my class all the advantages that Oxford has it in her power to offer, and I claim it as a right of which we have been unjustly deprived—unjustly for us and for Oxford too. . . . For, remember, democracy will be achieved with or without the assistance of Oxford; but if the university of Oxford continues to hold herself aloof from the working classes, then we shall end by thinking of her, not for what she is but for what she has been. . . . In point of fact workmen's sons come to Oxford to escape their class, not to relieve it. . . . We want her in future to inspire them, not with the desire of succeeding, but with that of serving society—we have need of you. But you have need of us.

J. R. MacTavish, a Scottish workman from the Clyde dockyards, at a Workers' Educational Association meeting in Oxford, 1907, in the presence of the President of the Board of Education

SELFISHNESS CORRUPTS . . .

Shortsighted is the philosophy which counts on selfishness as the master motive of human action . . . it is not selfishness that enriches the annals of every people with heroes and saints . . . Call it religion, patriotism, sympathy, the enthusiasm for humanity, or the love of God—give it what name you will; there is yet a force which overcomes and drives out selfishness; a force which is the electricity of the moral universe; a force beside which all others are weak. Everywhere that men have lived it has shown its power, and today, as ever, the world is full of it. To be pitied is the man who has never seen and felt it. And this force of forces that now goes to waste we may use for the strengthening and building up and ennobling of society, just as we now use physical forces that once seemed but powers of destruction. All we have to do is but to give it freedom and scope. The wrong that produces inequality; the wrong that in the midst of abundance tortures men with want or harries them with the fear of want; that stunts them physically, degrades them intellectually, and distorts them morally, is what alone prevents harmonious social development.

There are people into whose heads it never enters to conceive of any better state of society than that which now exists—who imagine that the idea that there could be a state of society in which greed would be banished, prisons stand empty, individual interests be subordinated to general interests, and no one seek to rob or oppress his neighbour, is but the dream of impracticable dreamers, for whom these practical level-headed men, who pride themselves on recognising facts as they are, have a hearty contempt. But such men, though some of them write books, and some of them occupy the chairs of universities, and some of them stand in pulpits—do not think.

If they were accustomed to dine in such eating houses as are to be found in the lower quarters of London and Paris, where the knives and forks are chained to the table, they would deem it the ineradicable disposition of men to carry off the knife and fork with which he has eaten.

Take a company of well bred men and women dining together. There is no struggling for food, no attempt on the part of any one to get more than his neighbour; no attempt to gorge or to carry off. On the contrary each one is anxious to help his neighbour before he partakes himself; to offer to others the best rather than pick it out for himself; and should any one show the slightest disposition to prefer the gratification of his own appetite to that of the others, or in any way to act the pig or pilferer, the swift and heavy penalty of social contempt and ostracism would show how such conduct is reprobated by common opinion.

All this is so common as to excite no remark, as to seem the natural state of things. Yet it is no more natural that men should not be greedy of food than that they should not be greedy of wealth. They are greedy of food when they are not assured that there will be a fair and equitable distribution which will give each enough. But when these conditions are assured, they cease to be greedy of food. And so in society, as at present constituted, men are greedy of wealth because the conditions of distribution are so unjust that instead of each being sure of enough, many are certain to be condemned to want. It is the 'devil catch the hindmost' of present social adjustments that causes the races and scramble for wealth, in which all considerations of justice, mercy, religion and sentiment are trampled under foot; in which men forget their own souls, and struggle to the very verge of the grave for what they cannot take beyond. But an equitable distribution of wealth, that would exempt all from the fear of want, would destroy the greed of wealth, just as in polite society the greed of food has been destroyed. Consider this existing fact of a cultivated and refined society, in which all the coarser passions are held in check not by force, not by law, but by common opinion and the mutual desire of pleasing. If this is possible for part of a community, it is possible for a whole community.

Henry George, Progress and Poverty, 1879

FELLOWSHIP

(The following is the closing passage of the Chairman's Address to the Labour Party Annual Conference of 26 June 1923.)

Let me remind you that there is a higher need even than government, whether it be the government of our tempers or the government of our tongues. It is not upon its plans or its programmes—not even upon its principles or its ideals—that a parliamentary party is ultimately judged. ... The success of the Labour Party in this country depends, more than on anything else, upon the spirit in which we hold our faith, the spirit in which we present our proposals, the spirit in which we meet our opponents in debate, the spirit in which we fulfil our obligations, the spirit in which, with inevitable backslidings, we live our own lives. We shall not achieve much, whatever changes we can bring about, unless what we do, is done in the spirit of fellowship. For we must always remember that the Founder of British Socialism was not Karl Marx but Robert Owen, and that Robert Owen preached not 'class war', but the ancient doctrine of human brotherhood—the hope, the faith, the living fact of human fellowship—a faith and a hope reaffirmed in the words of that other great British Socialist—William Morris—in *The Dream of John Ball*. 'Forsooth, brothers, fellowship is life and lack of fellowship is death; and the deeds that ye do upon the earth, it is for fellowship's sake that ye do them; and the life that is in it, that shall live on and on for ever and each one of you part of it, while many a man's life upon the earth from the earth shall wane.'

Sidney Webb, The Labour Party on the Threshold, 1923

OUR DEBT TO THE PAST

Here, [1892] I bring these disjointed recollections to a close, for to me the entrance of the first two Socialists into Parliament was the first faint signal of the dawn of a new era. Henceforward it was clear that given energy, will and perseverance all things were possible to the organised workers.

But before writing my final sentence I desire to pay a personal tribute to the unknown men and women, the rank and file of those early days, who gallantly played their parts in preparing the way for the great movement, which now counts its adherents by the million. Recognition is due to those who formed the tiny nuclei at the open-air meetings, held the flag around which the audiences gathered, sold literature, made the modest collections, and cheerfully performed the arduous task of electioneering. They never spoke of burdens or self sacrifice; to them work for the movement was a means of self-expression. In spite of quarrels, bitterness, weakness, personal failings—we were very human—and inadequacy of many kinds, their faces were towards the light, and they produced examples of courage in disheartening surroundings, unselfishness and loyalty to a cause, without achieving or expecting material reward, which gave us something infinitely precious: a firm faith in the abundant capacity of human nature to act from idealistic motives. To them, and the movement they helped to build, I owe a fourth gain: the discovery of a meaning and a purpose in the tangled medley of events we call life.

W. S. Sanders, *Early Socialist Days*, 1927

10. What's wrong with Socialism?

Nothing is so terrifying to the Socialist today as the folly of his opponents.
Bernard Shaw

A LETTER TO JOHN SMITH

DEAR MR SMITH, I am sorry to hear that you look upon Socialism as a vile and senseless thing, and upon Socialists as wicked or foolish men. Nevertheless, as you have good metal in you, and are very numerous, I mean to argue the point with you.

You are a staunch Liberal, and you pride yourself upon being a 'shrewd hard-headed, practical man'. You would not pride yourself upon that, for you are naturally over modest, had you not been told by political orators that you are that kind of man. . . .

Now, Mr Smith, if you really are a man of hard, shrewd sense, we shall get on very well. I am myself a plain, practical man. I base my beliefs upon what I know and see. . . .

In these letters I shall stick to the hardest of hard facts, and the coldest of cold reason; and I shall appeal to that robust common sense and English love of fair play for which, I understand, you are more famous than for your ability to see beyond the end of your free and independent nose at election times.

I assume, Mr Smith, that you, as a hard-headed, practical man, would rather be well off than badly off, and that, with regard to your own earnings, you would rather be paid twenty shillings in the pound than four shillings in the pound.

And I assume that as a humane man, you would rather that others should not suffer, if their suffering can be prevented.

If then, I assert that you are being defrauded, and that others, especially weak women and young children, are enduring much misery and wrong, and if I assert, farther, that I know a means whereby you may obtain justice, and they may secure peace, you will surely, as a kind and sensible man, consent to hear me.

If your roof were leaky, or your business bad, if there were a plague in your city, and all regular remedies had failed, you would certainly give a hearing to any creditable person who claimed to have found a cure.

I don't mean that you would accept his remedy without thinking about it; that would be foolish, but you would let him explain it, and if it seemed reasonable you would try it.

To reject an idea because it is new is not a proof of shrewd sense, it is a proof of bigoted ignorance. Trade unionism was new once, and was denounced by the very same people who now denounce the views I advocate. There were many prominent politicians and writers who declared the railway train and the telegraph to be impossible. There were many who condemned the Factory Acts. There were many who laughed at the idea of an Atlantic cable, and I remember when it was prophesied of the ballot that it would lead to anarchy and revolution.

To say that an idea is new is not to prove that it is untrue. The oldest idea was new once; and some of my ideas, as, for instance, the idea that justice and health are precious things—are considerably older than the House of Commons. . . .

I ask you, then, as a practical man, to forget me, and to consider my arguments on their merits.

But I must also ask you to forget yourself. . . . That means that when a problem is before you you should not let any personal prejudice or class feeling, come between that problem and your mind—that you should consider a case upon the evidence alone, as a jury should.

Forget, then, that you are a joiner or a spinner, a Catholic or a Freethinker, a Liberal or a Tory, a moderate drinker or a teetotaller and consider the problem as a *man*.

Robert Blatchford, *Merrie England,* 1895

IT'S ONLY HUMAN NATURE!

We will now proceed to consider some of the stock arguments against Socialism.

Non-Socialists are in the habit of saying that Socialism demands a complete change in human nature. They say Socialism is very pretty in theory, but that it is wrong because human nature is not good enough for Socialism. They tell us that we Socialists are mistaken because we have built up a scheme without first considering human nature. They are entirely mistaken.

The fact is that we Socialists have studied human nature, and that our opponents only object to Socialism because they do not understand human nature at all.

'Socialism', say these critics, 'is impossible because it would destroy the incentive of gain.' . . .

Now, the political economy of our opponents is built upon a false conception of human nature. In the first place, it recognises only one motive, which is sheer folly. In the second place, it assumes that the strongest motive is avarice, which is untrue. . . .

The last refuge of Gradgrind, when he is beaten by Socialistic argument, is the assertion that human nature is incapable of good. But this is not true. Men instinctively prefer light to darkness, love to hate, and good to evil.

The most selfish man would not see a fellow creature die or suffer if he could save him without personal cost or risk. . . .

Major Burke, of the Wild West, told me one day that on the prairies the cowboys went about finger on trigger, ever on the qui vive for an ambush. If a leaf stirred they fired, if a twig snapped they fired; and in about five cases out of a hundred they shot an Indian.

This is the state in which men live under a competitive commercial system. It is war. The hand of every man is against every man's hand. Men move finger on trigger, and fire at the falling of a leaf. But in a Socialistic state of society they would no more go armed and in fear of their fellow creatures, than did the Wild West cowboys in London.

Robert Blatchford, *Merrie England*, 1895

THE NEED FOR COMPETITION

Of all the many senseless and brutal theories which practical men support, the most fatuous and bestial is the theory of competition.

I use the word advisedly. You practical men are fond of scoffing at all humane systems of thought or government as mere 'theories'. It is one of the vainest of your vanities to believe that you have no theories at all.

Why, John, you practical men have as many theories as any Socialist. But the distinctive marks of all your theories are their falsity, their folly, and their utter impracticability.

For instance, your practical man swears by political economy. But it is by the political economy of the older writers. It is the science of the men who were only blundering over the construction of a rude and untried *theory*. The later and wiser political economy you practical men either do not know or will not accept. You resemble a railway director who should insist upon having his locomotives made to the exact pattern of Stephenson's 'Rocket'. Your economy isn't up to date, John. You cannot grasp a new idea—you are so practical.

One of the laws of your practical school is the law that 'Society flourishes by the antagonism of its individuals'.

That is the theory of competition. It means that war is better than peace, that a nation where every man tries to get the better of his neighbour will be happier and wealthier, more prosperous and more enlightened than a nation where every man tries to help his neighbour. . . .

Suppose two men had to get a cart up a hill. Would they get it up sooner if one tried to push it up whilst the other tried to push it down; or if both men tried to pull it up? . . .

Suppose a captain had to bring a ship from New York to Liverpool. Would he allow half a dozen men to fight for the post of helmsman or the whole crew to scramble for the job of setting sail?

No, he would set his crew in order, and send each man to his proper post.

When there is a fire panic in a theatre, how do people lose their lives? Is it not by all scrambling and fighting to get through the narrow doors? And the result of such a scramble. Is it not the blocking of the exit? But you must know very well that if the people kept cool, and went out quickly, and in an orderly way, they would all escape.

John, if a hundred men had a hundred loaves of bread, and if they piled them in a heap and fought for them, so that some got more than they could eat, and some got none, and some were trampled to death in the brutal scuffle, *that* would be competition. Were it not for competition the hundred men would all be fed.

That, John, is the theory of competition. What do you think of it?

And now let us be practical. You have fallen into the stupid error of supposing that competition is better than co-operation, partly because you have never seen anything but competition in practice, and partly because you have not very clear sight, nor very clear brains.

You know that when a railway company, or a salt company, or a coal company, has a monopoly the public gets worse served than when there are several companies in competition with each other.

And you suppose that because competition beats monopoly therefore competition is better than co-operation.

But if you were not rather slow, John, you might have noticed that co-operation and monopoly are not the same things. Co-operation is the mutual helpfulness of all; monopoly is the plundering of the many by the few.

Give one man a monopoly of the coal mines and coals would go up in price; but miners' wages would not.

But there is a great difference between making the collieries the property of one man, and making them the property of the whole people.

Now the Socialists propose to make them the property of the whole people. And they say that if that were done the price of coals would be the natural price. That is to say, it would be the price of the proper keep of the colliers.

Or, for you'll possibly understand this better, being a practical man, they say that the State could work the coal mines better and more cheaply —with less waste of labour—than could a private firm, or a number of firms in competition.

This is because a great deal of the time and energy of the private firms under competition is spent, not in the production and distributing of coals, but in the effort to undersell and overreach each other. . . .

Robert Blatchford, *Merrie England*, 1895

THE SURVIVAL OF THE FITTEST

One of the favourite arguments of the Gradgrinds in support of competition is the theory of the Survival of the Fittest.

They say that those who fail, fail because they are not fitted to succeed. They say that those who succeed, succeed because they are 'fit'. They say it is the law of nature that the weakest shall go to the wall, and to the wall with them—and no quarter.

The slumites live in the slums because they are unfit to live anywhere else. The Duke of Marlborough lives in a palace because the intellectual and moral superiority of such a man naturally forced him into a palace. . . .

But let me give you my own explanation of the law as to the survival of the fittest. Of two plants or animals, that one will survive which is fittest to endure the conditions in which both exist. The question of which man shall survive depends upon the conditions under which the men shall struggle for survival. . . .

In a nation of marauders, then, who live by spoliation and the sword, the fittest to survive would be a different type of man from him who gets first place in a nation of traders, where fierceness and strength of arm are less called for than tenacity and clearness of head.

It thus appears that when we say our poor are poor because they are not fitted to gain wealth, we mean that they are not 'fit' to gain wealth under the conditions of life now existing. But under different conditions of life they might succeed.

If then the present conditions of life in England are right, the poor are wrong; but if the present conditions of life are not right, the poor are *wronged*.

So much for the Survival of the fittest. So much for *Laissez Faire*.

The man who accepts *laissez faire* doctrine would allow his garden to run wild, so that the roses might fight it out with the weeds, and the fittest might survive.

Robert Blatchford, *Merrie England*, 1895

'HORDES OF OFFICIALS'

Another stock argument against Socialism is the assertion that it would destroy all intellectual progress. Here is a quotation from an article by the late Charles Bradlaugh:

'I object to Socialism because it would destroy the incentives which have produced amongst other things, the "clever" men who serve society in various fashions, as doctors, engineers, architects and teachers. I am inclined to doubt whether, if the enormous army of Socialist officials were rewarded at the like rate with the scavenger and the ploughman, the temptation on them might not be very great to help themselves to extra remuneration from the national stores.'

The first sentence in this passage displays a singular misconception of human nature; the second a grotesque misconception of Socialism.

We will dispose of the second sentence first. You will observe that Mr Bradlaugh spoke of the 'enormous army of Socialist officials'. He seems to have supposed, as so many suppose, that under Socialism we should be over-run with officials. . . . Now the fact is that under Socialism there would be as few officials, and as many workers as possible. I don't think you will find the officials in the Post Office more numerous than in any ordinary business house. But the surprising part of it is that a really shrewd man like Mr Bradlaugh should have failed to notice the enormous number of officials, the useless officials, too, who burden every department of trade under competition.

For what are all the clerks, travellers, agents, canvassers, salesmen, managers, capitalists, and other costly and needless people but an 'enormous army' of officials? Just glance back at the chapter on Competition, and then consider whether Socialism however badly managed, could possibly add to the number of overpaid and unnecessary non-producers.

Then Mr Bradlaugh was terribly shocked by the idea that a doctor should be paid at the same rate as a scavenger. This is chiefly due to two misconceptions of Mr Bradlaugh's. First of all, he had been so used to the recognised money standard of honour that he didn't seem able to realise that a man might, under Socialism, be honoured more for what he *was*, or for what he *did*, than for what he *got*. Secondly, he was so used to seeing such men as scavengers overworked, underpaid and generally despised that it did not occur to him as possible that under Socialism every worker would be treated justly and respected as a man.

. . . Mr Morley [a leading Liberal critic of Socialism] is convinced that if existence were no longer a sordid struggle for money the genius of the people would die out, and we should sink into barbarism and retain nothing but the bare necessaries of life. . . . Now, John, out of their own mouths shall these men be condemned.

Have you ever read any of the speeches and articles on the Payment of Members of Parliament? You have. What is the stock argument used against the payment of members?

It is the argument that to pay members would be to lower the tone and impair the quality of the House of Commons. It is the argument that *men of talent will serve the nation better for honour than for money*.

I think that here I have them on the hip. This argument is used by the same men who tell us that Socialism would degrade the nation by abolishing the incentive of gain.[1] . . .

They tell you one day that unless you pay clever men big wages they will cease to work.

They tell you another day that if you pay clever men at all, they will cease to work. . . .

The true artist: He to whom all creative work is due is mainly inspired, sustained and rewarded by a love of his art. He will take money, for he must live. He will take money, for money is the badge of victory. But with or without money, and with or without praise, he will worship the beloved mistress, art. . . .

Does Mr Morley ever read any Blue Books? Does he know *anything* about the condition of this country? 'Of the inhabitants of Glasgow, 25 per cent live in houses of one apartment. . . . No less than 14 per cent of the one-roomed houses and 27 per cent of the two-roomed houses, contain lodgers—strange men and women, mixed up with husbands and wives and children, within the four walls of small rooms. . . . There are thousands of these houses which contain five, six and seven inmates and hundreds which are inhabited by from eight to thirteen. Of all the children who die in Glasgow before they complete their fifth year, 32 per cent die in houses of one apartment, and not 2 per cent in houses of five apartments and upwards. . . . From beginning to rapid ending, the lives of these children are short parts in a wretched tragedy. . . .'

That is official testimony, from Dr Russell's pamphlet, and Mr Morley talks about 'necessaries' of life. Do you count fresh air, health, decency and cleanliness as necessaries? If you do, what say you to the barbarism

[1] Payment of members was introduced in 1911.

of Glasgow, of Liverpool, of London and of Manchester? Come, will you tell me how Socialism is going to ruin Ancoats, or lower the moral standard of Whitechapel, or debase the ideal of Black Country life? It will be time enough for our statesmen to despise the 'necessaries of life' when they have made it possible for the people to get them.

Robert Blatchford, Merrie England, 1895

'SOCIALISM MEANS SLAVERY'

To hear people talk about slavery under Socialism, you would suppose we had freedom now. . . .

Suppose you are out of work, can you have work for the asking? No. But under Socialism you could always have work. Is *that* a proof of slavery? Suppose under Socialism you were told that you must work or starve. Would that be any more despotic treatment than the treatment you get now? Tell your present employers that you do not wish to work and see what the alternative will be. You must work or starve now. The difference between present conditions, and the conditions of Socialism, are that you now work long hours for a bare existence, whereas in a Socialistic State you would work short hours for a life of honour and comfort.

Robert Blatchford, Merrie England, 1895

'IT'S THEIR OWN FAULT'

When Socialists complain of the misery of the poor they are often told by pressmen, parsons and politicians, that all the sufferings of the poor are due to their own vices and folly. . . . This is the very reverse of the truth. The misery of the people is due to the sins, negligences and ignorances of those who rob them of their earnings, and grow rich upon their moral ruin and physical destruction. Is it true that poverty is the result of idleness, of improvidence and of vice?

If it were, then we should always find that the idle, the vicious and the improvident were poor; and that the industrious, the thrifty and the temperate were well off. But it is a fact that many idle, vicious and improvident people are rich, and it is a fact that the poorest people in the world are the most industrious, and sober and thrifty. . . .

Between the navvy wheeling interminable barrows of clay over endless miles of planks at a fixed pittance, and the struggling author or painter living on dry bread and dreams in a garret, there is this immense difference, that whereas the navvy's work is a dull, monotonous, uninteresting task, with no motive but that of winning an animal subsistence, no exercise except for the physical powers, and no hope beyond a doubtful promotion to the post of ganger, the work of the painter or the writer, howsoever poor and obscure he is, is a labour of love; a labour that is in itself a pleasure, a recreation and an education. A work that employs and trains the highest faculties; that inspires the heart and brain with the brightest hopes; that holds out to the poorest and most insignificant of its drudges at least a chance, a little promise, however remote, of the highest honours and the most magnificent rewards.

It is all very well for the business man, the parson, the author, the engineer, the member of parliament, to abuse the workman as idle, thriftless and drunken; but let us do the workman justice. Let us remember that his work is neither exciting, pleasing, ennobling, nor remunerative. Often I have heard professional men say 'Talk about the working classes! What do they know of work? They never work as hard as I do. They have not the worry and strain that mental work involves. I am a manufacturer—a doctor—a lawyer—my work is never done.' All this is true. The doctor's work or the author's is never done. But remember that he loves it so much that he would not wish it ever done. He is so wrapped up in it, so wedded to it, that if it were done, if he were obliged to take off the harness and to go to grass in the prime of life, he would actually break his heart.

It is very nice for professional men to boast of their industry and love of work. They are doing the work of their choice. But take them away from the theatre or the desk, the pulpit, or the quarter-deck, and set them to carrying bricks up a ladder, stitching clothing, or scribbling out invoices, and see how they will enjoy that, and how industrious they will be. . . .

If a man's work is irksome, brutish, cheerless, and without hope or interest, the man grows jaded and dissatisfied. Getting no hope, no variety, no joy nor excitement out of the labour of his hands and brain, he seeks for change and relaxation elsewhere. He *must* have change and rest and pleasure. . . . Have you provided them with abundance of pure and innocent recreation for their leisure and refreshment? You have not. But you grant a great many public-houses licences I notice. You set them an example on the Stock Exchange and in the counting house and on the racecourse which they *may* follow.

Robert Blatchford, *Merrie England*, 1895

'IT DESTROYS THE INDIVIDUAL'

You have heard, very likely, of the thing called Individualism. You may have read articles or heard speeches in which Socialism has been assailed as an interference with the rights of the individual. You may have wondered why among the rights of the individual no place was given to the right to live; or that the apostles of Individualism should be so strangely blind to the danger of leaving private enterprise uncurbed. But you need not wonder about these things, for Individualism is a relic of savagery and its apologists would be agitating for the return of the good old individual right of carrying a stone club and living by promiscuous robbery and murder, were they not convinced that the law of supply and demand, although a more cowardly and brutal weapon than the cannibal's club, is infinitely more deadly and effective. . . .

One Individualist, Mr Levy, in an article written by him against Socialism a few years ago, says that—

'The Individualist denies to A and B the right of prescribing for C what will do him good, and forcing it down his throat by the aid of the policeman's truncheon. He denies that A and B have any right whatever to coerce C, *except to prevent him invading the rights of others, and to exact from him his share in the maintenance of the common liberties.*'

The italics are mine. On this point we are agreed. Our difference is as to what constitutes an 'Invasion of the rights of others'. I say, why punish the kind of thief we call a burglar, and not the kind of thief we call a sweater? Why hang the murderer who kills in the heat of passion and from motives of jealousy or revenge, and not the murderer who slays wholesale by the death-trap of the slums, and slays in cold blood, and from the bestial motive of gain? . . .

Now I think Individualism strengthens the hands of the rogue in his fight with the true man; and I think Socialism would fortify the true men against the rascals. I grant you that State Socialism would imply some interference with the liberty of the individual. But *which* individual? The scoundrel. Imagine a dozen men at sea in a boat with only two days' provisions. Would it be wise to consider the liberty of the individual? If the strongest man took all the food and left the others to starve would it be right or wrong for the eleven men to combine to bind him and divide all fairly? To let the strong or the cunning rob the weak or honest is Individualism. To prevent the rascal from taking what is not his own is Socialism.

Robert Blatchford, Merrie England, 1895

'THE RICH MAKE WORK FOR THE POOR'

From pressmen, writing for large daily papers, I quote three statements, all false and all foolish.

The first is that 'the luxury of the rich finds useful employment for the poor'.

The second that 'the expenditure of the rich confers upon the poor the two great blessings of work and wages'.

The third that 'a rich man cannot spend his money without finding employment for vast numbers of people who without him must starve'.

These statements, you will see, all amount to the same thing. The intelligent pressmen who uttered them, supposed that the rich man spent his own money, whereas he really spends the money of other people; that he found useful work for a number of men, whereas it is impossible to find useful work in making useless things; and that the men employed by the rich must starve were it not for his help, whereas if it were not for his hindrance they would all be doing useful instead of useless work.

All the things made or used by man may be divided into two classes, under the heads of necessaries and luxuries.

I should include under the head of necessaries all those things which are necessary to the highest form of human life.

All those things which are not necessary to the highest form of human life I should call luxuries, or superfluities.

For instance, I should call food, clothing, houses, fuel, books, pictures, and musical instruments necessaries; and I should call diamond ear-rings, race-horses, and broughams luxuries.

Now, it is evident that all those things, whether luxuries or necessaries, are made by labour. Diamond rings, loaves of bread, grand pianos and flat irons, do not grow on trees. They must be made by the labour of the people, and it is very clear that the more luxuries a people produce the fewer necessaries they will produce.

If a community consists of ten thousand people, and if nine thousand people are making bread and one thousand are making jewellery, it is evident that there will be more bread than jewellery.

If in the same community nine thousand make jewellery and only one thousand make bread, there will be more jewellery than bread.

In the first case there will be food enough for all, though jewels be scarce. In the second case the people must starve, although they wear diamond rings on all their fingers. In a well-ordered state no luxuries would be produced *until* there were enough necessaries for all. My Lady Dedlock 'finds useful employment' for Crispin, the shoemaker. She employs him to make Court slippers for her. Let us examine this transaction.

First, where does my lady get her money? She gets it from her husband, Sir Leicester Dedlock, who gets it from his tenant farmer, who gets it from the agricultural labourer, Hodge.

Then she employs Crispin to make Court slippers, and pays him with Hodge's money.

But if Crispin were not employed making shoes for my Lady he would be making boots for Hodge, or for the children of Hodge.

Whereas now Hodge cannot buy boots because he has no money, and he has not money because my Lady Dedlock has taken it.

... Every article of luxury has to be paid for not in *money* but in *labour*. Every glass of wine drunk by my lord, and every diamond star worn by my lady, has to be paid for with the sweat and tears of the poorest of our people.

... One more question. ... Will not the spread of Socialistic ideas tend to alarm the capitalist and so cause him to take his capital out of the country?

Take his capital out of the country! He might take himself out of the country, and he would doubtless take all the portable property he could carry. But the country could bear the loss. ...

This threat about the capitalist taking his capital out of the country is a common one. It is always used when workmen strike against a reduction of wages. It was used during the cotton strike and during the coal strike.

Now just fancy the millowners and the coalowners taking their capital out of the country. They might take some of their machinery; they could not take their mills, nor their mines. The threat is nonsense.

Imagine the landlords and capitalists, the shareholders and dividend-mongers, marching off with the farms, and fields and streets; the mills and mines; the railways and quarries and canals.

No; let the capitalist go when he will; he must leave England and the English behind him, and they will suffice for each other. It is the capitalist who keeps them apart, paralysing both, and helping neither.

A more idiotic assumption was never made than this assumption that the wasting of wealth by the idle rich is a good thing for the labouring poor. Follow it out to its logical conclusion, John Smith, and assure yourself that the drunkard is a benefactor to the workers because he finds much 'useful employment' for the coopers, hop-growers, maltsters and others who are doomed to waste their time in the production of the drink which slakes his swinish thirst.

Robert Blatchford, *Merrie England*, 1895

'THEY MAKE A GOOD THING OUT OF IT'

If any of our readers have an idea that Socialism is a paying trade, I hope they will do us the justice to abandon that idea at once. Socialism is in its infancy as a cause. Socialism is not popular. The Socialists are few in number. Twenty years hence all this will be changed, and then the dailies will discover that early Socialists, though crude thinkers, were useful in preparing the public mind for the great utterances of the press. In fact, we are preparing the ground for the harvest which other men shall reap. . . .

I know many Socialists and many Socialistic leaders. I know none who can make profit of it. *Most* of the leaders, such as Ruskin, Morris, Hyndman, . . . Shaw . . . would lose in money and position were Socialism adopted now. . . . We claim that we give our time and strength to the poor, and that we get but little in return but suspicion and envy and slander. . . .

Robert Blatchford, Merrie England, 1895

THE CASE OF HARDIE

During the first three years I was in Parliament I had no salary of any kind, having to earn every penny I got. During the whole of that time Mrs Hardie kept the home going and brought up our three children on a wage of 25/- a week. I earned much more, but, save the pittance named, every penny went in . . . helping the cause.

That is my reply to those who say I have made a 'good thing' out of the movement. There is no compulsion on me to work these long hours for such scant reward. I go on working because I love doing it. There are thousands of comrades doing the same, working men and women, who are devoting their lives to the cause without any hope or thought of reward. And this is the movement which so many of you call 'Materialistic' and would fain kill if you could!

Keir Hardie, 1911

CONTRARY TO HUMAN NATURE?

Whenever I hear the suggestion, that socialism is contrary to human nature, I want to ask the opposite question: Is capitalism contrary to human nature? Is it contrary to human nature to give the highest pay to those who do no work at all; to give the lowest pay to those who do the heaviest work? Is it contrary to human nature to pay the forty-three million of us who work, so little that we cannot buy enough to keep ourselves in employment? Is it contrary to human nature to keep several million people permanently idle while they and many others lack the very goods they ought to be producing? Is it contrary to human nature deliberately to destroy food, clothes and many other forms of wealth, in order to render the production of further wealth profitable again?

John Strachey, *Why you should be a Socialist*, 1938

SOCIALISM AND THE STANDARDIZED LIFE

A number of vague and inconsistent and confused ideas are mixed up in that phrase, but the underlying conception is a notion of life being lived according to rote and order. . . . An imaginary picture is raised in people's minds of men being allowed to shave only between certain hours . . . of artists being authorised to paint only such pictures as are authorised by a Ministry of Fine Arts; of poetic licence being converted into an actual licence for poets (issued by the local authority on the recommendation of two resident ratepayers, not being undischarged bankrupts or convicted of a punishable offence within the preceding five years); of the menu for each day of the week being scheduled (like the lessons in Church) in an act of Parliament. . . . Over and above all that is the fear that in an egalitarian society there will be, quite apart from external regulation, a minimum of colour, variety and oddness and a maximum of sameness and flatness. . . .

But the assumption, commonly made, that the existing economic organisation of society does in fact prevent the standardisation of life and that it produces, despite other evils, the maximum diversity of life and character, is a statement whose validity requires careful investigation. . . . In the first place . . . the very inequality of wealth which is brought about by the present state of affairs often leads to exactly the kind of standardisation in regard to personal matters, which is most dreaded under Socialism. . . . The existence of wealthy persons leading a fashionable life in a great city is far more prescribed than that of the poor. . . . Wealthy people tend on the whole to be even more alike than poor people not only in speech and dress, but also as regards their mental outlook and habits of life. . . . The costume of a man in well to do circles invited out to dinner in London or New York is prescribed as rigidly as the dress of a convict or a soldier. . . . At the English public schools the standardisation of life is carried to extreme limits and a boy does something which 'isn't done', that is, which isn't done by all the other boys, only at the peril of facing consequences of a particularly unpleasant kind. . . .

What Socialism is aiming at is to bring about an environment which will be far more conducive and stimulating to individual diversity and original effort, which springs from it, than is the present one. . . . Socialism alone offers the promise and the possibility of such an enrichment of human existence.

W. A. Robson, *Socialism and the Standardised Life*, 1926

THE PROFIT MOTIVE

As society is at present constituted nearly every man gets as much money as he can. What are the ordinary motives for this conduct? Plutocrat says 'I can make a fortune out of the cotton trade, and why should I not? If I don't make it some other man will; and perhaps the other man will be a rogue.' You see, men cannot trust each other. Under the operation of unfettered individual enterprise, life is a scramble. A man knows he could live on less than ten thousand a year, and he knows that multitudes are hungry. But if he forgoes the making of a fortune it will not benefit the poor. Some other man will seize on what he relinquishes, and the scramble will go on. So men amass wealth because they think they might as well do it as let another do it in their stead.

There is another thing. Plutocrat will tell you he has a wife and family to provide for. He knows the world too well to leave a widow and children to the tender mercies of his brother graspers. It is every man for himself and the weakest to the wall. So he will grind other people to make money to prevent other people from grinding his children. He is right in a great measure. It is his duty to provide for his wife and children. And under our present system of robbery and murder by individual enterprise the widow and the orphan will find none to pity and defend them unless they can pay for value received.

Again, in a commercial era and in a commercial nation wealth is the reward of merit, the crown of honour and the sign of virtue. . . .

It seems, then, that to deprive money grubbing of its power to mislead we must make great social changes. We must assure men that in *no* case should their children want. We must assure men that the possession of wealth will not bring them honour. We must assure men that justice will win them respect and not contempt, and that the good man who forbears to fill his coffer at the public expense need not fear to see some rascal render his generosity abortive. . . .

For the sake of love, for the sake of duty, for the sake of pity, for the sake of religion and for the sake of truth, men and women have resigned their bodies to the flames, have laid their heads upon the block, have suffered imprisonment, disgrace and torture and starvation. Who will do as much for *money*? . . .

It seems an amazing thing to me, this persistence in the belief that greed is the motive power of humanity. The refutation of that error is forever under our noses. You see how men strive at cricket; you see the intense effort and the fierce zeal which they display at football; you see men nearly kill themselves in boat races, on cycling tracks and running grounds; you know that these men do all this without the hope of a single penny of gain, and yet you tell me in the face of the powerful football combinations, and rowing clubs and cricket clubs and with a quarter of a million of volunteers amongst you, and with the records of Inkerman, and Lucknow and Marston Moor on your shelves, and with the walls of the hospitals, and the lifeboats of the Royal Humane Society, and the spires on your churches, and the convents of the Sisters of Charity, and the statues of your Cromwells, and Wellingtons, and Nelsons and Cobdens, all ready for you to knock your stupid heads against, that the only reliable human motive is—the desire for gain.

Robert Blatchford, Merrie England, 1895

SOCIALISM *IS* DOGMATIC

Gentlemen on the other side are very fond of calling me dogmatic. Perhaps I am dogmatic. But if you called in a professional auditor to audit your books, you would find him very dogmatic, about the balance. He would tell you that if you took £500 away from £550 there could only be a balance of £50. If you disputed the statement he would not argue about it. He would say: 'There are the figures; reckon it out for yourself.' I say the same to you. There is the reasoning. What else can you make of it?

A Robert Blatchford Calendar, 1912

11. Keep Left!

A Labour Government must be prepared to live dangerously.
R. H. Tawney

LEST WE FORGET

I contested Mid-Lanark in 1888 as an Independent Labour candidate, and out of 11,000 electors, got 617 votes. That election had the result of casting me out into the wilderness. Since then I have fought elections and been successful and at this hour I have a clear conscience—I say it in no spirit of vainglory—that I have been true and faithful to the interests of my class. That is all I claim. It has cost much. At 46 years of age I now feel worn out in body and very, very sad in spirit, not sad because of failure but sad because I feel that my work has cut me off from communion with my fellows. I have few friends and cannot, somehow, enter into the healthy and legitimate side of life. However, being what I am, I will endeavour in the future, as I have in the past, to steer a straight course.

People speak sometimes of what one makes out of the movement. If I were to die here and now I would leave my wife and family a legacy of debt bigger than I care to think about. As to the movement, however, if over any man was justified by success in his work, surely I am that man. When it is remembered what the movement was a dozen years ago, and a comparison is made with what it is now, there is cause of gratification and encouragement. No one knows better than I do the fearful temptations which beset the path of those who attempt to walk straight towards the goal of human emancipation. I venture to think that the worst is over and that those who are to come after will find it easier to follow the straight and narrow way because of those who have gone before.

Keir Hardie, 1902

KEEP FAITH

The turmoil of a contested election. Howls, curses, execrations, peltings with mud and stones; one poor, solitary figure knocked and buffeted about bodily and mentally, and yet compelled to go forward by he knew not what. One incident which helped I remember well. A baronet was

248

sent down from London, armed with plenipotentiary powers to make peace, and his offer took the form of . . . a guarantee of £300 a year so long as I remained in Parliament. The thing was so obviously a bribe that it removed the last traces of doubt or hesitation; nay, awoke a spirit of detestation which has never since yet been quite allayed.

Looking back over the way I have come I can honestly say I have never had reason to regret following the steep, straight path of duty; and, I may add, I have never yielded to the temptation to try the apparently easier way without having cause to rue it.

. . . Socialism is to me more of a certainty, also more of a necessity, than ever before. As for political independence, that must be maintained, even if it involves the loss at the next general election of every Parliamentary seat we now hold. We must keep faith with the brave souls whose toils have made the situation what it is.

Keir Hardie, 1906

TRADE UNIONISM IS NOT ENOUGH

This issue is not an issue between Liberals and Tories, it is an issue between Labourers and Capitalists. Neither of the Political Parties is of any use to the workers, because both the Political Parties are paid, officered and led by Capitalists whose interests are opposed to the interests of the workers. The Socialist laughs at the pretended friendship of Liberal and Tory leaders for the workers. These Party Politicians do not in the least understand what the rights, the interests, or the desires of the workers are; if they did understand they would oppose them implacably. The demand of the Socialist is a demand for the nationalisation of the land and all other instruments of production and distribution. . . . The Party leaders will not hear of such a thing. . . .

The older unionists think that Trade Unionism is strong enough in itself to secure the rights of the worker. This is a great mistake. The rights of the worker are the whole of the produce of his labour. Trade Unionism not only cannot secure that, but has never even tried to secure that. The most that Trade Unionism has secured, or can ever hope to secure for the workers, is a comfortable subsistence wage. They have not always secured even that much, and, when they have secured it, the cost has been serious. For the great weapon of Unionism is a strike, and a strike is at best a bitter, a painful, and a costly thing. . . .

You must remember, also, that the employers have copied the methods of Trade Unionism. They also have organised and united and in the future strikes will be more terrible and more costly than ever. The

Capitalist is the stronger. He holds the better strategic position. He can always outlast the worker, for the worker has to starve and see his children starve, and the Capitalist never gets to that pass. Besides, capital is more mobile than labour. A stroke of the pen will divert wealth and trade from one end of the country to the other; but the workers cannot move their forces so readily.

One difference between Socialism and Trade Unionism is that whereas the Unions can only marshal and arm the workers for a desperate trial of endurance, Socialism can get rid of the Capitalist altogether. The former helps you to resist the enemy, the latter destroys him.

Robert Blatchford, Merrie England, 1895

THE CLASSLESS PARTY

. . . Some hostile criticism has been evoked by the fact that certain of the office-bearers [in the Scottish Labour Party] are not *bona-fide* horny-handed sons of toil. These critics go on the assumption that a Labour Party should consist of the begrimed ones only. Those who argue thus are for the most part they who do not wish to see any Labour Party at all, and who hope to create prejudice against the new movement . . . by appealing to the prejudices of the working classes. . . . The Labour Party
. . exists for the purpose of 'educating the people politically, and securing the return to Parliament and all local bodies of members pledged to its programme'. If, therefore, any one, peasant or peer, is found willing to accept the programme and work with and for the Party his help will be gladly accepted.

Keir Hardie, 1888

THE WORKING CLASS AND THE LABOUR PARTY

. . . we shall, if need be, fall with them, but we shall not desert them, nor sacrifice their interests to any spirit of time-serving political expediency. We are of the workers; they are our kin; we are part of them; their battle is our battle; what hurts them hurts us; where they gain, we gain; and remembering the heroism of their toilsome lives, we shall, as a party, seek to create conditions in which the nobler aspirations which we know to be buried under the load of their poverty, or to be petrified by their sordid surroundings, shall have free play.

Keir Hardie, 1906

KNOW YOUR ENEMY

There are two classes in the community who are almost permanently ranged against us. The smug, selfish man, who finds himself fairly comfortable, and who desires to make his position secure. To him the defender of property can always appeal, certain of a willing response. . . .

Then there is the ignorant, besotted set, who vote Tory because of the strange vein of contrariness which runs through human nature. They have no property to conserve, no empire to defend . . . and they find a serf's pleasure in being on the same side as their masters.

Keir Hardie, 1895

COMPROMISE IS FATAL

Why should a Labour candidate be timid on the hustings? If a Liberal or a Conservative candidate holds, or professes to hold, advanced views, he glories in and makes a parade of them. He knows he stands to win thereby. He feels instinctively that he is under suspicion with the advanced section of the electorate, and, knowing also that the unthinking or timid party men are safe to vote for him, he is at special pains to win over the bold advanced spirits. It may be that the Labour candidate sees the situation from the other end. He enters the contest with the advanced men at his back, and feels that his business is to win over the cautious and timid electors to his side. Within limits, this is quite allowable, but it is none the less a very dangerous game to play. Once a man begins to play fast and loose with his principles, he gets on a slippery step, at the bottom of which is the slough of time-serving expediency. . . . What shall it profit a man though he gain a seat in Parliament and lose his own self-respect?

. . . The election contests now being waged [1906] prove that the candidate who courageously pursues a straightforward line of action, who has knowledge of the social problem and makes an intelligent use of it, is not in the least handicapped by being a Socialist; nay is rather helped thereby. It is the man who wobbles, who seems to face all points of the compass at once, who earns the contempt of friend and foe alike. The nation needs a strong lead; the eyes of the thoughtful of all classes are fixed upon the Labour candidate to see what hope for the future lies in him. If he temporises, and hesitates, when he should be firm and unbending; if he, because victory appears to be within his reach, nervously begins to unburden his candidature of principles which he thinks may offend some whose support he is anxious to secure, then he is sapping and undermining the foundation upon which alone an enduring movement can be built.

Keir Hardie. A call to the Labour Party on the eve of the 1906 election

Bibliography

Material used has been taken direct from the sources listed

Arch, Joseph, *The Story of His Life, Told by Himself*, 1876; G. Bell, 1920

Blatchford, Robert, *Merrie England*, Clarion Press, 1895; *Not Guilty: a Plea for the Bottom Dog*, Clarion Press, 1906; *My Eighty Years*, Cassell, 1931

Booth, Charles, *Life and Labour of the People in London*, Macmillan, 1892

Brittain, Vera, *Testament of Youth*, Gollancz, 1933

Clarke, William, 'Industrial Socialism' in *Fabian Essays in Socialism*, Allen and Unwin, 1889

Cole, G. D. H., *Life of William Cobbett*, Fabian Society, 1925; *The Simple Case for Socialism*, Gollancz, 1935

Cole, G. D. H. and Postgate, R., *The Common People*, 1746–1946, Methuen, 1946

Cooper, Lettice, *National Provincial*, Gollancz, 1938

Cripps, Sir Stafford, *Towards a Christian Democracy*, Allen and Unwin, 1945

Elliott, S. R., *England, Cradle of Co-operation*, Faber, 1937

Froissart, Jean, *Chronicles*, translated by Lord Berners, Macmillan, 1895

George Henry, *Progress and Poverty*, 1879, Modern Library, 1929

Glasier, R. B., *William Morris and the Early Days of the Socialist Movement*, Longmans, 1929

Gore, Charles, *Christ and Society*, Allen and Unwin, 1928

Gould, E. J., *Hyndman, Prophet of Socialism*, Allen and Unwin, 1925

Greenwood, Walter, *Love on the Dole*, Cape, 1933

Hall, F., and Watkins, P., *Co-operation*, Co-operative Union Ltd, 1937

Hamilton, Mary A., *Sidney and Beatrice Webb*, Sampson Low, 1932

Hammond, J. L. and B., *The Village Labourer* 1760–1832, Longmans, 1911; *The Town Labourer* 1760–1832, Longmans, 1917; *The Rise of Modern Industry*, Methuen, 1925

Hardie, Keir, *Speeches and Writings*, edited by Emrys Hughes, Forward Press, 1928

Holtby, Winifred, *South Riding*, Collins, 1936

Iremonger, F. A., *William Temple, His Life and Letters*, Oxford University Press, 1948

Jay, Douglas, *The Socialist Case*, Faber, 1947

Jenkins, Roy, *Mr Attlee*, Heinemann, 1948

Kingsley, Charles, *Yeast*, 'Fraser's Magazine', 1848

Kirkwood, David, *My Life of Revolt*, Harrap, 1935

Lansbury, George, *My Quest for Peace*, Michael Joseph, 1938

Lovett, William, *Life and Struggles of William Lovett*, 1876, G. Bell, 1920

Lyons, A. N., *Robert Blatchford*, Clarion Press, 1910

Martin, Kingsley, *Life of Thomas Paine*, Fabian Society, 1946

Masterman, C. F. G., *Life of F. D. Maurice*, Mowbrays, 1907

Mayhew, Henry, *London Labour and the London Poor*, Griffin, Bohn, 1861

More, Sir Thomas, *Utopia*, Clarendon Press, 1895

Morris, William, *Selected Works*, Nonesuch Press, 1946

Owen, Robert, *The Life of Robert Owen by Himself*, edited by Max Beer, Bohn's Library, 1920

Paine, Thomas, *The Rights of Man*, 1791, Dent, 1915

Prentice, A., *Historical Sketches of Manchester*, Gilpin, 1851

Prestige, G. L., *The Life of Charles Gore*, Heinemann, 1935

Robson, W. A., *Socialism and the Standardised Life*, Fabian Society, 1926

Sanders, W. S., *Early Socialist Days*, Hogarth Press, 1927

Shaw, G. B., *Essays in Fabian Socialism*, Constable, 1949

Spring, Howard, *Fame is the Spur*, Collins, 1940

Strachey, John, *Why you should be a Socialist*, Gollancz, 1938; *A Faith to Fight for*, Gollancz, 1941

Temple, William, *Christianity and Social Order*, Penguin, 1942

Tillett, Ben, *Memories and Reflections*, Long, 1931

Tressall, Robert, *The Ragged Trousered Philanthropists*, Richards Press, 1914

Wallas, Graham, *Life of Francis Place*, Allen and Unwin, 1925; *Human Nature in Politics*, Constable, 1908

Webb, Beatrice, *My Apprenticeship*, Longmans, 1946

Webb, Sidney, *The Labour Party on the Threshold*, Fabian Society, 1923

Webb, Sidney, and Beatrice, *History of Trade Unionism*, Longmans, 1894

West, J., *History of the Chartist Movement*, Constable, 1920

Wilkinson, Ellen, *The Town that was Murdered*, Gollancz, 1939

Williams, Francis, *Press, Parliament and People*, Heinemann, 1946

Woodward, W. E., *Thomas Paine*, Secker and Warburg, 1946

The *Holy Bible*

The Times, 2 August 1945

Daily Herald, 2 August 1945

The Listener, 8 April 1948

Hansard, House of Commons, fifth series, Vol. 468

Report of the Labour Party Annual Conference 1949

The English Hymnal

Songs of Praise

The following material has been taken from the sources stated

John Lilburne and Thomas Rainborough, from *The Good Old Cause*, edited by C. Hill and E. Dell, Lawrence and Wishart, 1949

Henry Hetherington, 'The Poor Man's Guardian', from *From Cobbett to the Chartists*, edited by Max Morris, Lawrence and Wishart, 1948

Thomas Hodgskin, from *The Early English Socialists*, by H. L. Beales, Hamish Hamilton, 1933

'The Political Register', from *The Autobiography of William Cobbett*, edited by W. Reitzel, Faber, 1933

'The Clarion', from *Labour's Turning Point*, edited by E. Hobsbawm, Lawrence and Wishart, 1948

William Morris's funeral oration over Alfred Linnell, from *The Pre-Raphaelite Tragedy*, by William Gaunt, Cape, 1942

T.U.C. Resolution of 1899, Electoral Conference Resolution of 1900, and the Constitution of 1918, from *Fifty Years' March* by Francis Williams, Odhams, 1949

Ernest Jones, 'The Song of the Lower Classes', from *A History of British Socialism* by Max Beer, Allen and Unwin, 1940

G. K. Chesterton, from *Life of G. K. Chesterton* by Maisie Ward, Sheed and Ward, 1944

The account of Hardie's conversion to Socialism, from *From Pit to Parliament*, D. Lowe, Labour Publishing Co., 1923

S. R. MacTavish, from *History of England*, Vol. VI, by E. Halévy, Benn, 1924

A selection of other books consulted

Barker, Sir E., *Political Thought* 1848–1914, Oxford University Press, 1928

Cole, G. D. H., *History of British Working Class Politics*, Routledge, 1946

Cole, Margaret, editor, *Makers of the Labour Movement*, Longmans, 1948

Ensor, R. C. K., *History of England* 1870–1914, Oxford University Press, 1936

Gray, Alexander, *The Socialist Tradition*, Longmans, 1946

Hovell, Mark, *The Chartist Movement*, Manchester University Press, 1925

Jefferys, J., editor, *Labour's Formative Years*, 1849–1879, Lawrence and Wishart, 1948

Stewart, J., *Life of Keir Hardie*, Cassells, 1921

Webb, Beatrice, *Our Partnership*, Longmans, 1948

Woodward, E. L., *The Age of Reform*, 1815–1870, Oxford University Press, 1939

Various, *Fabian Tracts*, Fabian Society, from 1889

Index of Authors